AUDUBON GUIDE

to the National Wildlife Refuges

South Central

AUDUBON GUIDE
to the National Wildlife Refuges

South Central
Arkansas · Kansas · Louisiana
Missouri · Oklahoma

By William Palmer
Foreword by Theodore Roosevelt IV

Series Editor, David Emblidge

A Balliett & Fitzgerald Book
St. Martin's Griffin, New York

AUDUBON GUIDE TO THE NATIONAL WILDLIFE REFUGES: SOUTH CENTRAL.
Copyright © 2000 by Balliett & Fitzgerald, Inc.

Cartography: © Balliett & Fitzgerald, Inc. produced by Mapping Specialists Ltd.
Illustrations: Mary Sundstrom
Cover design: Michael Storrings and Sue Canavan
Interior design: Bill Cooke and Sue Canavan

Balliett & Fitzgerald Inc. Staff
Sue Canavan, Design Director
Maria Fernandez, Production Editor
Alexis Lipsitz, Executive Series Editor
Anita Holmes, Editor
Rachel Deutsch, Associate Photo Editor
Kristen Couse, Associate Editor
Paul Paddock, Assistant Editor
Howard Klein, Editorial Intern

Balliett & Fitzgerald Inc. would like to thank the following people for their assis-
tance in creating this series:
At National Audubon Society:
    Katherine Santone, former Director of Publishing, for sponsoring this project
    Claire Tully, Senior Vice President, Marketing
    Evan Hirsche, Director, National Wildlife Refuges Campaign
At U.S. Fish & Wildlife Service:
    Richard Coleman, former Chief, Division of Refuges, U.S. Fish & Wildlife Service
    Janet Tennyson, Outreach Coordinator
    Craig Rieben, Chief of Broadcasting & Audio Visual, U.S. Fish & Wildlife
        Service, for photo research assistance
    Pat Carrol, Chief Surveyor, U.S. Fish & Wildlife Service, for map information
    Regional External Affairs officers, at the seven U.S. Fish & Wildlife Service
        Regional Headquarters
    Elizabeth Jackson, Photographic Information Specialist, National
        Conservation Training Center, for photo research
At St. Martin's Griffin:
    Greg Cohn, who pulled it all together on his end, as well as Michael
        Storrings and Kristen Macnamara
At David Emblidge—Book Producer:
    Marcy Ross, Assistant Editor
Thanks also to Theodore Roosevelt IV and John Flicker.

ISBN 0-312-24487-8
First St. Martin's Griffin Edition: March 2000

10 9 8 7 6 5 4 3 2 1

CONTENTS

LOUISIANA

MISSOURI

Foreword

America is singularly blessed in the amount and quality of land that the federal government holds in trust for its citizens. No other country can begin to match the variety of lands in our national wildlife refuges, parks and forests. From the Arctic Refuge on the North Slope of Alaska to the National Key Deer Refuge in Florida, the diversity of land in the National Wildlife Refuge (NWR) System is staggering.

Yet of all our public lands, the National Wildlife Refuge System is the least well known and does not have an established voting constituency like that of the Parks System. In part this is because of its "wildlife first" mission, which addresses the needs of wildlife species before those of people. That notwithstanding, wildlife refuges also offer remarkable opportunities for people to experience and learn about wildlife—and to have fun doing so!

The Refuge System was launched in 1903 when President Theodore Roosevelt discovered that snowy egrets and other birds were being hunted to the brink of extinction for plumes to decorate ladies' hats. He asked a colleague if there were any laws preventing the president from making a federal bird reservation out of an island in Florida's Indian River. Learning there was not, Roosevelt responded, "Very well, then I so declare it." Thus Pelican Island became the nation's first plot of land to be set aside for the protection of wildlife. Roosevelt went on to create another 50 refuges, and today there are more than 500 refuges encompassing almost 93 million acres, managed by the U.S. Fish & Wildlife Service.

The Refuge System provides critical habitat for literally thousands of mammals, birds, amphibians and reptiles, and countless varieties of plants and flowers. More than 55 refuges have been created specifically to save endangered species. Approximately 20 percent of all threatened and endangered species in the United States rely on these vital places for their survival. As a protector of our country's natural diversity, the System is unparalleled.

Setting NWR boundaries is determined, as often as possible, by the needs of species that depend on the protected lands. Conservation biology, the science that studies ecosystems as a whole, teaches us that wildlife areas must be linked by habitat "corridors" or run the risk of becoming biological islands. The resulting inability of species to transfer their genes over a wide area leaves them vulnerable to disease and natural disasters. For example, the Florida panther that lives in Big Cypress Swamp suffers from a skin fungus, a consequence, scientists believe, of inbreeding. Today's refuge managers are acutely aware of this precarious situation afflicting many species and have made protection of the System's biodiversity an important goal.

Clearly, the job of the refuge manager is not an easy one. Chronic underfunding of the System by the federal government has resulted in refuges operating with less money per employee and per acre than any other federal land-management agency. Recent efforts by some in Congress to address this shortfall have begun to show results, but the System's continued vulnerability to special interests has resulted in attempts to open refuges to oil drilling, road building in refuge wilderness areas, and military exercises.

The managers of the System have played a crucial role in responding to the limited resources available. They have created a network of volunteers who contribute tens of thousands of hours to help offset the lack of direct financing for the Refuge System. Groups like refuge "friends" and Audubon Refuge Keepers have answered the call for local citizen involvement on many refuges across the country.

I hope Americans like yourself who visit our national wildlife refuges will come away convinced of their importance, not only to wildlife but also to people. I further hope you will make your views known to Congress, becoming the voice and voting constituency the Refuge System so desperately needs.

—*Theodore Roosevelt IV*

Preface

Thank you for adding the *Audubon Guide to the National Wildlife Refuge System* to your travel library. I hope you will find this nine-volume series an indispensable guide to finding your way around the refuge system, as well as a valuable educational tool for learning more about the vital role wildlife refuges play in protecting our country's natural heritage.

It was nearly 100 years ago that Frank Chapman, an influential ornithologist, naturalist, publisher and noted Audubon member, approached President Theodore Roosevelt (as recounted by Theodore Roosevelt IV in his foreword), eventually helping to persuade him to set aside more than 50 valuable parcels of land for the protection of wildlife.

Because of limited funding available to support these new wildlife sanctuaries, Audubon stepped up and paid for wardens who diligently looked after them. And so began a century of collaboration between Audubon and the National Wildlife Refuge System. Today, Audubon chapter members can be found across the country assisting refuges with a range of projects, from viewing tower construction to bird banding.

Most recently, National Audubon renewed its commitment to the Refuge System by launching a nationwide campaign to build support for refuges locally and nationally. Audubon's Wildlife Refuge Campaign is promoting the Refuge System through on-the-ground programs such as Audubon Refuge Keepers (ARK), which builds local support groups for refuges, and Earth Stewards, a collaboration with the U.S. Fish and Wildlife Service and the National Fish and Wildlife Foundation, which uses refuges and other important bird habitats as outdoor classrooms. In addition, we are countering legislative threats to refuges in Washington, D.C., while supporting increased federal funding for this, the least funded of all federal land systems.

By teaching more people about the important role refuges play in conserving our nation's diversity of species—be they birds, mammals, amphibians, reptiles, or plants—we have an opportunity to protect for future generations our only federal lands system set aside first and foremost for wildlife conservation.

As a nation, we are at a critical juncture—do we continue to sacrifice wetlands, forests, deserts, and coastal habitat for short-term profit, or do we accept that the survival of our species is closely linked to the survival of others? The National Wildlife Refuge System is a cornerstone of America's conservation efforts. If we are to leave a lasting legacy and, indeed, ensure our future, then we must build on President Theodore Roosevelt's greatest legacy. I invite you to join us!

—John Flicker, President, National Audubon Society

Introduction
to the National Wildlife Refuge System

He spent entire days on horseback, traversing the landscape of domed and crumbling hills, steep forested coulees, with undulating tables of prairie above. The soft wraparound light of sunset displayed every strange contour of the Badlands and lit the colors in each desiccated layer of rock—yellow, ochre, beige, gold.

Theodore Roosevelt was an easterner. As some well-heeled easterners were wont to do, he traveled west in 1883 to play cowboy, and for the next eight years he returned as often as possible. He bought a cattle ranch, carried a rifle and a six-gun, rode a horse. North Dakota was still Dakota Territory then, but the Plains bison were about gone, down to a scattering of wild herds.

The nation faced a new and uneasy awareness of limits during Roosevelt's North Dakota years. Between 1776 and 1850, the American population had increased from 1.5 million to more than 23 million. National borders were fixed and rail and telegraph lines linked the coasts, but Manifest Destiny had a price. The ongoing plunder of wildlife threatened species such as the brown pelican and the great egret; the near-total extermination of 60 million bison loomed as a lesson many wished to avoid repeating.

Despite the damage done, the powerful landscapes of the New World had shaped the outlooks of many new Americans. From Colonial-era botanist John Bartram to 19th-century artists George Catlin and John James Audubon, naturalists and individuals of conscience explored the question of what constituted a proper human response to nature. Two figures especially, Henry David Thoreau and John Muir, created the language and ideas that would confront enduring Old World notions of nature as an oppositional, malevolent force to be harnessed and exploited. The creation in 1872 of Yellowstone as the world's first national park indicated that some Americans, including a few political leaders, were listening to what Thoreau, Muir, and these others had to say.

Roosevelt, along with his friend George Bird Grinnell, drew upon these and other writings, as well as their own richly varied experiences with nature, to take the unprecedented step of making protection of nature a social and political cause. Of his time in the Badlands, Roosevelt remarked "the romance of my life began here," and "I never would have been president if it had not been for my experiences in North Dakota." As a hunter, angler, and naturalist, Roosevelt grasped the importance of nature for human life. Though he had studied natural history as an undergraduate at Harvard, believing it would be his life's work, Roosevelt owned a passion for reform and had the will—perhaps a need—to be effective. Rather than pursuing a career as a naturalist, he went into politics. His friend George

Barren-ground caribou

Bird Grinnell, publisher of the widely read magazine *Forest and Stream,* champi-
oned all manner of environmental protection and in 1886 founded the Audubon
Society to combat the slaughter of birds for the millinery trade. Fifteen years later,
TR would find himself with an even greater opportunity. In1901, when he inher-
ited the presidency following the assassination of William McKinley, Roosevelt
declared conservation a matter of federal policy.

Roosevelt backed up his words with an almost dizzying series of conservation
victories. He established in 1903 a federal bird reservation on Pelican Island,
Florida, as a haven for egrets, herons, and other birds sought by plume hunters. In
eight years, Roosevelt authorized 150 million acres in the lower 48 states and
another 85 million in Alaska to be set aside from logging under the Forest Reserve
Act of 1891, compared to a total of 45 million under the three prior presidents. To
these protected lands he added five national parks and 17 national monuments. The
NWR system, though, is arguably TR's greatest legacy. Often using executive order
to circumvent Congress, Roosevelt established 51 wildlife refuges.

The earliest federal wildlife refuges functioned as sanctuaries and little else.
Visitors were rare and recreation was prohibited. Between 1905 and 1912 the first
refuges for big-game species were established—Wichita Mountains in Oklahoma,

the National Bison Range in
Montana, and National Elk
Refuge in Jackson, Wyoming.
In 1924, the first refuge to
include native fish was created;
a corridor some 200 miles
long, the Upper Mississippi
National Wildlife and Fish
Refuge spanned the states of
Minnesota, Wisconsin, Illi-
nois, and Iowa.

Still, the 1920s were dark
years for America's wildlife.
The effects of unregulated
hunting, along with poor
enforcement of existing laws,
had decimated once-abundant
species. Extinction was feared
for the wood duck. Wild turkey

Atlantic puffins, Petit Manan NWR, Maine

had become scarce outside a few southern states. Pronghorn antelope, which today
number perhaps a million across the West, were estimated at 25,000 or fewer. The
trumpeter swan, canvasback duck, even the prolific and adaptable white-tailed
deer, were scarce or extirpated across much of their historic ranges.

The Depression and Dust-bowl years, combined with the leadership of
President Franklin Delano Roosevelt, gave American conservation—and the
refuge system in particular—a hefty forward push. As wetlands vanished and fertile prairie soils blew away, FDR's Civilian Conservation Corps (CCC) dispatched
thousands of unemployed young men to camps that stretched from Georgia to
California. On the sites of many present-day refuges, they built dikes and other

Saguaro cactus and ocotillo along Charlie Bell 4WD trail, Cabeza Prieta NWR, Arizona

water-control structures, planted shelterbelts and grasses. Comprised largely of men from urban areas, the experience of nature was no doubt a powerful rediscovery of place and history for the CCC generation. The value of public lands as a haven for people, along with wildlife, was on the rise.

In 1934, Jay Norwood "Ding" Darling was instrumental in developing the federal "Duck Stamp," a kind of war bond for wetlands; hunters were required to purchase it, and anyone else who wished to support the cause of habitat acquisition could, too. Coupled with the Resettlement Act of 1935, in which the federal government bought out or condemned private land deemed unsuitable for agriculture, several million acres of homesteaded or settled lands reverted to federal ownership to become parks, national grasslands, and wildlife refuges. The Chief of the U.S. Biological Survey's Wildlife Refuge Program, J. Clark Salyer, set out on a cross-country mission to identify prime wetlands. Salyer's work added 600,000 acres to the refuge system, including Red Rock Lakes in Montana, home to a small surviving flock of trumpeter swans.

The environmental ruin of the Dust bowl also set in motion an era of government initiatives to engineer solutions to such natural events as floods, drought, and the watering of crops. Under FDR, huge regional entities such as the Tennessee Valley Authority grew, and the nation's mightiest rivers—the Columbia, Colorado, and later, the Missouri—were harnessed by dams. In the wake of these and other federal works projects, a new concept called "mitigation" appeared: If a proposed dam or highway caused the destruction of a certain number of acres of wetlands or other habitat, some amount of land nearby would be ceded to conservation in return. A good many of today's refuges were the progeny of mitigation. The federal government, like the society it represents, was on its way to becoming complex enough that the objectives of one arm could be at odds with those of another.

Citizen activism, so integral to the rise of the Audubon Society and other groups, was a driving force in the refuge system as well. Residents of rural Georgia applied relentless pressure on legislators to protect the Okefenokee Swamp. Many other refuges—San Francisco Bay, Sanibel Island, Minnesota Valley, New Jersey's Great Swamp—came about through the efforts of people with a vision of conservation close to home.

More than any other federal conservation program, refuge lands became places where a wide variety of management techniques could be tested and refined. Generally, the National Park system followed the "hands off" approach of Muir and Thoreau while the U.S. Forest Service and Bureau of Land Management, in theory, emphasized a utilitarian, "sustainable yield" value; in practice, powerful economic interests backed by often ruthless politics left watersheds, forests, and grasslands badly degraded, with far-reaching consequences for fish and wildlife. The refuge system was not immune to private enterprise—between 1939 and 1945, refuge lands were declared fair game for oil drilling, natural-gas exploration, and even for bombing practice by the U.S. Air Force—but the negative impacts have seldom reached the levels of other federal areas.

Visitor use at refuges tripled in the 1950s, rose steadily through the 1960s, and by the 1970s nearly tripled again. The 1962 Refuge Recreation Act established guidelines for recreational use where activities such as hiking, photography, boating, and camping did not interfere with conservation. With visitors came opportunities to educate, and now nature trails and auto tours, in addition to beauty, offered messages about habitats and management techniques. Public awareness of wilderness, "a place where man is only a visitor," in the words of long-time advocate Robert Marshall of the U.S. Forest Service, gained increasing social and political attention. In 1964, Congress passed the Wilderness Act, establishing guidelines for designating a host of federally owned lands as off-limits to motorized vehicles, road building, and resource exploitation. A large number of refuge lands qualified—the sun-blasted desert of Arizona's Havasu refuge, the glorious tannin-stained waters and cypress forests of Georgia's Okefenokee Swamp, and the almost incomprehensible large 8-million-acre Arctic NWR in Alaska, home to vast herds of caribou, wolf packs, and bladelike mountain peaks, the largest contiguous piece of wilderness in the refuge system.

Sachuest Point NWR, Rhode Island

Nonetheless, this was also a time of horrendous air and water degradation, with the nation at its industrial zenith and agriculture cranked up to the level of "agribusiness." A wake-up call arrived in the form of vanishing bald eagles, peregrine falcons, and osprey. The insecticide DDT, developed in 1939 and used in World War II to eradicate disease-spreading insects, had been used throughout the nation ever since, with consequences unforeseen until the 1960s. Sprayed over wetlands, streams, and crop fields, DDT had entered watersheds and from there the food chain itself. It accumulated in the bodies of fish and other aquatic life, and birds consuming fish took DDT into their systems, one effect was a calcium deficiency, resulting in eggs so fragile that female birds crushed them during incubation.

Partially submerged alligator, Anahuac NWR, Texas

Powerful government and industry leaders launched a vicious, all-out attack on the work of a marine scientist named Rachel Carson, whose book *Silent Spring,* published in 1962, warned of the global dangers associated with DDT and other biocides. For this she was labeled "not a real scientist" and "a hysterical woman." With eloquence and courage, though, Carson stood her ground. If wild species atop the food chain could be devastated, human life could be threatened, too. Americans were stunned, and demanded an immediate ban on DDT. Almost overnight, the "web of life" went from chalkboard hypothesis to reality.

Protecting imperiled species became a matter of national policy in 1973 when President Nixon signed into law the Endangered Species Act (ESA), setting guidelines by which the U.S. Fish & Wildlife Service would "list" plant and animal species as *threatened* or *endangered* and would develop a program for their recovery. Some 56 refuges, such as Ash Meadows in Nevada and Florida's Crystal River, home of the manatee, were established specifically for the protection of endangered species. Iowa's tiny Driftless Prairie refuge exists to protect the rare, beautifully colored pleistocene land snail and a wildflower, the northern monkshood. Sometimes unwieldy, forever politicized, the ESA stands as a monumental achievement. Its successes include the American alligator, bald eagle, and gray wolf. The whooping crane would almost surely be extinct today without the twin supports of ESA and the refuge system. The black-footed ferret, among the rarest mammals on earth, is today being reintroduced on a few western refuges. In 1998, nearly one-fourth of all threatened and endangered species populations find sanctuary on refuge lands.

More legislation followed. The passage of the Alaska National Interest Lands Conservation Act in 1980 added more than 50 million acres to the refuge system in Alaska.

The 1980s and '90s have brought no end of conservation challenges, faced by an increasingly diverse association of organizations and strategies. Partnerships now link the refuge system with nonprofit groups, from Ducks Unlimited and The Nature Conservancy to international efforts such as Partners in Flight, a program to monitor the decline of, and to secure habitat for, neotropical songbirds. These cooperative efforts have resulted in habitat acquisition and restoration, research, and many new refuges. Partnerships with private landowners who voluntarily offer marginally useful lands for restoration—with a sponsoring conservation group cost-sharing the project— have revived many thousands of acres of grasslands, wetlands, and riparian corridors.

Citizen activism is alive and well as we enter the new millennium. Protecting and promoting the growth of the NWR system is a primary campaign of the National Audubon Society, which, by the year 2000, will have grown to a membership of around 550,000. NAS itself also manages about 100 sanctuaries and nature centers across the country, with a range of opportunities for environmental education. The National Wildlife Refuge Association, a volunteer network,

Coyote on the winter range

keeps members informed of refuge events, environmental issues, and legislative developments and helps to maintain a refuge volunteer workforce. In 1998, a remarkable 20 percent of all labor performed on the nation's refuges was carried out by volunteers, a contribution worth an estimated $14 million.

A national wildlife refuge today has many facets. Nature is ascendant and thriving, often to a shocking degree when compared with adjacent lands. Each site has its own story: a prehistory, a recent past, a present—a story of place, involving people, nature, and stewardship, sometimes displayed in Visitor Center or Headquarters exhibits, always written into the landscape. Invariably a refuge belongs to a community as well, involving area residents who visit, volunteers who log hundreds of hours, and a refuge staff who are knowledgeable and typically friendly, even outgoing, especially if the refuge is far-flung. In this respect most every refuge is a portal to local culture, be it Native American, cows and crops, or big city. There may be no better example of democracy in action than a national wildlife refuge. The worm-dunker fishes while a mountain biker pedals past. In spring, birders scan marshes and grasslands that in the fall will be walked by hunters. Compromise is the guiding principle.

What is the future of the NWR system? In Prairie City, Iowa, the Neal Smith NWR represents a significant departure from the time-honored model. Established in 1991, the site had almost nothing to "preserve." It was old farmland with scattered remnants of tallgrass prairie and degraded oak savanna. What is happening at Neal Smith, in ecological terms, has never been attempted on such a scale: the reconstruction, essentially from scratch, of a self-sustaining 8,000-acre native biome, complete with bison and elk, greater prairie chickens, and a palette of wildflowers and grasses that astonish and delight.

What is happening in human terms is equally profound. Teams of area residents, called "seed seekers," explore cemeteries, roadside ditches, and long-ignored patches of ground. Here and there they find seeds of memory, grasses and wildflowers from the ancient prairie, and harvest them; the seeds are catalogued and planted on the refuge. The expanding prairie at Neal Smith is at once new and very old. It is reshaping thousands of Iowans' sense of place, connecting them to what was, eliciting wonder for what could be. And the lessons here transcend biology. In discovering rare plants, species found only in the immediate area, people discover an identity beyond job titles and net worth. The often grueling labor of cutting brush, pulling nonnative plants, and tilling ground evokes the determined optimism of Theodore and Franklin Roosevelt and of the CCC.

As the nation runs out of wild places worthy of preservation, might large-scale restoration of damaged or abandoned lands become the next era of American conservation? There are ample social and economic justifications. The ecological justifications are endless, for, as the history of conservation and ecology has revealed, nature and humanity cannot go their separate ways. The possibilities, if not endless, remain rich for the years ahead.

—John Grassy

How to use this book

Local conditions and regulations on national wildlife refuges vary considerably. We provide detailed, site-specific information useful for a good refuge visit, and we note the broad consistencies throughout the NWR system (facility set-up and management, what visitors may or may not do, etc.). Contact the refuge before arriving or stop by the Visitor Center when you get there. F&W wildlife refuge managers are ready to provide friendly, savvy advice about species and habitats, plus auto, hiking, biking, or water routes that are open and passable, and public programs (such as guided walks) you may want to join.

AUDUBON GUIDES TO THE NATIONAL WILDLIFE REFUGES

This is one of nine regional volumes in a series covering the entire NWR system. **Visitable refuges**—over 300 of them—constitute about three-fifths of the NWR system. **Nonvisitable refuges** may be small (without visitor facilities), fragile (set up to protect an endangered species or threatened habitat), or new and undeveloped.

Among visitable refuges, some are more important and better developed than others. In creating this series, we have categorized refuges as A, B, or C level, with the A-level refuges getting the most attention. You will easily recognize the difference. C-level refuges, for instance, do not carry a map.

Rankings can be debated; we know that. We considered visitation statistics, accessibility, programming, facilities, and the richness of the refuges' habitats and animal life. Some refuges ranked as C-level now may develop further over time.

Many bigger NWRs have either "satellites" (with their own refuge names) separate "units" within the primary refuge or other, less significant NWRs nearby. All of these, at times, were deemed worthy of a brief mention.

ORGANIZATION OF THE BOOK

■ **REGIONAL OVERVIEW** This regional introduction is intended to give readers the big picture, touching on broad patterns in landscape formation, interconnections among plant communities, and diversity of animals. We situate NWRs in the natural world of the larger bio-region to which they belong, showing why these federally protected properties stand out as wild places worth preserving amid encroaching civilization.

We also note some wildlife management issues that will surely color the debate around campfires and

ABOUT THE U.S. FISH & WILDLIFE SERVICE Under the Department of the Interior, the U.S. Fish & Wildlife Service is the principal federal agency responsible for conserving and protecting wildlife and plants and their habitats for the benefit of the American people. The Service manages the 93-million-acre NWR system, comprised of more than 500 national wildlife refuges, thousands of small wetlands, and other special management areas. It also operates 66 national fish hatcheries, 64 U.S. Fish & Wildlife Management Assistance offices, and 78 ecological services field stations. The agency enforces federal wildlife laws, administers the Endangered Species Act, manages migratory bird populations, restores nationally significant fisheries, conserves and restores wildlife habitats such as wetlands, and helps foreign governments with their conservation efforts. It also oversees the federal-aid program that distributes hundreds of millions of dollars in excise taxes on fishing and hunting equipment to state wildlife agencies.

congressional conference tables in years ahead, while paying recognition to the NWR supporters and managers who helped make the present refuge system a reality.

■ **THE REFUGES** The refuge section of the book is organized alphabetically by state and then, within each state, by refuge name.

There are some clusters, groups, or complexes of neighboring refuges administered by one primary refuge. Some refuge complexes are alphabetized here by the name of their primary refuge, with the other refuges in the group following immediately thereafter.

■ **APPENDIX**

Nonvisitable National Wildlife Refuges: NWR properties that meet the needs of wildlife but are off-limits to all but field biologists.

Federal Recreation Fees: An overview of fees and fee passes.

Volunteer Activities: How you can lend a hand to help your local refuge or get involved in supporting the entire NWR system.

U.S. Fish & Wildlife General Information: The seven regional headquarters of the U.S. Fish & Wildlife Service through which the National Wildlife Refuge System is administered.

National Audubon Society Wildlife Sanctuaries: A listing of the 24 National Audubon Society wildlife sanctuaries, dispersed across the U.S., which are open to the public.

Bibliography & Resources: Natural-history titles both on the region generally and its NWRs, along with a few books of inspiration about exploring the natural world.

Glossary: A listing of specialized terms (not defined in the text) tailored to this region.

Index

National Audubon Society Mission Statement

PRESENTATION OF INFORMATION: A-LEVEL REFUGE

■ **INTRODUCTION** This section attempts to evoke the essence of the place, The writer sketches the sounds or sights you might experience on the refuge, such as sandhill cranes taking off, en masse, from the marsh, filling the air with the roar of thousands of beating wings. That's a defining event for a particular refuge and a great reason to go out and see it.

■ **MAP** Some refuges are just a few acres; several, like the Alaskan behemoths, are bigger than several eastern states. The scale of the maps in this series can vary. We recommend that you also ask refuges for their detailed local maps.

■ **HISTORY** This outlines how the property came into the NWR system and what its uses were in the past.

■ **GETTING THERE** General location; seasons and hours of operation; fees, if any (see federal recreation fees in Appendix); address, telephone. Smaller or remote refuges may have their headquarters off-site. We identify highways as follows: TX14 = Texas state highway # 14; US 23 = a federal highway; I-85 = Interstate 85.

Note: Many NWRs have their own web pages at the F&W web site, http://www.fws.gov/. Some can be contacted by fax or e-mail, and if we do not provide that information here, you may find it at the F&W web site.

■ **TOURING** The **Visitor Center**, if there is one, is the place to start your tour. Some have wildlife exhibits, videos, and bookstores; others may be only a kiosk. Let someone know your itinerary before heading out on a long trail or into the backcountry, and then go explore.

Most refuges have roads open to the public; many offer a wildlife **auto tour,** with wildlife information signs posted en route or a brochure or audiocassette to guide you. Your car serves as a bird blind if you park and remain quiet. Some refuge roads require 4-wheel-drive or a high-chassis vehicle. Some roads are closed seasonally to protect habitats during nesting seasons or after heavy rain or snow.

Touring also covers **walking and hiking** (see more trail details under ACTIV-ITIES) and **biking.** Many refuge roads are rough; mountain or hybrid bikes are more appropriate than road bikes. When water is navigable, we note what kinds of **boats** may be used and where there are boat launches.

■ **WHAT TO SEE**

Landscape and climate: This section covers geology, topography, and climate: primal forces and raw materials that shaped the habitats that lured species to the refuge. It also includes weather information for visitors.

Plant life: This is a sampling of noteworthy plants on the refuge, usually sorted by habitat, using standard botanical nomenclature. Green plants bordering watery places are in "Riparian Zones"; dwarfed trees, shrubs, and flowers on windswept mountaintops are in the "Alpine Forest"; and so forth.

Wildflowers abound, and you may want to see them in bloom. We give advice about timing your visit, but ask the refuge for more. If botany and habitat relationships are new to you, you can soon learn to read the landscape as a set of interrelated communities. Take a guided nature walk to begin.

(Note: In two volumes, "Plants" is called "Habitats and Plant Communities.")

Animal life: The national map on pages 4 and 5 shows the major North American "flyways." Many NWRs cluster in watery territory underneath the birds' aerial superhighways. There are many birds in this book, worth seeing simply for their beauty. But ponder, too, what birds eat (fish, insects, aquatic plants), or how one species (the mouse) attracts another (the fox), and so on up the food chain, and you'll soon understand the rich interdependence on display in many refuges.

Animals use camouflage and stealth for protection; many are nocturnal. You may want to come out early or late to increase your chances of spotting them. Refuge managers can offer advice on sighting or tracking animals.

Grizzly bears, venomous snakes, alligators, and crocodiles can indeed be dangerous. Newcomers to these animals' habitats should speak with refuge staff about precautions before proceeding.

■ **ACTIVITIES** Some refuges function not only as wildlife preserves but also as recreation parks. Visit a beach, take a bike ride, and camp overnight, or devote your time to serious wildlife observation.

Camping and swimming: If not permissible on the refuge, there may be federal or state campgrounds nearby; we mention some of them. Planning an NWR camping trip should start with a call to refuge headquarters.

Wildlife observation: This subsection touches on strategies for finding species most people want to see. Crowds do not mix well with certain species; you

---

A NOTE ON HUNTING AND FISHING Opinions on hunting and fishing on federally owned wildlife preserves range from "Let's have none of it" to "We need it as part of the refuge management plan." The F&W Service follows the latter approach, with about 290 hunting programs and 260 fishing programs. If you have strong opinions on this topic, talk with refuge managers to gain some insight into F&W's rationale. You can also write to your representative or your senators in Washington.

For most refuges, we summarize the highlights of the hunting and fishing options. You must first have required state and local licenses for hunting or fishing. Then you must check with refuge headquarters about special restrictions that may apply on the refuge; refuge bag limits, for example, or duration of season may be different from regulations elsewhere in the same state.

Hunting and fishing options change from year to year on many refuges, based on the size of the herd or of the flock of migrating birds. These changes may reflect local weather (a hard winter trims the herd) or disease, or factors in distant habitats where animals summer or winter. We suggest what the options usually are on a given refuge (e.g., some birds, some mammals, fish, but not all etc..). It's the responsibility of those who wish to hunt and fish to confirm current information with refuge headquarters and to abide by current rules.

COMMON SENSE, WORTH REPEATING

Leave no trace Every visitor deserves a chance to see the refuge in its pristine state. We all share the responsibility to minimize our impact on the landscape. "Take only pictures and leave only footprints," and even there you'll want to avoid trampling plant life by staying on established trails. Pack out whatever you pack in. Ask refuge managers for guidance on low-impact hiking and camping.

Respect private property Many refuges consist of noncontiguous parcels of land, with private properties abutting refuge lands. Respect all Private Property and No Trespassing signs, especially in areas where native peoples live within refuge territory and hunt or fish on their own land.

Water Protect the water supply. Don't wash dishes or dispose of human waste within 200 ft. of any water. Treat all water for drinking with iodine tablets, backpacker's water filter, or boiling. Clear water you think is OK may be contaminated upstream by wildlife you cannot see.

may need to go away from established observation platforms to have success. Learn a bit about an animal's habits, where it hunts or sleeps, what time of day it moves about. Adjust your expectations to match the creature's behavior, and your chances of success will improve.

Photography: This section outlines good places or times to see certain species. If you have a zoom lens, use it. Sit still, be quiet, and hide yourself. Don't approach the wildlife; let it approach you. Never feed animals or pick growing plants.

Hikes and walks: Here we list specific outings, with mileages and trailhead locations. Smooth trails and boardwalks, suitable for people with disabilities, are noted. On bigger refuges, there may be many trails. Ask for a local map. If you go bushwacking, first make sure this is permissible. Always carry a map and compass.

Seasonal events: National Wildlife Refuge Week, in October, is widely celebrated, with guided walks, lectures, demonstrations, and activities of special interest to children. Call your local refuge for particulars. At other times of the year there are fishing derbies, festivals celebrating the return of migrating birds, and other events linked to the natural world. Increasingly, refuges post event schedules on their web pages.

Publications: Many NWR brochures are free, such as bird and wildflower checklists. Some refuges have pamphlets and books for sale, describing local habitats and species.

Note: The categories of information above appear in A and B refuges in this book; on C-level refuges, options are fewer, and some of these headings may not appear.

—*David Emblidge*

South Central
A Regional Overview

Water from half the North American continent flows toward the Gulf of Mexico through one of the greatest river systems in the world. Like a giant oak tree spreading its branches, the Mississippi River watershed stretches from the Rockies to the Appalachians and to the lake country of the northern United States. Each small branch connects to a larger branch, adding its share of water as the eternal pull of gravity draws it southward. It is the largest river system in North America, draining 1.25 million square miles. From Lake Itasca in Minnesota the river flows 2,350 miles south to the Gulf of Mexico. At the Gulf, Ol' Man River stops its rolling, each year dumping its sediment load of 724 billion cubic yards to create one of the largest and most fertile deltas in the world. The delta is a mix of marshes, mudflats, and tidal pools crisscrossed with a network of chutes and canals that resembles a bird's foot.

The rivers, streams, branches, creeks, sloughs, and bayous of the Mississippi system have a thousand names that read like a dictionary of American history: Rattlesnake and Maries Des Cygne (Kansas); Medicine Lodge and Washita (Oklahoma); Mingo and Squaw Creek (Missouri); Cache and Petit Jean (Arkansas); Tensas and Atachafalaya (Louisiana). This extraordinary river system gives the national wildlife refuges of the South Central region a common bond and defines their persona.

Along these rivers one of the greatest wildlife spectacles in America occurs during the spring and fall migrations, as millions of waterfowl, shorebirds, songbirds, and other migrants travel the Mississippi Flyway. Most of the 41 national wildlife refuges described in this book are nestled under the flyway.

The nine NWRs featured in Arkansas are traditional destinations for mallard, pintail, canvasback, and other migrating waterfowl. The four refuges in Kansas are diverse tallgrass prairies where shorebirds stop to rest and find food needed to fuel their continuing trip north or south. Louisiana has the most refuges (17), including islands in the Gulf of Mexico, the biggest tract of bottomland hardwood forest in America. The ever-present alligator adds to the thrill of touring any of Louisiana's refuges. Three of Missouri's five NWRs provide excellent auto-tour routes, bringing visitors in close contact with a myriad of plants and animals. Of Oklahoma's six refuges, one is the first federal land designated as a "wildlife preserve," and another produces selenite crystals that visitors may dig from the sand.

THEN AND NOW

The abundant natural resources of the region have always attracted humans. Native Americans sought food and shelter; the early French and Spanish explorers sought gold and furs; and European immigrants came to harvest timber and farm the rich soils.

American bittern   Traces of Native American culture can still be found on the South Central refuges. In Missouri, Mingo NWR has

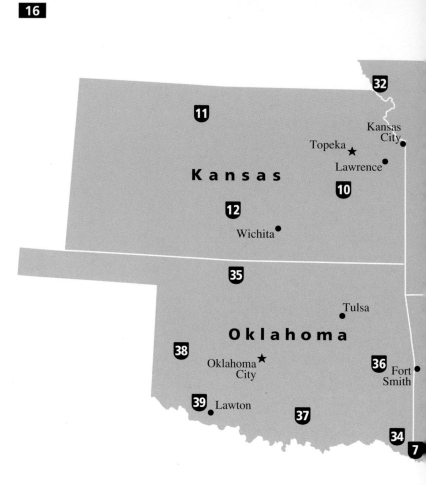

11

32

Kansas
City

Topeka ★
Lawrence

K a n s a s

10

12

Wichita

35

Tulsa

O k l a h o m a

38

Oklahoma ★
City

36 Fort
Smith

39 Lawton

37

34

7

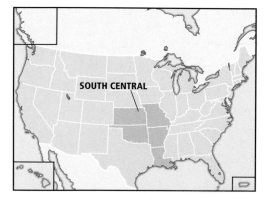

SOUTH CENTRAL

more than 99 recorded historic sites. D'Arbonne refuge, in Arkansas, holds the remains of three Indian villages. Oklahoma's Tishomingo NWR was named in honor of a Chickasaw chief, and Sequoyah refuge pays tribute to the native leader who developed the Cherokee alphabet.

Exploring northward from Mexico and the Caribbean, Spanish conquistadors roamed this region during the mid-1500s in search of gold and silver. Coronado crossed western Oklahoma in 1541 searching for the mythical Seven Cities, one of which was "Quivira" (an NWR carries this name today). The French moved southward from the upper Mississippi where the fur-trading enterprise flourished. By 1682 La Salle had claimed all the land drained by the Mississippi River for his king, Louis XIV, naming the region "Louisiane." About 120 years later, with the stroke of his quill pen in 1803, President Thomas Jefferson made the biggest real-estate purchase of all time when he paid Napoleon Bonaparte of France $15 million for about 800,000 square miles of territory, mostly unknown to whites, west of the Mississippi River. Thus, most of the South Central region as defined in this book joined the United States.

Almost immediately (1804), Jefferson sent Lewis and Clark on their epic voyage of discovery (looking, in vain, for a water route to the Pacific but recording, with great success, the natural history en route). They passed by what today are Swan Lake and Squaw Creek refuges in Missouri. Near Squaw Creek they were the first white men to see American white pelican.

President William McKinley declared what is now Wichita Mountains NWR a "wildlife reserve" in 1902, a full year before President Roosevelt made Pelican Island in Florida the first official national wildlife refuge. Breton Islands, off the coast of Louisiana, became the second national wildlife refuge in 1904. It was in Tensas River NWR, in Louisiana, that Roosevelt was captivated by a young black bear, an event from which the "teddy bear" was born.

Many refuges were added to the system following the Great Depression and after World War II; others were added during the period of renewed interest in the environment in the 1960s and 1970s. Some refuges were established to reduce

Red-winged blackbirds take flight.

downstream flooding by absorbing and then slowly releasing water. Today, refuges are still being added, often spurred by local environmentalists or by businesses seeking tax and other financial advantages on land they do not intend to develop.

In our time, much of the South Central region has been agricultural. Corn, soybeans, rice, pastureland, wheat, and timber plantations serve a multitude of purposes. In many areas, the NWRs preserve all that remains of the region's original natural environment.

GEOLOGY

The parent rocks and the geologic processes that break them down to form soil are the bases for all life. In ancient times, most of the South Central region was under a shallow sea, rich with life. Over a vast span of years, layers of sedimentary rocks (limestone, dolomite, shale) were deposited. Some buckling and uplifting of these layers produced the greatest elevations and most rugged areas of the region: the Flint Hills of Kansas, the Ozarks of Missouri, the Boston Mountains of Arkansas, and the Ouchita Mountains of Arkansas and Oklahoma. These are not major mountain ranges when compared with the Rockies, but for the hiker carrying a backpack, they are clearly more than hills. Rivers flowing through these mountains have carved wonderfully narrow valleys with steep bluffs.

Molten rock either cooled slowly beneath much older sedimentary layers or burst forth from beneath the sedimentary crust to form the St. Francois Mountains of Missouri and the Wichita Mountains of Oklahoma. Here, hard granites and rhyolites weather more slowly than the softer sedimentary rocks, producing strange, intriguing shapes.

In the lower half of the South Central region, the rocks lie far beneath the surface. They have been covered with windblown and river-carried sediments or their own weathered remains.

Whether deposited by wind or water, much of this covering came from ancient glaciers that blanketed a good deal of Kansas and northern Missouri. These glaciers ground hard rock into fine dust that became the stock for fertile soil. When the glaciers receded, rivers began eroding this rich soil and slowly deposited it over the sedimentary rocks to the south. Descendants of those rivers are still carrying sediments toward the Gulf of Mexico. Indeed, rivers, like people, are classified by their age. A youthful river is steep, with rapids and waterfalls. Rivers of the South Central region, however, are generally mature, with graceful curves and powerful in size and volume. Their leisurely meandering creates oxbow lakes like those at Arkansas's Holla Bend and White River refuges. Through annual flooding, some rivers create their own levees, and although it appears to defy gravity, it is possible for a river to be higher in elevation than the surrounding land. The swamps and marshes of Atchafalaya, Lacassine, and Sabine NWRs absorb and slowly release floodwaters, thus protecting downstream cities and towns.

Today, the most pervasive and strongest of nature's geologic forces continue to modify the region. The erosional forces of nature—wind, water, and freezing and thawing—are still gradually wearing away rock and trying to level the earth. One geologic event occurred suddenly and with great violence, however: a series of earthquakes that began at 2 a.m. on December 16, 1811. At least 2,000 aftershocks occurred over the next five months. The strength and size of the quakes were beyond imagination. Seismologists estimate that five registered at least 8.0 on the Richter scale. Only the quake that hit Anchorage, Alaska, in 1964 is believed to have been as strong. The quakes dramatically impacted a 50,000-square-mile area; moderately affected an area of 1 million square miles; and, to a lesser extent, were

Dark clouds roll over Clarence Cannon NWR in Missouri.

noticeable over an area of 2 million square miles. By comparison, the San Francisco earthquake of 1906 only moderately affected an area of 60,000 square miles.

It is said that when this earthquake struck, the "Mississippi River flowed backward," "the earth opened and swallowed people," and that "church bells as far away as Philadelphia were heard to ring." Known as the New Madrid earthquakes (so named for their epicenter), this cataclysm helped to form Reelfoot Lake in Kentucky and Big Lake (the heart of Big Lake NWR) in Louisiana. Although it is quiet today, most seismologists believe that someday the New Madrid fault will slip again.

CLIMATE

Warm, moist air from the Gulf of Mexico and cool, dry Canadian air meet eternally on the South Central battlefield. With such powerful fronts, weather changes suddenly and sometimes violently, resulting in severe thunderstorms, torrential rains, and hail. Systems usually pass through quickly but can "stall out" and produce prolonged droughts or floods. Much of the region lies in Tornado Alley. In tornado season (most frequent in spring), visitors to South Central refuges should keep an eye on the weather and keep their car radios tuned to local stations.

Like the man with one foot in the oven and one foot on a block of ice, the terms "average temperatures" and "average rainfall" are misleading in this region. Summer high temperatures may be unbearable, and winter low temperatures can be frigid. Southern Louisiana has the warmest and wettest climate (subtropical). It is one of the wettest states, averaging 57 inches of rain per year. Temperatures are moderated by the Gulf, by many inland lakes, bays, and rivers, and by prevailing

southerly winds. The January average temperature is 55 degrees. Summer temperatures average about 82 degrees—which sounds delightful until you adjust for the humidity and send the resulting heat index over the 100-degree mark. Hurricanes can occur from summer through fall, but one-half of them have hit in September.

The high plains of northwest Kansas have the coldest and driest climate of the South Central region. Strong winds and Canadian cold fronts can form blizzard-like conditions in the winter. Those same strong winds can combine with hot dry air in the summer to make a day outdoors feel like a blast furnace. Average temperature is near freezing in winter to the 80s in July. Rainfall is as little as 15 inches in northwest Kansas.

Other states in the region (Arkansas, Missouri, and Oklahoma) have temperatures and rainfall between these two extremes. Although there are hills in the region, their height is not great enough to affect the temperature or rainfall significantly.

The winds blow strong across the plains and prairies of Kansas, Oklahoma, and northern Missouri (remember the 1930s dust bowl). However, the region's modest hills slow the prairie winds as they enter the deciduous forests and pine forests of Missouri, Arkansas, and Louisiana.

NATURAL COMMUNITIES OF THE REGION

Natural communities result from the interaction of a region's geology and climate. The types of plants that can thrive in a given place and the animals that live on the plants and each other are present because the underlying forces of landscape and weather accommodate them.

Unlike political boundaries, there are no sharp edges to nature. Prairies melt into savannahs and savannahs melt into deciduous forest. You may find prairie species in deciduous forest and bottomland hardwood forest species in savannahs. Ecologists recognize dozens of natural communities in the South Central region. Most are named for geographical features: Great Plains, Southeastern Plains, Osage Plains, Northern Glaciated Plains, Gypsum Hills, Ozarks, Arbuckle Mountains, Sandstone Hills, Ouchita Mountains, Wichita Mountains, Mississippi Alluvial Plain, Arkansas Valley, Ouchita Mountains, West Gulf Coastal Plain, East Gulf Coastal Plain, and Big Rivers.

Visualize a large arc inscribed clockwise from the northwest corner of Kansas to the mouth of the Mississippi in Louisiana. This arc will pass through most of the major natural communities in the region as it cuts across the Great Plains of western Kansas, the tallgrass prairies of Kansas, Missouri, and Oklahoma, then the rugged hill country of the Ozarks in Missouri, eastern Oklahoma, Northern Arkansas and the Ouchitas of Arkansas and Oklahoma. At the southern end, the arc passes through the east and west Gulf Coastal Plains of Louisiana.

PLANT COMMUNITIES

Plant life in the South Central region varies from short grasses in the Great Plains to towering bottomland hardwood forests.

Great Plains and the prairies On the High Plains of western Kansas and the panhandle of Oklahoma is the shortgrass prairie, where the characteristic plants— buffalo grass and blue grama grass—are usually less than 3 feet tall. The tallgrass prairie dominates eastern Kansas, northern and western Missouri, and parts of Oklahoma and Arkansas. Big and little bluestem, Indian grass, and switchgrass are the most common grasses. Big bluestem may grow to more than 8 feet tall.

The tallgrass prairie is rich with wildflowers; late spring and early summer are the peak times for color. Purple coneflower and liatris imitate the morning sunrise with their pale purple hues. Black-eyed Susan, gray-headed coneflower, coreopsis, and compass plant mirror the bright yellow of the noonday sun. Butterfly weed and Indian paintbrush flame with the orange and red of a prairie sunset.

Savannah Where tallgrass prairie grades into deciduous forest, the landscape is reminiscent of African savannahs. Post and blackjack oaks dot these savannahs, while tall prairie grasses and forbs grow beneath them to provide a parklike atmosphere.

Forest East and south from the plains and prairies, drier conditions give way to higher rainfall in the Ozarks, Ouchitas, and Arbuckles. Here, deciduous forest becomes the climax natural community. Hickory, walnut, and oaks of all types (36 species include red, white, black, and scarlet) form most of the taller trees. The understory is rich with shorter trees and shrubs sporting showy spring blooms such as redbud, dogwood, shadbush, viburnum, wild plum, and wild cherry. Forest wildflowers must sprout, bloom, be pollinated, and form seeds between the end of winter and appearance of sunlight-blocking leaves on the trees. Therefore, they tend to be small but flourish in sheer numbers and vibrant colors, forming a carpet of white, yellow, purple, green, and blue on the forest floor.

In parts of southern Missouri, Arkansas, Oklahoma, and Louisiana, pine forests are prevalent. Native pines include longleaf and loblolly. Look for them on drier and thinner soils. Cypress and tupelo are the signature trees of permanently flooded portions of bottomland hardwood forests, commonly called swamps. Overcup and pin oaks grow on higher ground and provide mast crops for deer and waterfowl. In bottomland forests, fertile soil and abundant moisture nurture

Indian paintbrush, Wichita Mountains NWR, Oklahoma

many wildflowers. White spider lily, Louisiana blue iris, and copper iris add color to the swamps.

Coastal marsh In the coastal marshes of Louisiana, plant diversity depends on the salinity of the water. Cattails indicate freshwater and spartina indicates brackish waters.

ANIMAL LIFE

Diversity of plants brings an equal diversity of wildlife. The South Central region is a mecca for lepidopterists (butterfly and moth experts). At Sequoyah NWR in Oklahoma monarchs migrate and swallowtails flitter, while in the hardwood forests giant silk moths seek their mates on still, moist nights. Common species include several swallowtails, great spangled fritillary, question mark, comma, and painted lady butterflies. Promethea and luna moths gather around tulip trees in the southern swamps of Louisiana's refuges to lay eggs. Where there are insects, there are bats, and they can be seen at almost any refuge in early evening, making forays for mosquitoes, a favorite food.

Among fish, catfish is king, including common flathead and blue and the prized channel cat. Rivers and lakes feature bass, crappie, redear sunfish, green sunfish,

Raccoon

and bluegill. Many small streams have endemic fish, darters and shiners, and some that are endangered (Topeka shiner). Warmer waters down south host the giant alligator gar (up to 6 feet and over 100 pounds) and the bowfin (also called grinnel and dogfish). The Louisiana coast features speckled trout and redfish.

Abundant in southern sections are amphibians such as tiger, spotted, and marbled salamanders. Bullfrogs, spring peepers, and tree frogs are easily heard if not readily seen. Rare and lesser-known amphibians such as the bird-voiced tree frog and western lesser siren occupy special habitats at Missouri's Mingo NWR.

In southern Arkansas, southeast Oklahoma, or Louisiana refuges, you are sure to see the green anole. The local name for the lizard is chameleon, but its ability to change color is poor compared with the true chameleons of the Old World. Turtles (mud, map, painted, and sliders) seem to bask on every log in some refuges.

Nonpoisonous snakes are plentiful in the warmer portions of the region, and they vary in length, from the tiny 10-inch worm snake to the common 7-foot black rat snake. Their names are a spectrum of colors: scarlet snake, yellow-bellied water snake, blue racer, red-bellied snake, green snake. The shapes and patterns adorning them are equally fanciful: spotted, speckled, blotched, smooth, rough, and banded.

There are poisonous snakes in the region, too. Visitors should take sensible precautions. Cottonmouths live near waters south of the Missouri River; their cousin, the copperhead, slithers in the rolling hills. Timber rattlesnakes (and the southern subspecies, canebrake), pygmy, Massasauga, and western diamond-back rattlers are all present in the region.

But no other animal holds sway over the American alligator. Record length for this antediluvian beast is almost 20 feet. In all Louisiana and southern Arkansas refuges, alligators live wherever there is water: swamps, lakes, bayous, rivers, marshes, and ponds. Watch for them sunning themselves on banks or patrolling their kingdom, with only their eyes and nostrils above water. Visitors should be on the alert when around nests or young. Alligators have made a tremendous comeback from the days when they were hunted almost to extinction. Today they are so plentiful that species management requires a hunting season.

Birdwatchers love the South Central refuges. Migrating ducks and geese gather in spectacular numbers on many bodies of water found on NWRs. Waves of neotropical migrants head northward with the greening of spring. Look for them at Arkansas' White River NWR. Migrating shorebirds feed on insects and aquatic crustaceans in shallow water lakes found in mudflats at Quivira NWR (Kansas) and Great Salt Plains refuge (Oklahoma).

Wading birds (great blue heron, little blue heron, green heron, common, snowy, and cattle egrets) are plentiful. Many refuges provide ideal natural habitat where these colonial nesters form great rookeries to raise their young.

Almost every South Central refuge boasts of visiting bald eagles in winter. Many refuges have nesting eagles that visitors can easily observe from tour roads. Frequently seen raptors include northern harrier, red-tailed hawk, Cooper's and sharp-shinned hawks, and the kestrel.

White-tailed deer are perhaps the most sought-after mammals. Families love to watch deer wander into the fields in the mornings and evenings at Squaw Creek refuge in northwest Missouri. Many refuges offer a chance for deer hunting.

Aquatic mammals—muskrat, nutria, and beaver—are common. Playful river otters are making a comeback but are difficult to see. Opossum and raccoon are ubiquitous.

Bison and elk are the featured animals at Wichita Mountains refuge. Several other NWRs have prairie dog towns. Elusive bobcats roam the southern swamps. The rare Louisiana black bear is making a comeback, and Tensas River and Atachafalaya refuges are crucial to its recovery. And some mammals are new to the region: The nine-banded armadillo, common in Oklahoma, is expanding its range northward.

GETTING UNDER WAY

Like the pieces of a jigsaw puzzle, each refuge in this book is unique, with its own shape, history, resident plants and animals, recreational opportunities, and mission. Each refuge has dedicated professionals working long hours to ensure the preservation of the nation's natural heritage. The refuges in Arkansas, Kansas, Louisiana, Missouri, and Oklahoma interlock with other national wildlife refuges and state, federal, and private lands to provide a bright future for America's wildlife.

Come out to explore. Follow the fall migration of geese south across several refuges. Or trace the spring migration of warblers north from Lacassine to Pond Creek to Mingo. Watch endangered least terns nest at Great Salt Plains and Quivera. Canoe silently through the largest bottomland hardwood forest in America at Atachafalaya. Sound a highball call to lure a flock of mallards into a set of decoys at White River. Camp in the heart of the great prairie of North America and listen to the song dog's yips, yowls, and howls. Ramble through bottomland forest for a close look at delicate wildflowers. Or join the effort, as a volunteer, to develop the newer refuges or to inform visitors about the older ones.

If the biggest challenge we face as a society is learning to meet our demands wisely for natural resources, while ensuring that there will be plentiful resources for future generations, then your participation in the national wildlife system, as visitor or volunteer, will make a good contribution toward that end. Go out and enjoy.

Bald Knob NWR
Augusta, Arkansas

Northern pintails

Four broad paths through the sky serve as routes by which waterfowl migrate from their northern summer homes to their wintering grounds in warmer climates. These routes, from west to east, are known as the Pacific, Central, Mississippi, and Atlantic flyways. Wildlife refuges located along these pathways were established to provide rest, food, and habitat for migrating waterfowl. Bald Knob NWR, located in central Arkansas, is one such stop along the Mississippi Flyway.

HISTORY

This 14,800-acre refuge, which takes its name from the nearby town of Bald Knob, was purchased from the John Hancock Insurance Company in 1994 as a part of the North American Waterfowl Management Plan. This treaty between Canada, the United States, and Mexico determines the overall management of waterfowl that migrate through the three nations.

Bald Knob borders the Little Red River. Originally, the area consisted of extensive tracts of bottomland hardwood forests interspersed with swamps, sloughs, and oxbow lakes. These forested bottomlands and wetlands were a veritable paradise for waterfowl and other wildlife.

During the period between 1950 and 1970, farmers, attracted to the region's rich soil, drained the swamps and converted the bottomland forests to farmland. Today nearly three-fourths of the refuge remain agricultural.

The refuge consists of two units, the smaller Mingo Creek Unit and the larger Farm Unit, a portion of which is designated a waterfowl sanctuary.

GETTING THERE

Bald Knob is located about 60 mi. northeast of Little Rock. From Little Rock take US 67 North, then US 64 East to the town of Bald Knob. At Bald Knob, follow Rte. 367 South through town to Coal Chute Rd., then take Coal Chute Rd. 2 mi. to the refuge.

■ **SEASON:** General refuge: open year-round; waterfowl sanctuary closed mid-Nov. through Feb. Portions of the refuge may be closed at any time due to flooding.
■ **HOURS:** Dawn to dusk.
■ **FEES:** None.
■ **ADDRESS:** Bald Knob NWR, Rte. 2, Box 126-T, Augusta, AR 72006
■ **TELEPHONE:** 501/724-2458

TOURING BALD KNOB

Access to the refuge can be limited and difficult because of poor roads and frequent flooding. Most visitors to the refuge are hunters and fishers, equipped to deal with these difficult problems. ATVs may be used on existing trails and provide the only access other than by foot to the Mingo and much of the Farm Unit.

WHAT TO SEE

Bald Knob lies in the shadow of the Ozark Mountains at the edge of the great Mississippi Alluvial Plain. The terrain is generally flat. The Little Red River borders the refuge to the south and east. Overflow Creek meanders through the center of the refuge.

The climate at Bald Knob is generally mild, with warm to hot summers and cool winters. March to May is the rainy period.

It is along the banks of the creek and river that Bald Knob's tracts of bottomland forest lie. The rest of the refuge is agricultural fields. Fortunately, reforestation programs are under way to restore 4,000 acres of croplands to native trees, among them oaks, bald cypress, gum, and pecan.

As part of a cooperative waterfowl management program, local farmers plant rice, milo, millet, and other crops in refuge fields. The farmers leave a portion of the crops in the fields for waterfowl and harvest the remainder.

In the fall these fields and the shallow waters of the waterfowl sanctuary attract large flocks of waterfowl and other birds. Three species of geese—blue and snow, white-fronted, and Canada—winter at the refuge. Dabbling ducks are also plentiful. Northern pintail are especially attracted to Bald Knob, and the refuge boasts the largest wintering population in Arkansas. As many as 20 bald eagles and a few peregrine falcons, both endangered, also use the refuge during the winter months.

During spring and fall migration the shallow waters of the waterfowl sanctuary team with shorebirds and waders, among them long-legged herons and egrets. Summer residents include common yellowthroats, eastern bluebirds, white-eyed vireos, and brightly colored prothonotary warblers.

In addition to the varied birdlife, visitors are sure to see white-tailed deer and raccoons throughout the year and perhaps a glimpse of a bobcat, otter, or beaver. There is also a good diversity of reptiles, amphibians, and invertebrates.

ACTIVITIES

Although access to the refuge is limited, outdoor enthusiasts with ATVs or those prepared to bushwhack will find many opportunities to observe and photograph wildlife. It's a significant wintering area for mallards, so duck hunting can be excellent. So can hunting for deer, squirrel, rabbit, quail, and raccoon. In addition, there are limited opportunities to fish for bass, catfish, crappie, and bream.
■ **PUBLICATIONS:** Refuge brochure with map; refuge hunting and fishing regulations.

Big Lake NWR
Manila, Arkansas

Big Lake wetlands

It is a clear sunrise on a winter morning at Big Lake NWR. The sky is a shimmering pink hue, the kind of sky that portends an approaching cold front. The Canada geese that roosted the night before on a huge lake in the center of the refuge seem uneasy, perhaps sensing the coming cold. They make nervous little jerking motions, almost taking flight several times. The "goose talk" is constant. Finally, a few geese rise off the water. Others soon follow, forming wavy lines and classic V-formations across the morning sky. The geese head to distant grain fields to feed and store up energy for the cold weather ahead.

Left behind are an assortment of diving ducks, including a large flock of canvasbacks. These big, handsome ducks were once common in the area but became scarce as nesting and feeding grounds declined. Now rebuilding their numbers, they continue diving, oblivious to the coming front and the goings of the geese.

HISTORY

The serenity of the scene today belies the turbulent origins of this 11,038-acre refuge in northeastern Arkansas. Long forgotten is that terrible Sunday night, December 15, 1811, when the first of a series of earthquakes shook the entire Mississippi Alluvial Plain, causing land to drop and basins and lakes to form (see Regional Overview). Before the quakes, the Little River meandered freely here through great expanses of bottomland hardwood forest, and early pioneers hunted the plentiful game that thrived in this environment.

In the late 1800s, the region experienced new changes. Loggers seeking ties for the nation's developing railway system cleared the area of most of its trees. Later, farmers drained the land and converted the rich bottomland to cotton fields. Waterfowl and other wildlife began to disappear.

In 1915, in response to concerns over the rapid loss of habitat and wildlife, President Woodrow Wilson, by executive order, made Big Lake and surrounding lands a preserve. Acquisition of additional tracts brought the refuge to its present size.

Because of its importance as a stopover for migrating and wintering waterfowl and neotropical birds, a 5,000-acre tract, essentially the northern half of the refuge, was designated a National Natural Landmark in 1974, with 2,100 of those acres added to the Wilderness Preservation System in 1976.

GETTING THERE

The refuge is located on AR 18, approximately 15 mi. west of Blytheville and 30 mi. east of Jonesboro. From the south, take AR 77 North to AR 18 and turn east to the refuge. Or take US 55 North to Rte.140 West, then go north on Rte. 181 to AR 18 West.

■ **SEASON:** General refuge open year-round except periodically when flooded. Lake closed from late Oct. to early March.

■ **HOURS:** Refuge: dawn to dusk. Office: weekdays, 7 a.m.–3:30 p.m.

■ **FEES:** None.

■ **ADDRESS:** Big Lake NWR, P.O. Box 76, Manila, AR 72442

■ **TELEPHONE:** 870/564-2429

TOURING BIG LAKE

■ **BY AUTOMOBILE:** Two gravel roads run atop the levees that skirt the refuge. The first 3.5 miles of the west side road is an auto drive that leads to the Timm's Point Observation Area. The drive is closed to automobiles beyond this point.

■ **BY FOOT:** There are no established hiking trails, but you can walk anywhere within the refuge. If you plan to get off the road, wear boots and use insect repellent.

■ **BY BICYCLE:** Biking is permitted but may be tough going on the refuge gravel roads.

■ **BY CANOE, KAYAK, OR BOAT:** In spring as much as 99 percent of the refuge can be under water, so you'll need a canoe or flat-bottomed johnboat to get around. There are two concrete boat launch areas. To get to the wilderness area in the northeast sector of the refuge, boat up the Little River.

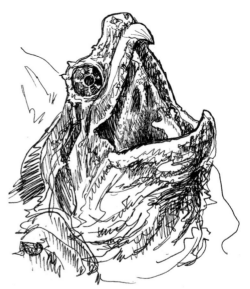

WHAT TO SEE

■ **LANDSCAPE AND CLIMATE** Big Lake occupies most of the southern half of this large refuge. It is an amoeba-shaped body of water with numerous fingers and waterways that twist and turn, creating many islands and fingerlike peninsulas. The northern half of the refuge consists mainly of bottomland hardwood forests.

Alligator snapping turtle

American lotus grows in Big Lake NWR.

The Little River flows through the center of this forested section into Big Lake. Between the river and the eastern boundary is the wilderness area.

Several large flood-control ditches were built to funnel water through the refuge from the surrounding farmland. This caused sedimentation and pollution problems. Ditch 81, on the west side of the refuge, was constructed to divert some of the floodwaters around the refuge and correct the problems.

The climate is mild with warm to hot summers and cool winters. March to May is the rainy period, when flooding is typical.

■ PLANT LIFE

Forests Bottomland hardwoods grow on the slightly elevated, less swampy areas of the refuge. Typical species include swamp cottonwood, sycamore, red maple, and several varieties of oak (see sidebar).

Croplands A small area (only about 30 acres) at the south end of the refuge is planted annually in corn, milo, soybeans, and cowpeas as supplemental food for waterfowl.

Wetlands Most of the refuge is swamp. In the lowest-lying areas, stands of black willow and buttonbush, an aquatic shrub, grow in the shady muck and water beneath towering bald cypress and water tupelo (see sidebar). Pondweed, duckweed, and wigeon grass grow in the water beneath the trees, and smartweed flourishes in the more open areas.

Open waters Open water, most of which is Big Lake itself, accounts for 2,000 acres of the refuge. Big Lake is shallow, with an average depth of only 3 feet. It is populated with a variety of aquatic plants, including sago and pondweed.

■ ANIMAL LIFE

Birds In winter the refuge provides habitat for many species of migratory waterfowl, peaking usually in December and January. Ducks are most profuse, averaging 70,000 a season, and include teal, northern pintail, northern shoveler, wigeon, ring-necked, lesser scaup, and the cocky ruddy duck with upright tail and bright blue bill. Large numbers of Canada geese also collect here to feed and roost.

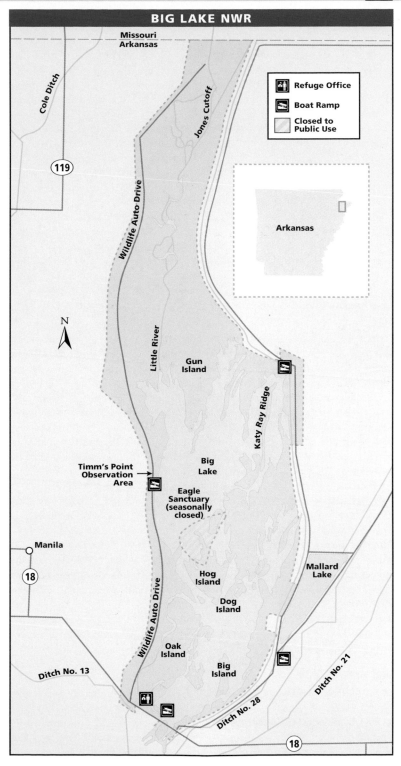

WHAT'S THAT TREE? Big Lake is a good place to hone your skills at tree identification through the seasons. Take, for example, the red maple, often found in bottomland forests. This well-named tree is easy to identify in all seasons. Just think red: In winter the buds are red, swelling to a brilliant scarlet by winter's end. Flowers too are generally red. In summer leafstalks are red, while in autumn the foliage turns predictably crimson or burgundy.

Its spreading branches and dark trunk make the black willow easy to recognize in winter. In summer it's the only willow whose narrow leaves are uniformly green on both sides. What gives the sycamore away is its smooth but constantly peeling, mottled-colored bark that exposes muted patches of brown, green, and gray. The bark of the short-lived swamp cottonwood is characterized by deep furrows and in spring its cottony seeds are easily recognized. The majestic bald cypress can be distinguished by its feathery needles, fibrous reddish-brown bark, and, in deep water, knobby "knees," that penetrate the water's surface. The peculiar growths aid in transpiration. The tupelo, sometimes called sour gum, is recognized by its swollen base and long, straight trunk. It is unique in the tree world because it begins to decay from the top down at an early age, making it the only tree that gets shorter as it gets older!

In spring and fall a colorful array of songbirds and a number of warblers pass through the refuge. Bachman's warbler, a small yellow bird with a black bib, is probably extinct, but breeding populations may have persisted in the area into the 1940s. Local Audubon chapters make several field trips each spring to Big Lake in hopes of spotting the warbler.

Bald eagles and ospreys nest on the refuge as well as a number of hawks. Common resident species include pileated woodpeckers, barred and screech owls, great blue herons, killdeer, dickcissels, indigo buntings, prothonotary warblers, summer tanagers, hooded mergansers, and wood ducks. The wood ducks produce as many as 2,500 hatchlings a year. In all, birders have recorded 227 species of birds at the refuge.

Mammals It is not surprising that an abundance of beavers and muskrat call this watery habitat home. White-tailed deer, squirrels, river otters, nine-banded armadillos, and rabbits are also common, and bobcats are seen occasionally.

Reptiles and amphibians Among the reptiles found in and around the lake are a variety of snakes, including the eastern cottonmouth. Turtles are common and include the alligator snapping turtle, a behemoth reptile (the record weight is more than 200 pounds) with a unique wormlike appendage attached to its tongue that it uses to lure unsuspecting fish into its jaws.

Invertebrates Among the wide variety of insects and other invertebrates living in the refuge are dragonflies, damselflies, mayflies, and stoneflies—all of which are terrestrial as adult insects but have totally aquatic larvae.

ACTIVITIES

■ **CAMPING AND SWIMMING:** Camping and swimming are not allowed on the refuge.

■ **WILDLIFE OBSERVATION:** Good places to observe wildlife include Timm's Point, Bright's Landing, the viewing platform off Rte. 305, and the roads to each of these spots. If you have a spotting scope, from Timm's Point look to the east and a

Wetlands swamp

little south for an eagle's nest at the far tree line about a half mile away. Also watch for turkeys along the auto-tour road and herons and egrets feeding in the swampy fields.

With a boat you can explore the hidden backwaters of the refuge where, if you move slowly and quietly, you may find all kinds of wildlife.

■ **PHOTOGRAPHY:** From Timm's Point photographers can capture scenics and photographs of waterfowl coming in to roost for the evening or, with luck, an osprey or eagle diving for fish.

■ **HIKES AND WALKS:** Stop at the first parking area on the auto tour and walk the muddy road a short distance for a landlubber's view of cypress swamp. Walk quietly and you may surprise a raccoon foraging at the water's edge.

■ **SEASONAL EVENTS:** None.

■ **PUBLICATIONS:** Refuge brochure with map; refuge hunting and fishing regulations.

HUNTING AND FISHING Hunting on Big Lake is a management tool that provides wildlife population data. Hunting for **squirrel** is allowed from the state's fall season through Oct. **Raccoon** may be hunted the last half of Oct. **Deer** hunting (archery) is allowed from Nov. through Dec. **Rabbit** may be hunted mid-Sept. through Oct., while **coyote** and **beaver** may be taken during any refuge hunt with appropriate hunting device.

Fishing (**bass, catfish, crappie** and **sunfish**) permitted, March through Oct. **Frogging** permitted, mid-April through Oct.

Cache River NWR
Augusta, Arkansas

Male mallard

Watching mallards on the slow-moving Cache River is not unlike witnessing a three-ring circus. In ring number one, groups of mallards scurry about, quacking, chuckling and otherwise engaging in "duck talk"; in ring number two, they chase each other as one tries to steal a food morsel from another; in ring number three, the ducks act like clowns "tipping-up" their backsides as they plunge heads under water to search for food. Behind the scenes, tremendous efforts have gone into ensuring a safe habitat for these engaging creatures.

HISTORY

Cache River NWR, which stretches some 100 river miles along the Cache River basin in eastern Arkansas, was established in 1986 to protect significant wetland habitats and provide feeding and resting areas for migratory waterfowl. It comprises some of the largest remaining tracts of bottomland hardwood forest in the Mississippi Alluvial Plain and is an especially critical area for mallards. Up to 10 percent of the 3.5 million mallards that use the Mississippi Flyway each year winter in Cache River.

In 1989 Cache River, along with adjoining White River NWR, was designated a "Wetland of International Importance" by the Ramsar Convention, a meeting of international scientists who gather periodically in Ramsar, Iran, to identify critical wetlands throughout the world and work toward their protection.

GETTING THERE

The office is located at Dixie on AR 33 approximately 16 mi. south of Augusta. Access to the refuge is limited, but gravel and dirt side roads from Rtes. 17, 33, 37, and 38 provide some access. Contact the office for a current map and road conditions.

■ **SEASON:** General refuge open year-round, however, areas in the lower half are classified as waterfowl sanctuaries and are closed from mid-Nov. through Feb.

- **HOURS:** Refuge: sunrise to sunset. Refuge office: 7:30 a.m.–4 p.m. weekdays.
- **FEES:** None.
- **ADDRESS:** Cache River NWR, Rte. 2, Box 126-T, Augusta, AR 72006
- **TELEPHONE:** 870/347-2614

TOURING CACHE RIVER

Touring Cache River can be difficult. It has no main roads, no campsites, few facilities, few access points, and no trails. In addition, large parts of the refuge are subject to flooding, and some areas can be reached only by crossing private lands. Always check with landowners and obtain permission before attempting to cross these lands. The easiest way to visit this beautiful refuge is by boat. Visitors can paddle the entire length of the Cache River.

WHAT TO SEE

The refuge is not one tract of land but a string of tracts within the floodplain of the Cache River from its confluence with the White and Bayou DeView rivers. Currently the refuge includes some 45,000 acres, but its boundary is ever-changing as land acquisitions along the meandering Cache, White, and Bayou DeView rivers continue.

As one of the few remaining areas in the lower Mississippi River Valley not drastically altered by channelization and drainage, the Cache River basin remains a wild place, offering visitors a glimpse of what the entire region must have looked like prior to settlement. It includes 32,300 acres of stunning bottomland forests, cypress-tupelo swamps, and associated sloughs and oxbow lakes plus 4,500 acres of cropland and 5,200 acres of reforested land. Reforestation is a high priority as managers work to relink remaining but fragmented forests and improve habitat by planting hardwood trees that once covered the land—native oaks, bald cypress, gum, and pecan.

The climate in this part of Arkansas can be hot and humid in the summer, and winter temperatures can be below freezing.

Although the refuge is best known as wintering grounds for tens of thousands of mallards, many other wildlife species make Cache River their home for all or part of the year. Year-round residents include an abundance of mammals—white-tailed deer, coyotes, beaver, bobcat, river otters, muskrat, nutria, armadillo, squirrel, rabbit, opossum, and a few black bears. Wild turkeys, doves, and quail are also full-timers.

The cypress-tupelo swamps provide good habitat for reptiles and amphibians. Turtles here include smooth and spiny softshells, snapping turtles, and western chicken turtles. Southern leopard frogs and bullfrogs, the largest frog in America, lounge at the water's edge.

During spring and fall migrations huge flocks of neotropical migrants, wading birds, snipe, and woodcock come to the refuge seeking food and shelter. The legendary flocks of mallards arrive in the fall along with other waterfowl and are followed by majestic bald eagles.

ACTIVITIES

Although access to the Cache River NWR is limited, the outdoor enthusiast willing to make the effort can find many opportunities to hike, canoe, hunt, fish, or photograph and observe wildlife.

- **PUBLICATIONS:** Refuge brochure with map; refuge hunting and fishing regulations.

Felsenthal NWR
Crossett, Arkansas

View from Felsenthal Dam

Throughout the day and night, wildlife of one kind or another is active in the Felsenthal NWR bottomland forest. But it is at dusk when the forest seems most alive. On an early summer evening, the air is warm and still. The damp, water-soaked soil and vegetation in the magnificent forest give off a rich, earthy smell. Beneath a canopy of tall oaks and water hickories, darkness comes early. Diurnal creatures seek a safe and comfortable place to sleep, while nocturnal creatures begin to stir. The night resonates with the sounds of their stirrings.

In refuge ponds, spring peepers trill. Bullfrogs, leopard frogs, and green frogs add their distinctive voices to the swamp choir. Birds of the night begin their haunting calls. The eight-note cry of the barred owl sounds like "*who cooks for you, who cooks for you-alllll.*" A bat, difficult to identify in the failing light, breaks through the leafy canopy, twisting and turning in an acrobatic pursuit of mosquitoes and other insects. A raccoon leaves its den and ambles along the sodden forest floor looking for acorns and grubs.

HISTORY

Felsenthal is a huge, wild, watery place in the Mississippi Delta region of southeast Arkansas. Some 8 miles wide and 13 miles long, this 65,000-acre refuge contains huge tracts of bottomland hardwoods and smaller tracts of pine and oak on the higher ridges.

The refuge was established in 1975 to provide habitat for migratory waterfowl and other wildlife and to protect a rich cultural history. Archaeologists have found significant and well-preserved artifacts from excavated sites left behind by Caddo Indians who hunted, fished, and trapped the area some 5,000 years ago. Seasonal fishing camps, temple mounds with ceremonial plazas, and villages with up to 200 structures have been uncovered.

The Felsenthal staff also manages three other wildlife refuges in southern

Arkansas—Overflow, Pond Creek, and the Oakwood Unit. The latter is not open to the public.

GETTING THERE

The main entrance is located on US 82 about 5 mi. west of Crossett and 45 mi. east of El Dorado.

■ **SEASON:** Refuge: open year-round, but some of the more sensitive waterfowl areas are closed from mid-Nov. to late Jan.

■ **HOURS:** General refuge: open dawn to dusk. Visitor Center open weekdays, 7 a.m.–3:30 p.m. and Sun., 1–5 p.m.

■ **FEES:** None.

■ **ADDRESS:** Felsenthal NWR, P.O. Box 1157, Crossett, AR 71635

■ **TELEPHONE:** 870/364-3167

■ **VISITOR CENTER:** A diorama depicts several of Felsenthal's important plant and animal communities. A cutaway of a tree enables you to see inside a wood-pecker's nest. Press a button and an archaeologist comes to life to explain Felsen-thal's prehistoric and more recent Indian history.

TOURING FELSENTHAL

■ **BY AUTOMOBILE:** There are more roads in the refuge than can be explored in one day, including 15 miles of gravel roads open to cars and 65 miles of unim-proved trails open seasonally to high-flotation ATVs. Use of some trails in the more remote parts of the refuge is restricted to wildlife-related activities such as hunting. A few roads may be gated because of flooding or to protect wildlife.

Two roads near the Visitor Center are suitable for touring. The 5.7-mile Pine Island Road winds through pines and hardwoods and ends at a boat ramp. Shallow Lake Road leads 3.8 miles to a boat launch and a primitive campground on the west side of the refuge.

■ **BY FOOT:** Many miles of unimproved roads, gated roads closed to vehicles, and ATV trails may be hiked throughout the year. In addition, there are two des-ignated hiking trails; one is handicapped-accessible.

■ **BY BICYCLE:** Bicycling is permitted on most of the roads open to cars.

■ **BY CANOE, KAYAK, OR BOAT:** The ideal way to visit this refuge is by boat. Shallow-draft boats, especially canoes, kayaks, and small johnboats, will carry you through the quiet backwaters. Larger boats with motors are better suited to Felsenthal Pool and the Ouchita River. Twelve boat ramps provide access to these waterways.

WHAT TO SEE

■ **LANDSCAPE AND CLIMATE** The refuge lies within the Felsenthal Basin, the remnant of an enormous lake that once extended south into Louisiana. The edges of the basin rise to pine- and hardwood-covered uplands and open fields. Throughout the low-lying areas a meandering, amoeboid system of rivers, creeks, sloughs, swamps, and shallow lakes cuts through large tracts of bottomland hard-wood forests.

At the center of the refuge where the Saline and Oauchita rivers meet is a large cypress swamp, most of which is designated as a waterfowl sanctuary during November through January each year. At the southern end lies Felsenthal Pool, actually a seasonally flooded forested region whose water levels can be manipu-lated by refuge staff. In the winter the pool can expand to 36,000 acres, making it the world's largest greentree reservoir. During the dry summer months the reser-

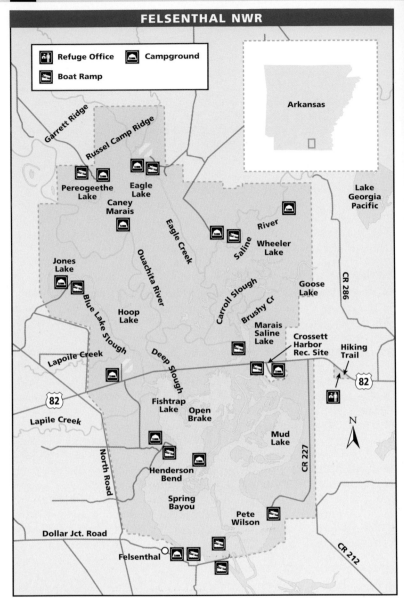

FELSENTHAL NWR

voir covers about 15,000 acres. The periodic flooding creates an excellent habitat for waterfowl in winter.

Felsenthal has a humid subtropical climate. Average rainfall is more than 58 inches. December and January are usually the wettest months. Temperatures are moderate for most of the year, although temperatures can exceed 100 in July and drop into the teens in January. Delightful autumn weather begins in September and often continues into December. Springs are long and pleasant.

■ PLANT LIFE

Forests Bottomland hardwoods comprise 40,000 acres with pine and upland hardwoods making up 10,000 acres. Oaks are the dominant trees in the bottom-lands and are interspersed with moss-draped cypress, tupelo, hickories, and other water-tolerant trees. Buttonbush, never more than 6 feet tall, grows thick and dense in wet or flooded areas and provides excellent habitat for common yellowthroats and other water-loving birds.

Loblolly and shortleaf pines dominate the upland forests. Here a smattering of hardwoods add seasonal color, from the white blooms of the flowering dogwood in the spring to the burgundy-crimson foliage of the red maple and sweet gum in the fall. The loblolly can be huge, with trunks up to 5 feet in diameter and 80 to 100 feet tall. The bark consists of broad, flat, bright reddish-brown plates; the needles are pale green. This tree has also been called rosemary, probably due to the rosemary-like aroma of its resinous boughs and foliage.

The bluish shortleaf pine is protected by a thick bark of large, irregular, rosy-orange plates. These pines grow tall and straight. In forests, where competition for light is fierce, the tree usually develops only a thin crown. When the tree grows in uncrowded conditions, it develops fuller foliage. Because of its straight, easy-to-saw trunk, the tree has always been popular at the sawmill.

Open waters There is a total of 15,000 acres of open water in the refuge, some covered with American lotus. This plant has a large, pale-yellow flower that may be as much as 8 inches in diameter. Its large bowl-shaped leaves (1 to 2 feet in diameter) rise a foot or two above the water and provide shade and protection for aquatic life. Watch for baby wood ducks as they swim beneath the leaves.

■ ANIMAL LIFE

Birds During spring and fall, myriad migratory songbirds stop briefly at the refuge to feed before finishing their long journeys south. For other birds, such as northern parula, prothonotary warbler, and the American redstart, Felsenthal is the end of the journey and serves as a summer home.

Waterfowl begin arriving in September, with 20 species wintering here. Mallards are the most common species, but blue-winged teal, black duck, gadwall,

Bottomland hardwood forest in winter

Red-cockaded woodpecker

and ring-necked duck also winter over. Bald eagles commonly follow the water-fowl to the refuge in winter.

Great blue herons and great, snowy, and cattle egrets nest on the refuge. So do the yellow-crowned and black-crowned night-herons. Both species of night-herons are stockier than their wading bird cousins. The black-crowned prefers to roost in small groups in brushy areas and small trees, while the yellow-crowned is something of a loner. Watch for these birds as they leave their roost to feed as darkness approaches.

The refuge also supports an abundance of year-round residents. Wood ducks, once on the verge of extinction largely due to loss of nesting trees, find plenty of tree cavities for nesting in the flooded hardwood forests here, and endangered red-cockaded woodpeckers nest in pine forests (see sidebar). Many wading birds, raptors, bobwhite quail, wild turkeys, and mourning doves are seen in all seasons.

The chuck-will's-widow (southern relative of the whip-poor-will) is a summer resident (meaning it nests on the refuge). As evening approaches it begins its nightly chant. Listening carefully, you count as the bird says its name over and over and over. *"Chuck-wills-widow"*—52, *"Chuck-wills-widow"*—53, *"Chuck-wills-*

RED-COCKADED WOODPECKER Felsenthal has the highest known concentration in Arkansas of the endangered red-cockaded woodpecker, a small bird with a black-and-white barred back and white cheek patches. The male sports a small red tuft on its head.

These birds nest in colonies, often in grassy parklike stands of mature pines. If you are lucky enough to spot one bird, you have a good chance to see several. At Felsenthal it's easy to identify trees with nests because the refuge staff marks them with white bands.

The red-cockaded woodpecker has an unusual way of protecting its nest from snakes and other predators. Instead of digging a cavity in dead trees like most woodpeckers do, it chooses living pines. As the woodpecker drills, sap oozes from the fresh wound forming a thick gooey substance around the nest entrance. This sap is irritating to would-be predators (think how turpentine, made from pine sap, can irritate your hands). Unfortunately, the sap is no deterrent to flying squirrels who can "fly" directly through the entrance unscathed and often take over the woodpecker cavities during nesting season or bad weather.

widow"—54, and on and on it goes. The calls come so fast that it does not seem that the bird will get its breath.

According to the official refuge check list, 228 species of birds have been seen on or near the refuge.

Mammals Felsenthal waters are filled with aquatic plants and creatures that attract raccoons, river otter, mink, and beaver. Other mammals you might chance upon here are skunks, rabbits, raccoons, gray and fox squirrels, opossum, gray and red foxes, coyotes, and white-tailed deer. The upland regions are home to secretive bobcats and black bears.

The propensity of the large beaver population to fell trees and build dams sends shudders through refuge managers. With no significant predators and a high reproductive rate, the beaver population is increasing. As it does, it threatens to destroy or alter thousands of acres of valuable bottomland forests. Managers have initiated a massive beaver control effort to protect the bottomland hardwoods.

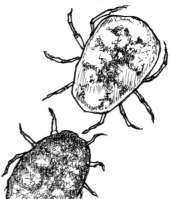

Reptiles and amphibians A variety of snakes, turtles, lizards, frogs, and salamanders finds their niche in the diverse habitats of Felsenthal. Biologists estimate that approximately 100

The Felsenthal wetlands attract ticks in summer.

American alligators also live at Felsenthal, which is on the northern edge of the large reptile's range. Since alligators prefer brushy, weedy, out-of-the-way areas, it is possible that their actual number is higher.

Invertebrates Periodic flooding encourages a proliferation of insects, crustaceans, and mollusks. Crayfish, an important food for many wetland creatures, are abundant in refuge waters and particularly favored by night-herons, whose thick bills can easily crush the mudbugs.

FELSENTHAL HUNTING AND FISHING SEASONS

Hunting
(Seasons may vary)

	Jan	Feb	Mar	Apr	May	Jun	Jul	Aug	Sep	Oct	Nov	Dec
deer (modern gun)	▫	▫	▫	▫	▫	▫	▫	▫	▫	▫	■	▫
deer (muzzle-loader)	▫	▫	▫	▫	▫	▫	▫	▫	▫	■	▫	▫
deer (bow)	■	▫	▫	▫	▫	▫	▫	▫	▫	■	■	■
quail	■	▫	▫	▫	▫	▫	▫	▫	▫	▫	■	■
rabbit	■	▫	▫	▫	▫	▫	▫	▫	▫	■	■	■
squirrel	■	▫	▫	▫	▫	▫	▫	▫	■	■	■	■
raccoon	■	▫	▫	▫	▫	▫	▫	▫	▫	■	■	■
oppossum	■	▫	▫	▫	▫	▫	▫	▫	▫	■	■	■
duck	▫	▫	▫	▫	▫	▫	▫	▫	▫	▫	■	■
goose	▫	▫	▫	▫	▫	▫	▫	▫	▫	▫	■	■
coot	■	▫	▫	▫	▫	▫	▫	▫	▫	■	■	■
beaver	■	■	■	■	■	■	■	■	■	■	■	■
nutria	■	■	■	■	■	■	■	■	■	■	■	■
coyote	■	■	■	■	■	■	■	■	■	■	■	■
feral hog	■	■	■	■	■	■	■	■	■	■	■	■

Fishing

	Jan	Feb	Mar	Apr	May	Jun	Jul	Aug	Sep	Oct	Nov	Dec
largemouth bass	■	■	■	■	■	■	■	■	■	■	■	■
crappie	■	■	■	■	■	■	■	■	■	■	■	■
bluegill	■	■	■	■	■	■	■	■	■	■	■	■
catfish	■	■	■	■	■	■	■	■	■	■	■	■

Duck, goose, and coot hunting is usually permitted, Nov. through Dec., except during deer hunts. Woodcock season is set each year by the Federal government. The trapping of furbearers is allowed mid-Nov. through Jan. Beavers, nutria, coyote, free-roaming hogs may be taken during any daytime season with appropriate hunting device. Please check with the refuge for specific dates for the hunting seasons shown above.

Fishing is permitted in most refuge waters year-round. The mobility-impaired may fish for channel catfish in the half-acre woodland pond behind the office/Visitor Center. Frogging is permitted from May through Dec.

Unfortunately, during the warm summer months, Felsenthal, like most wetlands, is also an ideal habitat for pesky ticks, chiggers, and mosquitoes. To help prevent tick bites, keep your pants legs tucked into your shoes and wear light-colored pants so that dark-colored ticks will show up and can be removed before they attach themselves. Many people prefer to wear rubber boots— although hot in the summer, they do help keep out ticks.

ACTIVITIES

■ **CAMPING:** Ten primitive camping areas (no facilities) are dispersed throughout the refuge. Two campgrounds with full facilities are nearby: Crossett Harbor RV Park on Route 82 and Grand Marais Campground in Felsenthal.

■ **WILDLIFE OBSERVATION AND PHOTOGRAPHY:** Several good areas to spot and photograph waterfowl include the Felsenthal Dam, anywhere along Route 82, the two hiking trails, and the boat launch area at Pine Island. Staff-led

The beaver at work

day-long field trips provide opportunities to see and photograph red-cockaded woodpeckers (see sidebar).

■ **HIKES AND WALKS:** Walking the 1-mile trail at the Visitor Center is a good introduction to the refuge. The trail identifies the major trees found here and gives interesting information about them. One particularly curious tree, the Hercules' club, is covered with scary-looking spiky projections. Its menacing-looking bark was used in earlier days as an aspirinlike painkiller. The first half of the trail is handicapped-accessible.

Sand Prairie Trail begins at the south end of Crossett Harbor RV Park and makes 1- and 3-mile loops mostly through upland forests. Periwinkle and Mallard trails, part of the Sand Prairie Trail system, are color-coded, well-marked, and easy to follow. Along the way, signs provide interpretive information. A variety of vociferous birds are your constant companions here. Little blue herons perched in trees keep a beady eye out for movement in a small pond. Redheaded woodpeckers drill holes in dead trees farther down the trail. (The trail is closed during refuge quota deer hunts and is sometimes flooded, so check at the Visitor Center before using.)

A spring walk down any forest road will be accompanied by birdsong from all directions. The rapid trill of the pine warbler is one song that can be heard almost any time of the year. Look for this olive-gold songster in pine trees anywhere from the ground to the treetops as it searches for insects.

■ **SEASONAL EVENTS:** May: Birding and Native Plant Event; May: Mayhaw picking.

■ **PUBLICATIONS:** Refuge brochure with map; refuge hunting and fishing regulations; bird list; Sand Prairie Trail guide.

Holla Bend NWR
Dardanelle, Arkansas

The grassy floodplains of Holla Bend NWR attract migratory waterfowl.

After the first frosts of winter, the grasses in north-central Arkansas become dormant and brown; once-scarlet leaves fall, and bottomland hardwood forests are left stark and barren against the scudding winter sky. It is not an easy season. Still, for many, the cold months provide an opportunity to get outdoors and explore and discover the wintry world. There are no leaves to hide resident birds, no tall grass to conceal the coyote. It is a time when nature invites you into her home saying, "Look at me. See what I am up to."

At Holla Bend NWR nature is up to quite a bit. Between November and March large flocks of Canada geese and snow geese come to the refuge, announcing their arrival with furious honking. With them come ducks, herons, and egrets. Following close behind are gulls, bald eagles, hawks, and pelicans. At Holla Bend, all find a welcoming environment.

HISTORY

On its path to meet the great Mississippi River, the Arkansas River cuts across a broad, rolling valley between the Ozark Plateau and the Ouachita Mountains. At Holla Bend, where the river once made a tremendous sweeping curve, more than 65 families farmed the land. But rivers have a habit of flooding. In 1927 a particularly disastrous flood swept over the region and buried the fertile farmlands under deep layers of sand. No longer able to make a living, the farmers moved out.

In 1954, to control flooding and improve navigation, the U.S. Army Corps of Engineers straightened the Arkansas River, bypassing Holla Bend and creating an artificial oxbow lake. In 1957, at the urging of local sportsmen and conservationists, the Corps transferred this 7,055-acre area to the Department of the Interior to be managed as a refuge for migrating and wintering waterfowl.

The staff at Holla Bend NWR also manages Logan Cave NWR in northwest Arkansas. It is not open to the public.

GETTING THERE

Holla Bend is located about 10 mi. southeast of Russellville. From Russellville, take AR 7 South through Dardanelle, then Rte. 155 East 6 mi. to the refuge.

■ **SEASON:** Open year-round except on occasion when closed due to flooding.
■ **HOURS:** Refuge: opens at daylight and usually closes at dusk. (Hours are posted at the entrance gate.) Office open weekdays, 7 a.m.–3:30 p.m., except on holidays.
■ **FEES:** Entrance fee $4 per car.
■ **ADDRESS:** Holla Bend NWR, Rte. 1, Box 59, Dardanelle, AR 72834
■ **TELEPHONE:** 501/229-4300

TOURING HOLLA BEND

■ **BY AUTOMOBILE:** About 10 miles of flat secondary roads wind through the refuge. An interpretive auto tour follows the Arkansas River, then cuts across farm fields and bottomland hardwood forests before completing an 8-mile loop. (No ATVs are allowed.)
■ **BY FOOT:** Four trails, basically mowed paths through the grass, branch off the main roads and provide access to remoter areas of the refuge. An observation tower overlooks the old river channel to the east and fields to the west.
■ **BY BICYCLE:** Biking is allowed on the auto tour, other dirt roads, and grassy trails.
■ **BY CANOE, KAYAK, OR BOAT:** Boating is permitted on refuge ponds and lakes from mid-March through October. Two concrete boat ramps provide access to the old river channel and Lodge Lake. There are no boat ramps to the Arkansas River. Boaters must enter the Arkansas River at Dardanelle.

WHAT TO SEE

■ **LANDSCAPE AND CLIMATE** When the Corps rerouted the Arkansas River, it cut off a 6-mile meander loop. The old loop and the bottomland inside it are now Holla Bend NWR. The Arkansas River forms the northern border of the refuge. A levee parallels the Arkansas and protects bottomlands from flooding. The old river channel, on the south and east sides, has filled with water, creating a ribbon of swampy, shallow lakes and ponds. The low-lying center remains largely agricultural with a few natural lakes and ponds, mudflats, and remnants of bottomland forest. In the distance, forming a picturesque backdrop, are Mt. Nebo, Petti Jean, and White Oak mountains.

The climate is generally mild. South winds prevent severe winters. Temperatures occasionally drop below zero degrees, but only for short times. Spring and fall are long and pleasant. July and August can be very hot and humid. The average annual precipitation is 54 inches.

■ **PLANT LIFE**
Forests Bottomland forests of black willow, water oak, and

Southern flying squirrel

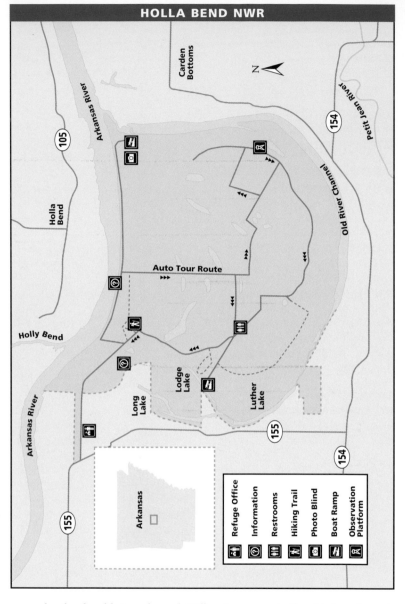

HOLLA BEND NWR

pecan border the old river channel. Willow trees grow in the old river channel, providing observation towers for belted kingfishers as they watch the water below for small fish. Eastern red cedars, called junipers locally, grow in dense rows atop several old levees that cross the refuge.

Croplands Local farmers are contracted to plant soybeans, milo, corn, and winter wheat in the many farm fields. They harvest the soybeans and milo and leave the corn and wheat in the fields for use by waterfowl, deer, turkey, and quail.

Open water During the summer, the field ponds are either drained or dry up naturally. This allows the growth of plants whose seeds are important food for waterfowl. Refuge staff may also plant millet, another good seed-producing plant,

Painted bunting

when the growth of natural plants is not adequate. In the winter, these areas are flooded from rains or by irrigation.

■ ANIMAL LIFE

Birds Birding can be interesting at Holla Bend because, along with the common eastern species, some unusual western species are found here. Golden eagle, prairie falcon, greater roadrunner, western meadowlark, and Harris' sparrow are all species that are more commonly found to the west of Holla Bend.

Waterfowl, however, is the main refuge attraction. Both Canada and snow geese are abundant in winter, as are mallards. Northern pintail, blue- and green-winged teal, and gadwall also flock to the refuge.

In summer brushy areas with scattered trees are home to nesting painted buntings, arguably the most colorful bird in North America, with blue head, red belly, and greenish-yellow back. Scissor-tailed flycatchers hunt the fields, exposing their salmon-pink underwings as they gracefully turn and dive in pursuit of insects. Resident nesting species include northern mockingbird, brown thrasher, loggerhead shrike, and field sparrow.

Mammals Twenty-seven species of mammals have been recorded on the refuge. Most common are white-tailed deer, mink, bobcat, southern flying squirrel, eastern fox squirrel, eastern cottontail, striped skunk, and coyote.

Although nocturnal and rarely seen, the opossum is right at home in this largely agricultural refuge. It is the only marsupial in the United States. It carries its babies in its pouch for about two months. After that, the young may ride on mom's back, holding on to her ratlike tail with their tiny prehensile tails.

Reptiles and amphibians Reptiles and amphibians are plentiful in the refuge. Gray treefrogs use the pads on their toes to cling to trees and leaves while American toads and varieties of Fowler's and Woodhouse's toads search for insects on the ground. (The refuge lies on the boundary where the range of these two species overlap. Interbreeding produces toads with characteristics of both species.)

SNOW GOOSE OR BLUE GOOSE? Once, blue geese and snow geese were considered separate species. Today, scientists consider these birds to be two color phases of the same species, the lesser snow goose. Its scientific name is *Chen caerulescens*.

The white phase is pure white with black wingtips. The blue phase has a white head and neck, a dark brown back, and varying amounts of white underneath. Immature snow geese are grayish while young blue geese are mostly light brown. The two phases interbreed frequently, producing variants, or animals somewhere between the two phases. It is possible for two snow geese to mate and produce a blue goose and vice-versa. The same parents may give birth to both phases in the same brood. Confused about what to call that goose? Simple: Just call it a snow goose and you will be correct.

The five-lined skink, with its bright blue tail, and the large broad-headed skink, with its bright orange-red head (males only), are representative lizards. Aquatic snakes and turtles are also plentiful on the refuge.

ACTIVITIES

■ **WILDLIFE OBSERVATION:** The best months to visit Holla Bend are November through March. It is then you'll see the large numbers and variety of waterfowl. Good observation points are anywhere on top of the levees along the south side of the Arkansas River. This elevation allows you to be eye-to-eye with flying birds. There is also an observation tower from which you may see bald eagles across the old river channel or geese in the fields.

The auto tour also offers opportunities to see wildlife. Along the roadway you sometimes see white-tailed deer and turkeys, and often in winter you may spot ducks in the small, shallow field ponds.

Snow geese

HOLLA BEND HUNTING AND FISHING SEASONS

Hunting (Seasons may vary)	Jan	Feb	Mar	Apr	May	Jun	Jul	Aug	Sep	Oct	Nov	Dec
deer (bow)										■	■	
turkey (bow)										■	■	
rabbit (bow)										■	■	
squirrel (bow)										■	■	
coyote (bow)										■	■	
armadillo (bow)										■	■	
beaver (bow)										■	■	
raccoon (gun)	■											
Fishing												
largemouth bass	■	■	■	■	■	■	■	■	■	■	■	■
crappie	■	■	■	■	■	■	■	■	■	■	■	■
bluegill	■	■	■	■	■	■	■	■	■	■	■	■
catfish	■	■	■	■	■	■	■	■	■	■	■	■

Raccoon hunting (with a gun) permitted, Thurs., Fri., and Sat. nights in Jan. Refuge hunting permit, $12.50.

Fishing in ponds and lakes permitted, March through Oct.; in the old river channel, mid-March through Oct. Frogging (bullfrog) is allowed Fri. and Sat. nights until 1 a.m. in May.

Walk the thick stands of junipers in winter to find long-eared owls. The best way to locate them is to look for whitewash (a white stain from their droppings) on branches and trunks.

■ **PHOTOGRAPHY:** Opportunities abound for picture taking along the auto tour. Portable blinds are permitted. Catch the geese at sunset flying back for the night with the surrounding hills as background.

■ **HIKES AND WALKS:** From the auto tour, you can pull over just beyond the observation tower and walk down to the river. Here you may flush wood ducks, watch pied-billed grebes as they dive, and try to guess where they will resurface, or catch a flock of yellow-rumped warblers taking a bath.

■ **PUBLICATIONS:** Refuge brochure with map; refuge hunting and fishing regulations.

Overflow NWR
Crossett, Arkansas

Morning mist rises off the water at Overflow WNR.

As the sun rises on a late fall day at Overflow NWR, the air is filled with the call of wood ducks. *Whoo—eeek.* It's a welcome sound. These colorful crested ducks, once nearly eradicated in this region, fly through woods in search of acorns, here at the refuge in abundance.

HISTORY

Overflow Creek is a shallow, meandering creek that flows through the Mississippi alluvium of southeastern Arkansas. Overflow NWR, which straddles the creek, was established in 1980 to protect bottomland hardwood forest for the benefit of wintering and resident waterfowl, neotropical migrants, and other wildlife. The refuge currently includes about 12,300 acres.

Like so many floodplains in Arkansas, most of the lands along Overflow Creek were logged, drained, and converted to farmland long ago. Years of intensive farming and other development left the soil in poor condition. As a result the turbidity of the river increased and the abundant wildlife decreased. Now Overflow is undergoing an aggressive program to revitalize the area. Two areas at either end of the refuge are designated waterfowl sanctuaries. Modern management practices are paying off. Today, spectacular concentrations of waterfowl collect on the refuge in winter.

GETTING THERE

Overflow is located about 8 mi. west of Wilmot and 20 mi. southeast of Crossett. From Crossett, take AR 82 East 8 mi. and then AR 52 West 9 mi. to the west side of the refuge. There are seven access points to the west side off CR 342. From Wilmot, take AR 173 West from which there are several access points to the east side. Most access points are at ATV trailheads, but you'll need a map.

■ **SEASON:** General refuge open year-round. However, the South Sanctuary is closed all year while the North Sanctuary is open only in Oct. to hunters and other visitors.

■ **HOURS:** Refuge: dawn to dusk. Refuge headquarters (located at Felsenthal NWR in Crossett) open weekdays, 7 a.m.–3:30 p.m.

■ **ADDRESS:** Overflow NWR, c/o Felsenthal NWR, P.O. Box 1157, Crossett, AR 71635

■ **TELEPHONE:** 870/364-3167

TOURING OVERFLOW

No improved roads traverse the interior, so travel within the refuge is limited to boating along Overflow Creek or hiking along ATV trails. ATVs are allowed on designated trails only during certain times of the year.

WHAT TO SEE

While most refuge land is low-lying, the western edge rises to an escarpment that separates the Mississippi Alluvial Plains from the Coastal Plains. Close to 3,000 acres in the floodplain is managed as moist soil units and agricultural fields. The rest consists of bottomland hardwood forest dominated by red oaks. Bald cypress and tupelo gum are found along waterways while overcup oak and bitter pecan thrive in less swampy areas. Willow oak, a tree with willowlike leaves and the acorn of an oak, delta post oak, and Nuttall oak are common on the low ridges and flats, while a few loblolly pines and upland hardwoods occur on the higher elevations along the western boundary.

Overflow is a humid, subtropical place with mildly warm to hot summers and cool winters. December and January are usually the wettest months. Delightful autumn weather begins in September and often continues into December. Springs are also long and pleasant.

Overflow's diverse wetlands provide food and shelter for vast numbers of birds and other wildlife. Wintering populations of waterfowl often exceed 100,000, mainly mallards, but also northern pintail, green and blue-winged teal, and geese.

Blue-winged teal

In summer, various shorebirds, wading birds, marsh and water birds ply the refuge waters for food, among them coots, moorhens, rails, and the endangered interior least tern. Peak populations of these species occur during migration periods (March–April and July–August).

Birds of prey including northern harriers, red-tailed hawks, broad-winged hawks, Mississippi kites, barred and screech owls, and a few bald eagles and peregrine falcons, both endangered, find plenty to hunt throughout much of the year in this watery habitat.

Small mammals that call the refuge home include rabbits, squirrels, opossums, and nutria. Beavers are plentiful, but don't look for the traditional beaver lodge. Unlike beavers in mountain streams, most beavers here build homes in tunnels or under brush piles along creek banks and sloughs.

Coyotes, raccoons, and foxes are the most common carnivores while black bears are sighted annually either on or near the refuge. White-tailed deer forage in the reforested areas and feral hogs can be found rooting out crops and native plants, often causing great damage.

As the process to restore water quality continues, animals dependent on clean water become more abundant. Amphibians like the marbled and spotted salamander lurk in muck at the water's edge, and cottonmouths and common water snakes alternately bask in the sun or glide through refuge waters.

ACTIVITIES

Although travel within the refuge is limited, those who boat along Overflow Creek will have opportunities to spot animals in, on, and along the river. And for landlubbers, there are opportunities for hiking, hunting, trapping, wildlife observation, and photography.

■ **PUBLICATIONS:** Refuge brochure with map; refuge hunting regulations.

Pond Creek NWR
Horatio, Arkansas

Wood duck

It's one of the lesser-known refuges in the region, but Pond Creek NWR is a joy to discover. The refuge consists of watery bottomland hardwood forests and old pine plantations.

HISTORY

Pond Creek became the 501st National Wildlife Refuge in 1994. It was established to protect wetland habitat for the benefit of migratory waterfowl, neotropical songbirds, and breeding and nesting wood ducks. Currently, the refuge includes 27,300 acres, but the U.S. Fish & Wildlife Service hopes to acquire an additional 3,000 acres.

The refuge was originally named Cossatot NWR after the Cossatot River, which flows beside it. However, local residents who had always called the region Pond Creek Bottoms, after the small creek that meanders through it, objected. In 1997, the refuge was returned to its original name.

GETTING THERE

Pond Creek is located off AR 71 approximately 30 mi. north of Texarkana and 10 mi. southeast of DeQueen. The best way to reach the refuge is to go southwest from the town of Horatio on Central Rd. Several gravel roads lead to the heart of the refuge.

■ **SEASON:** Open year-round, although some areas may be closed due to flooding or to protect wildlife.

■ **HOURS:** Refuge: dawn to dusk. Office (at Felsenthal NWR in Crossett) open weekdays, 7 a.m.–3:30 p.m.

■ **FEES:** None.

■ **ADDRESS:** Pond Creek NWR, % Felsenthal NWR, P. O. Box 1157, Crossest, AR 71635

■ **TELEPHONE:** 870/364-3167

TOURING POND CREEK

There are no developed facilities or Visitor Center at Pond Creek. However, several improved gravel roads and designated ATV trails provide access to the refuge. Canoeing the Little River is an ideal way to experience the pristine habitat. The river moves surprisingly fast for a southern stream, cutting through high banks and bottomland hardwood trees. Boating is also possible on the Cossatot River and the small ponds and lakes.

WHAT TO SEE

■ **LANDSCAPE AND CLIMATE** Most of Pond Creek is an area of mature bottomland hardwoods lying between the confluence of the Little and the Cossatot rivers in Arkansas' Coastal Plain region. The refuge's namesake, Pond Creek, flows southwest through the refuge and takes the unusual practice of dividing in two. Part of the creek empties into the Little River and part into the Cossatot. Numerous natural oxbow lakes occur throughout the refuge and are popular fishing areas.

Pond Creek has a mild, moist climate with a full range of seasons. Winters are generally short, wet, and mild, although occasional ice storms do occur. Temperatures in the high 90s are typical in summer. Flooding after heavy rains is common throughout the year. The best time to visit is October to May.

■ **PLANT LIFE** The tracts of bottomland hardwood forest nearest the rivers consist of several species of oak, sweetgum, black gum, hackberry, willow, green ash, bitter pecan, sycamore, cottonwood, cypress, and tupelo gum. Approximately 600 acres of the refuge was converted to pine plantations by the previous owners. These old pine plantation areas are obvious—for never in nature do pines grow

Egret

in such straight rows. The plantations were created by the Weyerhaeuser Company on former hardwood bottomland and are populated with loblolly pine. One refuge management objective is to convert these plantations to native hardwoods.

■ ANIMAL LIFE

Birds The flooded green-timber and dead-timber areas provide excellent wintering habitat for waterfowl, primarily ducks—mallards, gadwall, green-winged teal, and ring-necked ducks. Bald eagles are sighted during the winter as they follow migrating waterfowl.

Wading birds, including great blue, little blue, and green herons; cattle, snowy, and great egrets; and black-crowned and yellow-crowned night-herons frequent these wetlands. Refuge managers have identified at least four wading-bird rookeries.

In spring and fall the area is an excellent stopover for songbirds and other migrants including warblers. Look for the American redstart in the tops of hardwood trees. The male of this species is black with splashes of bright on its wings and tail. Its habit of flitting like a butterfly reveals the bright-orange patches and prompted its name.

Mammals The watery refuge is ideal habitat for the raccoon. This well-known masked mammal rests by day and hunts crayfish, frogs, insects, and small rodents at night. The little bandit also fancies wild fruit and is not above raiding the farmer's sweet corn or your cooler if you carelessly leave it in the open. Other mammals calling the refuge home are white-tailed deer, squirrel, rabbit, opossum, gray fox, coyote, beaver, armadillo, bobcat, and numerous species of rodents.

ACTIVITIES

Although there are no developed facilities at Pond Creek, there are opportunities galore to hike, bike, photograph and observe wildlife, hunt, fish, and trap. Five primitive campgrounds (no facilities) are located in the southern part of the refuge.

■ **PUBLICATIONS:** Refuge hunting regulations.

Wapanocca NWR
Turrell, Arkansas

Wapanocca NWR in spring

The centerpiece of Wapanocca NWR is Wapanocca Lake, a 6,600-acre, sparkling body of water ringed by towering bald cypress trees and willows. Throughout the year, this gleaming lake attracts diverse wildlife. In fall masses of migrating waterfowl begin to arrive. By deepest winter the lake bustles with the comings and goings of up to 150,000 ducks and 50,000 geese. Bald eagles roost in the naked cypress trees around the lake, where they can keep an eye out for weak or sick ducks.

In summer the lake's open waters appear deserted, but that's simply not so: Beautiful, multicolored wood ducks and elegant hooded mergansers swim between the cypress trunks at the lake's edge, their broods close behind. Painted turtles pull themselves up onto slippery logs to sun. Snakes glide through the water, gently rippling the surface. Fish and snapping turtles lurk below.

HISTORY

Wapanocca NWR lies just 4 miles west of the Mississippi River in northeast Arkansas. Throughout time, the flooded alluvial plains have been a wintering place for large flocks of migrating waterfowl. At the beginning of the 19th century there was a widescale effort to drain the swamps, harvest the timber, and plant corn. Ducks and geese continued to use the area, however, finding corn to their liking. Then, in the mid-1800s, agricultural practices changed throughout the South. Farmers replaced corn with cotton. Sadly, the loss of habitat and grain crops here and throughout the entire region meant a decline in the numbers of waterfowl.

Fortunately, Wapanocca Lake and about 3,000 of the surrounding acres were purchased by a group of businessmen in the late 1800s (for 50 cents an acre!) to be used as a hunting club. In 1961 the U.S. Fish & Wildlife Service bought the club with money from the sales of federal duck stamps to provide and protect habitat for migrating waterfowl. Today the refuge consists of 5,485 acres.

GETTING THERE

Wapanocca is located approximately 16 mi. north of West Memphis. From West Memphis, take I 55 or AR 77 north, then go east approximately 2 mi. on AR 42 to the refuge.

■ **SEASON:** Open year-round, although some portions are periodically closed to protect wildlife.

■ **HOURS:** Refuge: open dawn to dusk. Headquarters open weekdays from 7 a.m.–4 p.m.

■ **FEES:** None.

■ **ADDRESS:** Wapanocca NWR, P. O. Box 279, Turrell, AR 72384

■ **TELEPHONE:** 870/343-2595

■ **VISITOR CENTER:** Features Indian artifacts found on the refuge, a relief map that can be helpful in navigating the nature drive, and dioramas of the changing seasons and a fish-eye view of life underwater.

TOURING WAPANOCCA

■ **BY AUTOMOBILE:** A 6-mile auto trail begins on a levee bordered by cypress swamp on one side and a slough on the other. The road then passes through a crop field, winds through mature bottomland hardwood forests, and then eases back into the sunlight of an old field that has recently been planted with trees. It ends at a picturesque cypress swamp that shelters ducks year round.

■ **BY FOOT:** While there are no hiking trails per se, miles of field roads including the nature drive are suitable for walking. A side spur off the drive leads to a lakeside observation platform.

■ **BY BICYCLE:** Biking is allowed on the relatively flat nature drive and field roads.

■ **BY CANOE, KAYAK, OR BOAT:** A public boat ramp, located 2 miles south of the headquarters along AR 77, provides access to the lake but is open only during the refuge fishing season.

WHAT TO SEE

■ **LANDSCAPE AND CLIMATE** Wapanocca Lake is a shallow old 600-acre oxbow (5 feet at its deepest) that was once part of the meandering Mississippi River. Large tracts of cypress swamp and bottomland hardwood forest cover the lowlands surrounding the lake. Fields and croplands interspersed with small impoundments make up the slightly elevated areas east of the lake. Today, there are no natural streams or creeks feeding the lake.

White-fronted goose

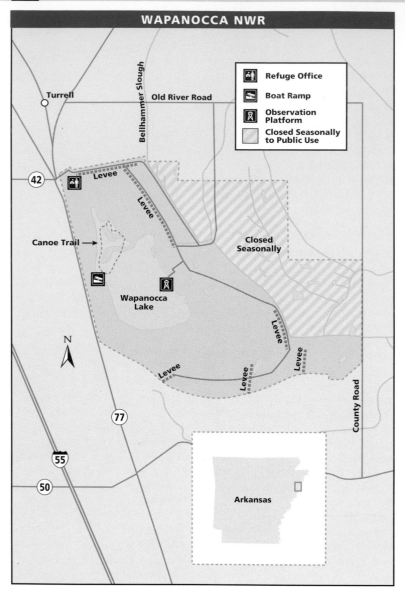

WAPANOCCA NWR

	Refuge Office
	Boat Ramp
	Observation Platform
	Closed Seasonally to Public Use

Turrell

Bellhammer Slough

Old River Road

42

Levee

Levee

Canoe Trail →

Closed Seasonally

Wapanocca Lake

Levee

Levee

Levee

Levee

N

77

55

50

County Road

Arkansas

However, water levels in the lake and surrounding impoundments can be artificially managed through a system of canals, levees, and flood gates.

The climate is mild with long springs and falls, hot summers, and cool winters that sometimes get cold enough for the lake to freeze. The average annual precipitation is 42 inches, much of which comes between March and May. Tornadoes are always possible, especially in warm seasons.

■ PLANT LIFE

Forest One-third of the refuge is a remnant of a once extensive bottomland hardwood forest, part of which is seasonally flooded. The tree canopy is tall, ranging from 90 to 140 feet. In areas of seasonal flooding, the understory is poorly

The Wapanocca auto trail winds through bottomland hardwood forest.

developed, giving the tall forest an open, or parklike, appearance. Common trees include oak, willow, and Nuttall oak. The straight-trunked, lobed-leafed pin oak is at the southern edge of its range here. It takes its name from short pinlike spurs that cover its main branches.

Croplands Local farmers cultivate 1,300 acres of the refuge on a cooperative basis. They harvest part of their crop—corn, millet, and wheat—and leave the rest in the field for waterfowl and other wildlife.

Wetlands A swamp composed mainly of bald cypress and willow surrounds the lake.

Open waters Nearly 2,000 acres of freshwater impoundments cover the refuge. They include the 600-acre Wapanocca Lake, 1,200 acres of adjoining swamp and hardwood forest, and nineteen shallow ponds. The ponds are seasonally flooded and then drained to allow the growth of natural foods that attract waterfowl. In summer American lotus often carpets large portions of the shallow lake and must be controlled by refuge staff. Coontail and duckweed, both favored by waterfowl, are also abundant on the lake.

■ ANIMAL LIFE

Birds Almost every duck and goose species that uses the Mississippi Flyway can be found at Wapanocca. Mallards are the most common duck, but gadwall, wigeon, pintails, and ruddy ducks are also abundant. Ruddy ducks spend half their time diving below the lake's surface, straining the soft muck for snails, insect larvae, and aquatic plants. Canadas are the most common geese, but some white-fronted and snows also congregate at the refuge.

During the spring migration, the trees are filled with neotropical migrants, including brightly colored orioles, indigo buntings, and a variety of warblers, who pause often from their feeding to fill the air with song.

Nesting birds include hooded mergansers, horned larks, Carolina wrens,

Eastern cottontail rabbit

pileated and redheaded woodpeckers, prothonotary warblers, and wood ducks. The wood ducks produce 1,000 or more young "woodies" on the refuge each year.

Mammals Easily seen land mammals include raccoons, squirrels, rabbits, opossum, and white-tailed deer while coyotes and bobcats are more illusive. Muskrats, beaver, and nutria become visible in the swamp areas along the levee in November.

Reptiles and amphibians Many reptiles and amphibians flourish in this wetland environment including the cottonmouth water moccasin (see sidebar).

Invertebrates Look for invertebrates—insects, mollusks, crustaceans—anywhere on the refuge. Many people ignore these animals, but they are vital to the wetland habitat and some are quite colorful. The broad-winged skipper, a small orange and brown butterfly, has a characteristic jerky or "skipping" way of flying and is often spotted around the lake observation area. Because its antennae are hooklike, not clublike with swollen tips, it is sometimes taken for a moth.

ACTIVITIES

■ **WILDLIFE OBSERVATION AND PHOTOGRAPHY:** The best places to view and photograph wildlife are from a boat on the lake or a car along the auto tour.

The slough along the auto tour is chock-full of ducks in the winter and you can get quite close to them. In summer the surrounding trees fill with songbirds. The picturesque cypress swamp at the end of the drive and the ponds in the fields along the way are good places for spotting wading birds. Pure white egrets and powdery-blue great blue herons often pose like statues as they fish the shallow water. Often puddle ducks and darting little shorebirds share the shallow waters with them. Red-tailed

HUNTING AND FISHING
There are seasons on **squirrel, rabbit**, and **raccoon**. Deer hunting is not allowed.
Fishing for **warm-water species** is permitted mid-March through Sept.

COTTONMOUTH WATER MOCCASIN No reptile better symbolizes the swamps, bayous, and sloughs of the South Central region than the cottonmouth water moccasin. These brown to black, heavy-bodied serpents are pit vipers, poisonous snakes that have a heat-sensitive "pit" between their eye and nostril for locating prey.

Water moccasins can be distinguished by their broad, flat-topped heads that are noticeably wider than their necks. They are usually patternless, but may have dark body crossbands and/or a light-bordered, dark cheek stripe. When swimming, they often hold their head erect above the water.

The snake likes to sun itself on logs. If encountered, it will either crawl away slowly or stand its ground. When provoked, the snake will form a loose coil, throw its head up and back, and open its mouth wide, revealing the cottony-white lining that gives the snake its name. It may vibrate its tail, and, if the tail brushes against a dry leaf, the sound will be something like a rattlesnake's rattle.

The bite of the cottonmouth can be lethal. If you do see one, give it a wide berth, and let it go on its way. If you should get bitten, seek medical help immediately.

hawks are found along the drive, too, and, if you are lucky, you will see one in a screaming dive as it tries to capture a mouse or snake in its talons.

Canada geese are at their highest numbers in January. They roost on Wapanocca Lake at night, and photographers can capture them at sunrise as they leave the lake to feed or as they return to the lake in the evening.

■ **HIKE AND WALKS:** A short walk begins at a parking area on the nature drive and leads to an observation platform on Wapanocca Lake. On warm summer evenings listen for the chorus of katydids and crickets and watch for the blinking yellow-green glow of fireflies as you amble toward the lake.

■ **PUBLICATIONS:** Refuge brochure with map; refuge fact sheet; bird list; Calendar of Wildlife Events; refuge hunting regulations; refuge fishing regulations.

Cottonmouth water moccasin

White River NWR
DeWitt, Arkansas

A black bear stops for a drink.

The ancient Egyptians revered the annual spring flooding of the Nile. To them, floods signaled the coming of spring and new life and were not something to be feared and loathed. Ecologists these days agree, having found that flooding is naturally beneficial and provides essential nutrients to soils and promotes the growth of plants.

In the bottomland forests of White River NWR, flooding has other benefits as well. Spring and winter floods provide food for phytoplankton, which in turn provide food for small invertebrates, which in turn provide food for fish and other animals. And so it goes up the food chain. Spring waters also inundate grass, shrubs, and small trees, thus providing a safe spawning grounds for millions of fish and a safe nursery where their young can hide from predators. When flood waters recede, the fish seek residual waters in lakes and ponds. This introduces new populations of fish. Because of the nutrients provided by life-giving floods, biologists calculate that there are up to five times more wildlife species in bottomland than in upland forests.

HISTORY

The early 1900s marked a lowpoint for bottomland forests throughout Arkansas. Land clearing and farming had destroyed thousands upon thousands of acres. Then in 1935 the tide turned. White River NWR was established to preserve 113,380 acres of pristine forestland and migratory waterfowl habitat.

The Arkansas-Idaho Land Exchange Act of 1992 added another 40,749 acres of bottomland habitat to the refuge, and other additions have increased the refuge to 160,000 acres. The refuge now extends for 90 river miles along the White River in east-central Arkansas and joins Cache River NWR to the north. White River, and other publicly owned lands in the White River Basin, have been designated "Wetlands of International Importance" under the Ramsar Convention.

GETTING THERE

Access to the refuge is by way of Rtes. 1, 17, 44, and 85. Because the refuge is large and complex, you'll need a map. The U. S. Geological Survey maps or maps from the Corps of Engineers are excellent. Some commercial maps are available at sporting goods stores.

■ **SEASON:** AR 1 divides the refuge into two operational units, north and south. Most of the North Unit is open year-round. The South Unit is open from early March through Oct. or Nov., although the levee on the east side is open all year. Winter and spring flooding commonly limits road access.

■ **HOURS:** General refuge: open all hours. Office open weekdays from 7:30 a.m.– 4:30 p.m.

■ **FEES:** None.

■ **ADDRESS:** White River NWR, 321 West 7th St., P. O. Box 308, DeWitt, AR 72042

■ **TELEPHONE:** 870/946-1468

TOURING WHITE RIVER

When touring White River, know that you will always be at the mercy of water. In December, as much as 90 percent of the refuge may be flooded, and it is not uncommon for 85 percent of the refuge to remain under water for 6 months of the year.

■ **BY AUTOMOBILE:** There are 90 miles of gravel roads through White River, but access can only be described as difficult and tricky. Many roads are unmarked while some are in poor condition due to flooding.

You can explore the east side of the South Unit from a levee reached by going north from DeWitt on AR 1, turning right on AR 316, then right on AR 318 for about five miles to the levee. From the levee, several secondary roads lead into the refuge shown on the map in the hunting regulations brochure

To explore the west side of the South Unit, take AR 1 south of DeWitt to AR 44, then go east through Tichnor to a secondary road named Jack's Bay. Turn right and go one mile to the refuge entrance. Jack's Bay Recreation Area is about four miles from this entrance.

The west side of North Unit can be reached from AR 33, west of Stuttgart. The east side of the North Unit can be reached from AR 17, north and south of Holly Grove.

You may see some trees marked with purple paint. In Arkansas, this is a legally binding method of saying "private property," "no trespassing," or "do not enter."

■ **BY FOOT:** There are no improved trails, but many miles of unimproved trails and roads closed to vehicles make hiking possible. Always carry a map and a compass and wear insect repellent.

■ **BY CANOE, KAYAK, OR BOAT:** A boat is the only way to fully experience the pristine nature of the refuge and to comprehend its size and scope. Both motorized and nonmotorized boats are allowed on the White River and its chutes and ponds. Touring kayaks are an ideal way to see the backwaters, while motorized boats are good for the main river channel.

Any time you are boating remember that flood waters can be dangerous. The currents are swift and may contain high numbers of pathogens. Free boat ramps that provide access to the White River are found at St. Charles, Clarendon, Aberdeen, Preston Ferry, Indian Bay, Moon Lake, Weber, Hudson's Landing, Jack's Bay, and Lock #1. Many smaller refuge lakes have dirt ramps for boat access. Fee boat ramps are found at Maddox Bay and East Lake.

WHITE RIVER NWR

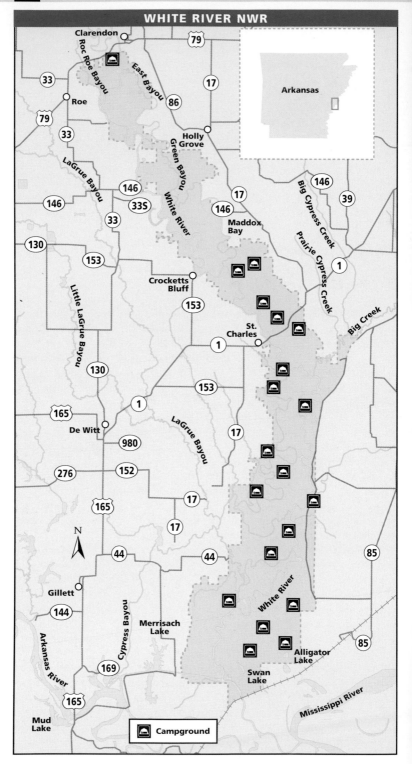

Arkansas

Campground

Bottomland hardwoods grow along the White River.

WHAT TO SEE

■ **LANDSCAPE AND CLIMATE** White River NWR occupies a long swath in Arkansas' Mississippi Alluvial Plain. The terrain is flat and the soil moist and fertile, a perfect environment for magnificent bottomland hardwood forests. The White River flows southward through the heart of the refuge before it adds its water to the Mississippi River. Hundreds of small lakes and miles of interlacing streams, sloughs, and bayous are all found in the refuge. A man-made levee parallels the river on the east side.

The climate is warm and moist. Average yearly precipitation is 49 inches, most of which comes in the winter.

■ **PLANT LIFE**

Forest The refuge contains 150,000 acres of forest, mostly prime bottomland hardwoods, making it one of the largest remaining tracts in the Mississippi River Valley. Overcup, Nuttall, and willow oaks grow tall and wide here.

The forests are selectively harvested to provide a diverse and quality wildlife habitat. Water levels are managed in controlled areas to encourage growth of native wetland species.

Cropland Crops—winter wheat, rice, corn, and milo as well as native grasses— are grown on 900 acres of the refuge for the benefit of Canada geese and other migrating birds.

Wetlands In areas of standing water the bald cypress tree is king. These ancient trees dot the waters throughout the refuge.

Open water The White River twists and turns for 90 miles through the 50-mile-long refuge creating hundreds of lakes, oxbows, and sloughs; numerous tributary streams also dissect the refuge. There are 356 natural and man-made lakes to explore, almost one for each day of the year. They total 4,000 acres of surface water. Generally the lakes are relatively shallow and tree-lined, but each lake has its own personality.

■ **ANIMAL LIFE**

Birds Between 150 to 350 thousand ducks, depending on populations and

PROTHONOTARY WARBLER The prothonotary warbler, a bird with a striking yellow-gold head, neck, and chest, is a common nester throughout most of the South Central region except western Oklahoma and Kansas. Early scientists named it after a group of Roman Catholic Church officials (notaries) who wore similarly colored robes. It is also nicknamed the "golden swamp warbler."

This beautiful bird prefers dark, swampy, mature forests with standing water. It is one of only two warblers that nest in hollow tree cavities. It may use a woodpecker hole or even a man-made nest box.

Different individuals have different voices. Their song is a "*sweet-sweet-sweet-sweet-sweet...*," or "*tweet-tweet-tweet-tweet-tweet....*," each note being repeated loudly from 5 to 12 times. The clear call is easily recognized on a spring morning.

Prothonotary warbler

weather conditions, and up to two thousand Canada geese winter at White River. They begin arriving in October and reach peak numbers in late December. This refuge has the largest concentration of wintering mallards in the Mississippi Flyway, but gadwall, wigeon, and green-winged teal are also abundant.

Dozens of bald eagles follow the migrating waterfowl each winter, and biologist have observed four active bald eagle nests, with each nest usually producing two young each year.

Migrating warblers (more than 24 species have been recorded) travel through the refuge during spring migration. Throw in the permanent residents, other neotropical migrants, and a few vagrants and unusual birds and the list of birds seen on the refuge numbers 234.

Mammals White River supports a healthy population of white-tailed deer, and because the many oaks usually produce a good crop of mast, some deer reach a weight of 250 pounds or more. Black bears, nearly eradicated from Arkansas by the time the refuge was acquired, now number more than 300. These bears are very mobile, consistently swimming across lakes, bayous, and even the White

River in their daily excursions. They have adapted to the seasonal flooding by denning in trees, sometimes 60 feet high, from late winter until spring when the flood waters recede. It is in these tree dens that they give birth to their young.

Other mammals found at White River include gray and fox squirrel, river otter, mink, gray and red foxes, and coyotes. Bobcats do well in this habitat.

Reptiles and amphibians The refuge reptile and amphibian checklist registers 47 reptiles and 20 amphibians. Because the refuge is on the northern limit of the American alligator's range, refuge managers believe some alligators are nesting here.

Cottonmouths, common water snakes, and many aquatic turtles find the refuge to their liking. So do bullfrogs. Look for them as they sit on mud banks (always ready to leap after food or escape from predators).

Invertebrates The refuge supports an impressive array of insects and other invertebrates. The threatened and endangered rare pink mucket mussel lives here as do more common mussels, clams, and snails. The common crayfish is abundant and provides food for raccoons, herons, ducks, frogs, snakes, and even each other. The refuge is also home to the usual assortment of ticks, chiggers, and mosquitoes.

ACTIVITIES

■ **CAMPING:** There are 27 primitive camping areas throughout the refuge. During the muzzle-loader and modern gun deer hunts, camping is by permit only.

■ **WILDLIFE OBSERVATION:** White River is a great place to observe ducks. Driving the levee is usually a good place to see them in the winter. But because the refuge is large and waterfowl move around, it is a good idea to check with the refuge staff to locate the birds. Seeing a sky full of ducks at sunrise or sunset can be a memorable experience.

■ **PHOTOGRAPHY:** Photo opportunities abound at White River, but because wildlife is dispersed over a large area, the photographer must work to take advantage of them. The refuge permits the use of portable photo blinds.

■ **SEASONAL EVENTS:** A Youth Fishing Rodeo is held each June, and a Youth Waterfowl Hunt is held in December.

■ **PUBLICATIONS:** Refuge brochure; refuge fact sheet; map; refuge hunting, fishing, and camping regulations.

HUNTING AND FISHING In the North Unit, **deer** hunting is permitted, with guns, muzzle-loaders, bow and arrow; seasons can vary and change annually. Hunting for **rabbit**, **squirrel**, **raccoon**, and **opossum** is allowed. Waterfowl may be hunted; call for details on waterfowl season. **Beaver**, **coyote**, **nutria**, and **free-roaming hogs** may be taken during any daytime season.

In the South Unit, deer hunting is permitted, with modern guns, muzzle-loaders, bow-and-arrow; seasons vary and change annually. **Turkey**, rabbit, squirrel, and raccoon, and opossum hunting is permitted. Seasons on **duck** and **coot** to be set. Beaver, coyote, nutria, free-roaming hogs may be taken during any daytime season.

Fishing (**bluegill**, **crappie**, **largemouth bass**, **catfish**) is permitted year-round in the North Unit and March through Nov. in the South Unit.

Flint Hills NWR
Hartford, Kansas

Dove Roost Trail at Flint Hills NWR

In the twilight just before sunrise a thin mist hangs over the upper reservoir. It is difficult to distinguish the shapes of waterfowl that roosted on the quiet waters overnight. Yet the experienced hunter or birder can identify the birds by their honks, squeaks, quacks, and whistles.

From a large congregation of birds at the lake's center comes a conversation of rich, loud "*quack, quacks.*" Hen mallards. Answering the lusty quacks, less audible and squeaky "*kwek-kweks.*" Male mallards.

A smaller group not far away issues a series of distinctly whistled "*whew-where-whews.*" Male wigeons. Replying, a few quiet "*quacks,*" not as full-bodied as the mallards'. Wigeon females.

Near the lake's edge a small flock of birds is barely discernable under eerie-looking snags that pierce the morning mist. But their low, rasping croaks give them away. Common mergansers.

Flint Hills is a good place to learn the ways of waterfowl. The 18,500-acre refuge in eastern Kansas attracts tens of thousands ducks and geese each year.

HISTORY

Flint Hills was established as a sanctuary for migratory waterfowl in 1966. Despite its name, the refuge is not located in the limestone-capped Flint Hills traversing central Kansas north to south.

The refuge straddles the Neosho River at the headwaters of the John Redmond Reservoir. The huge reservoir was created by the U.S. Army Corps of Engineers for flood control. The Corps actually owns the land occupied by the refuge and partners in its management.

GETTING THERE

KS 130 cuts through the northwestern portion of the refuge and provides a number of access points. The headquarters is located just off KS 130 in the town of Hartford. From Burlington, turn west on Kennebec St. and follow it into town.

■ **SEASON:** Main refuge open year-round, but a portion is closed in winter to protect wildlife and portions close periodically due to flooding.

■ **HOURS:** General refuge open from sunrise to sunset. Office open weekdays, 8 a.m.–4:30 p.m.

■ **FEES:** None.

■ **ADDRESS:** Flint Hills NWR, P.O. Box 128, 530 W. Maple, Hartford, KS 66854

■ **TELEPHONE:** 316/392-5553

TOURING FLINT HILLS

■ **BY AUTOMOBILE:** There are 40 miles of gravel and blacktop roads through Flint Hills refuge.

■ **BY FOOT:** Three trails are open to foot traffic. Hiking is also permitted on the developed roads.

■ **BY BICYCLE:** Biking is permitted on the three trails as well as developed roads.

■ **BY CANOE, KAYAK, OR BOAT:** Boating is allowed on refuge waters in areas open to the public, including parts of John Redmond Reservoir, several small ponds, and some marshy areas. Water levels determine the possibility of boating.

WHAT TO SEE

■ **LANDSCAPE AND CLI-MATE** The Neosho River meanders through a broad, low-lying valley nestled between low cuestas. The steplike hills are actually weathered remnants of beds of limestone and shale laid down by shallow seas millions of years ago. The refuge occupies the part of the valley just above the John Redman Reservoir and actually takes in the reservoir's upper reaches.

The refuge consists of a variety of habitats from shallow marshes and hardwood forests to tallgrass prairie and crop-lands. Because it lies smack in the flood pool of the John Red-

Warbling vireo

mond Reservoir, as much as 90 percent of the refuge can be flooded at times.

Flint Hills has a continental climate. Temperatures are generally moderate, though extremes occur in winter and summers. Blizzards are possible. Strong winds are characteristic of Kansas. Severe thunderstorms and tornadoes can occur anytime from early spring to late fall; however, they are most likely to occur in May and June.

■ **PLANT LIFE**

Forests Just under a quarter of the refuge (5,000 acres) is forested with soft-woods. In low areas subject to frequent flooding, cottonwood, maple, locust, and willow are common. The box elder, another water-loving tree, also thrives here.

FLINT HILLS NWR

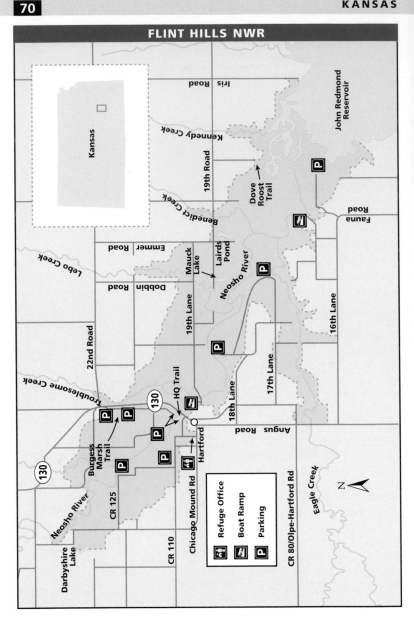

	Refuge Office
	Boat Ramp
	Parking

This fast-growing, short-lived tree with elderlike leaves and boxlike wood grows on muddy stream banks and sometimes reaches heights of 70 feet.

On higher ground away from the river, dominant species include oak, sugar maple, ash, pecan, hackberry, locust, walnut, elm, and bitternut hickory. Two native trees, the pecan and walnut, produce nuts valued by wildlife and humans alike.

Grasslands Tallgrass prairie (with grasses over 5 feet tall) was once common throughout this region. Now, only 300 acres of native grassland (big and little bluestem, prairie cordgrass, switch grass) remain. However, some of the abandoned cropland is being restored to prairie by refuge staff.

Croplands Presently 4,000 acres of former forest and grassland are farmed under contract with local farmers. Crops such as wheat, soybeans, corn, and sorghum are planted and a percentage is left in the fields for wildlife.

Wetlands About 5,000 acres of wetlands and marshes are found on the refuge. Refuge managers, in partnership with Ducks Unlimited, are constructing man-made dikes to restore or create new wetlands.

Open waters The amount of open water on the refuge can vary dramatically depending on water levels and flooding conditions. The upper end of John Redmond Reservoir and 36 small ponds provide several thousand acres of the open water on which waterfowl prefer to roost at night. The Neosho River, which flows through the refuge into the reservoir, provides a riverine habitat.

■ ANIMAL LIFE

Birds More than 40,000 ducks and 200,000 geese pass through this refuge in spring and fall. A few stay until the John Redmond Reservoir freezes. The majority of ducks are mallards, but northern pintails, blue-winged teals, wigeons, redheads, canvasbacks, and several mergansers frequent the refuge as well. Snow and Canada are the predominant geese. Other migrants that stop here include bald eagles, white pelicans, a wealth of sandpipers, assorted other shorebirds, and songbirds.

In spring and summer, upland sandpipers nest on the refuge and often perch on fence posts. This bird looks like a cross between a shorebird and a dove. Its breathy call is a perfect imitation of the old-fashioned wolf whistle.

A number of songbirds nest on the refuge including eastern bluebirds, blue-gray gnatcatchers, northern mockingbirds,

Upland sandpiper

Bell's, warbling, and red-eyed vireos, northern cardinals, and indigo buntings. The yellow-chested, black-bibbed dickcissle, named after its song (a combination of "*dicks*" and "*cissels*"), arrives in May. Soon after, the male begins to court the female by belting out his song from the tops of swaying grasses and wildflowers. After mating, the pair makes a well-camouflaged nest in the grass.

Mammals Flint Hills is also a haven for white-tailed deer, squirrels, and raccoons which can often be seen from the walking trails. Coyotes and bobcats prowl the woods, marshes, and grasslands for food at night.

Reptiles and amphibians The stoutly built tiger salamander burrows in moist ground throughout the refuge and can sometimes be seen at night after heavy rains. Western box turtles often bask in the sun in the morning and then

seek grassy retreats during the heat
of the day.

Invertebrates Like any prairie
region, Flint Hills has it share of
grasshoppers, including spur-
throated, green valley, and two-
striped.

ACTIVITIES

■ **CAMPING:** There are no developed campgrounds on the refuge,
but primitive camping is allowed. In
addition, the Corps of Engineers has
developed camping sites on John
Redmond Reservoir land, 15 miles
southeast.

**HUNTING AND FISHING Water-
fowl** hunting is usually permitted
from Nov. through Dec., but specific dates are set annually. Hunting
for **deer, pheasant, turkey, crow,
prairie chickens, quail**, and **squirrel** is permitted; call the refuge for
details.

Fishing is permitted (for **white
bass, channel catfish**) north of
Neosho River, March through Oct.,
and south of the river year-round.
Frogging (**bullfrogs**) is allowed
from July through Oct.

■ **WILDLIFE OBSERVATION:**
In the fall, the drive to Horseshoe and Half Mile marshes is good for viewing ducks
and geese. Search the mudflat near Goose Bend Marsh for shorebirds. Depending
on water conditions, the marsh could have wading birds or nesting mallards. On
Garner Road also watch for wild turkeys and prairie chickens.

Waterfowl, wading birds, and several rails, including sora, king, and Virginia,
often collect at Burgess Marsh in the northwestern part of the refuge. A trail
through the marsh can be reached from KS 130.

■ **HIKES AND WALKS:** Headquarters Trail is actually several short trails leading through bottomland hardwood forest along the Neosho River. In summer look
for bright songbirds in this area. Dove Roost Trail at the southern end of the refuge
is a short loop (1 mile) around a fishing pond where belted kingfishers feed. You
can view the reservoir from an observation point along the trail.

■ **SEASONAL EVENTS:** December: Annual Christmas bird count; January:
Eagle Tour held jointly with the Audubon Society.

■ **PUBLICATIONS:** Refuge brochure with map.

SATELLITE REFUGE

■ **MARAIS DES CYGNE NWR** Marais des Cygnes NWR, 67 miles south of
Kansas City, has 7,300 acres, with another 2,000 acres proposed for acquisition.
The refuge is administered from the Flint Hills NWR but has a small staff on-site.

All but the northeast quarter of the refuge, which is a sanctuary, is open to
the public. However, the refuge includes many private inholdings, so you'll need
a map.

This biologically diverse refuge contains fine expanses of marsh, swamp, and
bottomland hardwoods as well as mudflats, shallow-water pools, and croplands.
An abundance of wildlife inhabit this refuge for all or part of the year including
large numbers of migratory waterfowl, shorebirds, and neotropical migrants.
More than 300 species of birds have been observed here, with 113 species nesting.

Mussels are good indicators of the water quality, and several mussel species
are present in the wetlands within the refuge. One, the flat-floater mussel (formerly called the heel-splitter mussel), is on the state's threatened species list.

■ **ADDRESS:** Rte. 2, Box 185 A, Pleasanton, KS 66075
■ **TELEPHONE:** 913/352-8956

Kirwin NWR
Kirwin, Kansas

A windmill rises above the grasslands of Kirwin NWR.

Kirwin NWR, in western Kansas, is a wonderful place to observe wildlife. Scanning the land for signs of life, you see deer, in ones, twos, even small herds, grazing in the thick grass. Overhead, ferruginous hawks circle or flee as they are harassed by kingbirds and blackbirds. As night approaches, the huge sky fills with more stars than a city-dweller can dream of, and coyotes cry out into the dark vastness.

HISTORY

Before European settlers arrived here, the free-flowing North Fork of the Solomon River met Bow Creek in the valley between these grassy hills. Great herds of bison roamed the area, drinking the river waters and feeding on the mixed grasses. Native Americans lived in harmony with the bison.

This balance was first upset when farmers began to settle the area. Later, the river was dammed, creating a reservoir in the valley's center. Native prairie plants and fertile farmlands went underwater, but ducks and geese, formerly uncommon, now arrived in great numbers during migration.

Kirwin, the first national wildlife refuge in Kansas, was established in 1954 to protect and provide habitat for migratory birds and resident animals. The 10,778-acre refuge is a joint project between the Bureau of Land Reclamation, which owns the land and manages the dam and water levels, and the U.S. Fish & Wildlife Service, which manages the land and wildlife resources.

GETTING THERE

Kirwin is located in north-central Kansas. From Hays, take US 183 North to Glade, then KS 9 East 6 mi. to the refuge entrance.

■ **SEASON:** Refuge open year-round.

■ **HOURS:** General refuge: 24 hours daily. Refuge office open weekdays, 7:30 a.m.–4 p.m.

WHOOPING CRANES Throughout the fall birders all along the Central Flyway watch expectantly for the arrival of one of the nation's most spectacular birds, the endangered whooping crane. Weather conditions dictate where these huge birds stop in their annual flight from their breeding grounds in Canada to their wintering grounds in Texas. Every two to five years they put down at Kirwin.

Whoopers often hang out with sandhill cranes and are sometimes confused with them. Both are long-legged wading birds with red crowns. But the birds are easily distinguished. Sandhills are smaller, less than 4 feet tall, and gray or bluish-gray. Whooping cranes are about a foot taller, gleaming white, have black-tipped wings, and wear a tell-tale bustle.

Once on the edge of extinction (there were 15 birds in 1941), through advanced management practices, strict enforcement of hunting laws, and habitat protection, whoopers are making a comeback. But their future is still uncertain.

- **FEES:** None.
- **ADDRESS:** Kirwin NWR, RR 1, Box 103, Kirwin, KS 67644
- **TELEPHONE:** 785/543-6673

TOURING KIRWIN

- **BY AUTOMOBILE:** About 30 miles of dirt, rock, and paved roads traverse the refuge. To get from north to south, you must leave the refuge.
- **BY FOOT:** You are free to walk anywhere on the refuge and on three short interpretive trails.
- **BY BICYCLE:** Biking is permitted on all roads open to vehicles.
- **BY CANOE, KAYAK, OR BOAT:** Boating is permitted on the east side of the reservoir, unless otherwise designated. The Solomon River arm on the west side is closed to motorized boating all year and to nonmotorized boating most of the year. At Kirwin, the term "boat" includes float tubes, inflatable rafts, inner tubes, and all other floating devices. There are two boat ramps.

WHAT TO SEE

- **LANDSCAPE AND CLIMATE** Kirwin is located in the Smoky Hills region of north-central Kansas at the edge of the Great Plains. In these hilly dissected uplands, sculpted by the many creeks and rivers flowing through them, the lush tallgrass prairies of the east meet the shortgrass prairie of the west. Trees are largely confined to the valleys; the almost treeless uplands were originally grassland, but now many are plowed fields or pasture.

The climate is hard with extremes of temperature, strong winds, and a great deal of sunshine. Weather can change suddenly and sometimes violently, causing blizzards, hail, thunderstorms, or tornadoes. Winter temperatures can drop to 20 degrees below zero. Summers are hot.

- **PLANT LIFE**
Forests Trees in the refuge grow where water is available—along waterways, rivers and streams, and the banks of the reservoir. They are mostly cottonwoods, willow, and green ash.

The honey locust is also found here and in spring the sweet fragrance of its creamy-white blossoms fill the air. Its beanlike fruits are favored by deer, rabbits, squirrels, and bobwhites.

Grasslands Staff at the refuge are rotating cropland with a mixture of native grasses. Species being restored include big and little bluestem, Indian grass, switch grass, and sideoats grama grass.

Big bluestem, an extremely tall, gangly grass, is the dominant grass of the tall-grass prairie. Switch grass is almost as tall. Because its leaf blades are long and tender, big bluestem is the preferred food of most large grazing animals. Little bluestem, only two or three feet tall, is the dominant species of the mixed-grass prairie (grasses range between two and four feet). It produces an abundance of tillers that quickly form compact sod. Grama grass, a short clump-forming grass, is typical of the shortgrass prairie (grasses are less than two feet tall).

Croplands Through a cooperative farming program, local farmers grow corn, wheat, and milo on refuge lands. The farmers harvest a portion of the crops and leave the rest in the field for the thousands of migratory ducks and geese that use the area in spring and fall.

Wetlands When the reservoir becomes low, small wetland areas ranging from marsh to mudflats appear at the water's edge. In some years brush grows up quickly. When the lake again fills, the flooded brush provides outstanding habitat and food for fish.

Open waters The North Fork of the Solomon River and Bow Creek, which feed Kirwin Reservoir, are intermittent streams that dry up in periods of drought. This causes the reservoir's water levels to fluctuate from year to year. At normal water levels, the clear blue water of Kirwin Reservoir covers 5,097 acres. Just before the Great Flood of '93, the reservoir reached an all-time low of only 900 acres.

■ ANIMAL LIFE

Birds Kirwin attracts large numbers of migratory waterfowl. Ducks and geese begin arriving in the fall. Some stay for a while before moving on, but as many as

Whooping cranes can often be found in the company of the smaller gray sandhill cranes.

Piping and semipalmated plovers feed in refuge mudflats.

20,000 Canada geese and 10,000 or more mallards winter at the refuge. Spring migration has less spectacular concentrations, but a variety of waterfowl stops by including white-fronted geese, mallards, northern pintails, and lesser scaup.

Water birds and shorebirds also pass through in spring and fall. Sandhill cranes are seen commonly and the endangered whooping crane puts in an occasional appearance (see sidebar). When the reservoir is low and mudflats are exposed, an abundance of shorebirds can be seen feeding in the muck, including semi-palmated, piping, and snowy plovers, long-billed curlews, American avocets, and upland sandpipers.

With the melding of tall and shortgrass prairies at Kirwin comes an intermingling of eastern and western species. Both eastern and western kingbirds are here, as are eastern and western meadowlarks, and eastern and Say's phoebes.

Northern bobwhites, ring-necked pheasants, lesser prairie chickens, and the Rio Grande subspecies of the eastern wild turkey all find places to nest in the refuge. Wading birds nest in several rookeries found on the refuge. In all, a total of 197 bird species have been recorded at Kirwin.

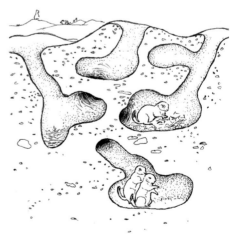

Prairie dog town

Mammals The grasslands provide a plethora of seeds for rodents. The spot called "Dog Town" on the map is indeed a "dog town," but not a town for Labrador retrievers. It is a 35-acre prairie dog town!

Prairie dogs are an integral part of a prairie ecosystem in natural balance.

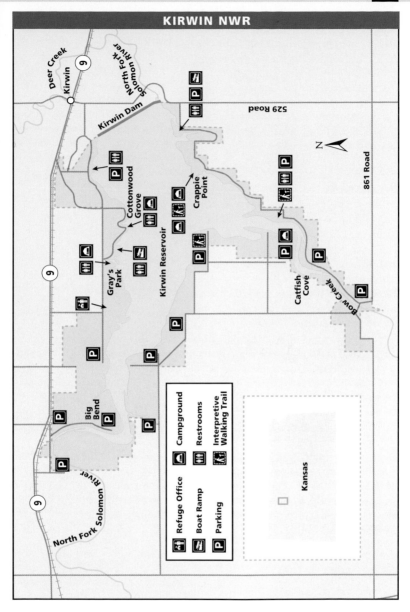

KIRWIN NWR

They forage grasses and herbs around their town which stimulates growth and makes plant nutrients available to other grazers. When abandoned, their burrows are often used by burrowing owls or rattlesnakes.

Other rodents who find homes here include both Franklin's and 13-lined ground squirrels, plains pocket gophers, and Ord's kangaroo rats.

Coyotes, red and gray foxes, beaver, raccoons, mink, opossum, eastern and spotted skunks, and bobcats are some of the carnivores that prey on Kirwin's many rodents. With luck, you may observe a badger working feverishly to dig a prairie dog from its den.

Reptiles and amphibians Long and severe winters keep the number of reptiles and amphibians on the refuge to a minimum, but 31 species have been found there. The western plains garter snake, the large, but harmless bullsnake, and prairie rattlesnake are typical prairie snakes. Folklore tells us that the olive-green prairie rattler lives in harmony with prairie dogs since it sometimes uses their burrows, but this is untrue. The prairie rattler preys on prairie dogs.

ACTIVITIES

■ **CAMPING:** Tents and RVs are allowed in four designated primitive camping areas for up to seven consecutive days. A camp must be removed from any specific campground for a minimum of 72 hours before it can be moved back to the same campground.

■ **SWIMMING:** Swimming, float tubing, and water skiing are permitted in the areas where motorized boating is allowed. There is no designated swimming beach.

HUNTING AND FISHING
Duck hunting and light and dark **geese** hunting are permitted during designated seasons. Hunting for **fox squirrel, deer, pheasants, quail, prairie chicken, cottontail rabbits,** and **turkey** is permitted at various times of the year. The dates and seasons vary year by year; check with refuge managers for current regulations.

Fishing is permitted in the reservoir and North Fork of the Solomon River and Bow Creek year-round (**walleye, bass, black crappie,** and **channel catfish**).

■ **WILDLIFE OBSERVATION:** Watching wildlife at Kirwin is easy. The wildlife comes into the open where it can be seen easily. Keep your eyes open for mule deer and jackrabbits on the prairie and white-tailed deer and the eastern cottontail in brushy areas.

The marshy area at the western end of the reservoir is a delightful place to spot ducks, geese, shorebirds, and wading birds. Beyond the marsh, American white pelicans sometimes fish shallow waters.

■ **PHOTOGRAPHY:** A good spot to take panoramic shots of the refuge is from the overlook just north of the refuge headquarters.

■ **HIKES AND WALKS:** A short interpretive nature trail allows you to walk the trails of "Dog Town." Interpretive signs explain prairie dog ecology. Two other short interpretive trails are found at Crappie Point and the Kiln.

■ **PUBLICATIONS:** Refuge brochure with map; children's wildlife checklist; bird list; mammal list.

Quivira NWR
Stafford, Kansas

A grasslands view from Migrant Mile Trail

Birders working on their bird life-lists will find a bonanza in Quivira NWR. Located in the geographic center of the country and strategically situated along the Central Flyway, this large wetland complex attracts thousands upon thousands of migratory birds each year. In spring and fall the skies literally fill up with waves of birds.

Half the shorebirds of North America are believed to stop here or in nearby Cheyenne Bottoms—among them, phalaropes, long-billed curlews, sandpipers, godwits, and several species of plovers. The curlew sandpiper, a rare curved-bill sandpiper that many birders would like to add to their life-list, is seen feeding in mudflats here. Huge numbers of waterfowl also stop by in spring and fall, including Canada and white-fronted geese, plus more than a dozen species of ducks. Quivira is also a major staging area for sandhill cranes, whooping cranes, peregrine falcons, bald and golden eagles, and other raptors. In October the bugling cries of the majestic whoopers ring out over the huge expanses of marsh and waterlogged fields.

Migratory birds have been stopping at Quivira for centuries. Some stay only a day or two and go on. Others remain to nest, including avocets, stilts, snowy plovers, upland sandpipers, herons, egrets, white-faced ibises, the endangered interior least tern, and four species of rails—black, king, Virginia, and sora.

HISTORY

Quivira was named for an Indian tribe living in the area in 1541 when Coronado came through during his long search for gold, treasures, and the fabled "Seven Cities of Cibola." Although Coronado found no gold, he did find thriving Indian villages, fertile grasslands and marshes, large, shallow salt lakes, and abundant wildlife. The name Quivira symbolized for him the bounteous natural life he saw.

Native Americans had long hunted waterfowl and other wildlife in the region.

Early settlers followed suit. By the turn of the century, commercial hunters discovered the region's bounty and provided wagonload after wagonload of waterfowl to restaurants in Kansas City and cities farther east.

The loss of prime waterfowl habitat to development over the years prompted sportsmen to band together to buy land for private hunting clubs. Sometimes these clubs made improvements. At Quivira, sportsmen diverted the flow of Rattlesnake Creek directly into Little Salt Marsh to maintain the aquatic habitat.

After Quivira was established as a wildlife refuge in 1955, additional canals were dug in hopes of ensuring a steady water supply. With the ongoing loss of wetlands throughout the United States, this 22,135-acre refuge is more vital to migrating birds today than ever before.

GETTING THERE

Quivira is located in the Kansas heartland about 30 mi. from Hutchinson. From Hutchinson, take US 50 West to Zenith, then go north on Zenith Rd. for 8 mi. (continuing as it becomes dirt) to refuge headquarters.

■ **SEASON:** Open year-round.

■ **HOURS:** General refuge open daylight hours. Visitor Center, on the south end of the refuge, open weekdays, 7:30 a.m.–4 p.m., and selected weekends during the spring and fall migration seasons.

■ **FEES:** None.

■ **ADDRESS:** Quivira NWR, RR 3 Box 48A, Stafford, KS 67578

■ **TELEPHONE:** 316/486-2393

TOURING QUIVIRA

■ **BY AUTOMOBILE:** Approximately 20 miles of roads are open for driving. From the south end of the refuge, the main road follows the east side of Little Salt Marsh and then continues north through cropland and seasonally flooded water units. At the north end of the refuge the road connects to a four-mile wildlife drive that passes Big Salt Marsh and salt flats.

■ **BY FOOT:** There are two interpretive trails, both handicapped-accessible. There are also miles of roads closed to vehicles that visitors may follow into the remote areas of the refuge.

■ **BY BICYCLE:** Bicycles are permitted on any road open to automobiles and roads closed to other vehicles, but in some places deep sand make peddling difficult.

■ **BY CANOE, KAYAK, OR BOAT:** Boating is not allowed at Quivira.

WHAT TO SEE

■ **LANDSCAPE AND CLIMATE** Quivira is a complex of large salt marshes, mudflats, croplands, and sand prairie lying in a transition zone where the Central Lowlands meet the Great Plains. In this region of flat to rolling terrain, the lush tallgrass prairie of the eastern plains blends into the more arid mixed and shortgrass prairie of the west. Much of the original prairie is gone, but a few pieces remain intact and look much as they did a century and a half ago before farmers tilled the soil.

The climate is variable with strong winds, cold winters, and warm summers. Rainfall is sparse here, and many streams are diverted to provide irrigation water for agricultural crops. Severe thunderstorms are likely from May to June.

■ **PLANT LIFE**

Forest Forests do not exist here, but there are stands of sandplum and cotton-

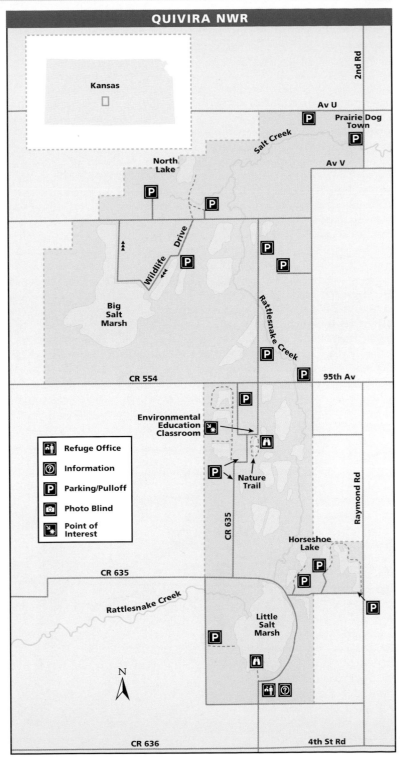

QUIVIRA NWR

Kansas

2nd Rd

Av U

Prairie Dog Town

Salt Creek

North Lake

Av V

Wildlife Drive

Big Salt Marsh

Rattlesnake Creek

CR 554

95th Av

Environmental Education Classroom

Nature Trail

Raymond Rd

CR 635

Horseshoe Lake

CR 635

Rattlesnake Creek

Little Salt Marsh

N

CR 636

4th St Rd

Refuge Office

Information

Parking/Pulloff

Photo Blind

Point of Interest

wood and scattered occurrences of cedars, locusts, and mulberry. The small (about 10-acre) forested plots that dot the area were planted by pioneers to provide a source of firewood. Homesteaders could also claim additional land if they planted trees.

Grassland About 50 percent of the refuge is grassland (more than 13,000 acres). Some of these grasslands are pristine —the sod has never been turned by a plow. Others were created by seeding old farm fields or by allowing natural succession to occur. Prairie management involves prescribed burning and letting cattle graze for short periods of time in grassy areas to stimulate growth, a function performed in the past by grazing bison.

Cropland More than 1,300 acres are planted in crops—milo and wheat. Farmers leave a portion of the milo and cow peas in the field for wildlife and harvest the rest. However, farmers harvest all of the winter wheat because geese prefer to eat spilled wheat in stubbled fields rather than standing wheat that could hide predators.

Wetlands Water is at a premium in this part of Kansas, and water management is a key concern for refuge managers. Water enters Quivira through Rattlesnake Creek, flows into Little Salt Marsh, and is then diverted through a network of canals to managed wetland units and marshes totaling more than 6,500 acres in all. The continuing demands of agriculture on the region's water resources is a constant threat to the refuge's water resources.

Open waters The 1,500-acre Big Salt Marsh and the 900-acre Little Salt Marsh are both shallow lakes, only 4 to 5 feet deep when full. The salt in these marshes comes from groundwater that rises to the land's surface after passing through salt layers deep within the earth. As the water in the lakes evaporates during the dry summer months, salt concentrations rise. In 1991, when drought reduced Big Salt Marsh to about 20 acres, biologists measure the salt concentrations in the remaining water at three times that of seawater. Plants that live in the salt marsh include cattail, cordgrass, needlerush, salt grass, and bulrush.

Two dozen other smaller lakes lie in the refuge, including North and Horseshoe lakes, that are managed to provide aquatic habitat for migratory waterfowl.

■ ANIMAL LIFE

Birds In all, Quivira's bird list consists of an impressive 311 species. The list of full-time bird residents includes Swainson's and red-tailed hawks, black-billed magpies, Bell's vireos, ring-necked pheasants, greater prairie chicken, wild turkeys, and northern bobwhites, to name a few. But it is the large collection of shorebirds that makes Quivira NWR truly a birder's paradise.

Black-billed magpie

American avocets

The endangered interior least tern nests at Quivira. These small white, black-capped terns prefer to nest on bare beaches and river sandbars. However, flood-control efforts have reduced the number of bare sandbars occurring along rivers. Quivira's unvegetated salt flats at the north end of the refuge provide a suitable nesting alternative. Unfortunately, since the tern's nests are merely small scraped-out depressions in the ground, any amount of flooding can destroy them. To mitigate this problem, refuge staff and volunteers have built small mounds of rock and gravel throughout the flats as nesting platforms for the tern. Fortunately, the terns are accepting these mounds.

Some of the shorebirds that flock to Quivira each year appear to have come straight out of a Lewis Carroll fable. Take, for instance, the dowitcher. This shorebird has a long bill that is quite out of proportion with its body and medium long legs. The woodcock suffers from a similarly odd configuration. This bird has a long bill that is out of keeping with its short neck, short legs, and chunky body. In addition, the woodcock's large, dark eyes are mounted on the top of its head. Some birds have peculiarly shaped bills. The long bills of the long-legged avocet and godwit are upturned, while those of the whimbrel, long-billed curlew, and white-faced ibis are down-curved.

In truth, these odd configurations actually add up to very efficient feeding mechanisms. Dowitchers probe the mud by rapidly pumping their beaks up and down like the needle of a sewing machine. Woodcocks plunge their bills straight into the mud to grab food morsels. The American avocet sweeps its beak back and forth like a scythe, working the water's surface for insects.

Mammals Quivira is home to many mammals associated with grasslands and marshlands—black-tailed prairie dogs, white-tailed deer, raccoons, muskrat, badgers, and beaver are common. So are coyotes, who quickly learned that the small tern nesting mounds in the salt flats held an egg meal. Biologists tried various means of thwarting the coyote's marauding ways, including building electric fences around the tern nesting areas. At first these fences were not a deterrent. Some coyotes broke through them, electric shock or no. Then biologists decided to try some Pavlovian training. Before the terns arrived in the spring, they coated

Coyote on the hunt

the electric wires with a pungent mix of cat food, dog food, and cooking oil. Each time the coyotes stopped to smell the wire, they got a good jolt. Now the coyotes no longer bother the terns.

Reptiles and amphibians A fair number of snakes are found at Quivira, including the bullsnake, the great plains rat snake, and two kinds of rattlesnakes, the prairie rattlesnake and the Massasauga rattlesnake. The Massasauga is fairly common and can often be seen crossing roads in spring and fall as it migrates to and from its overwintering areas in moist lowland areas. It is a short, thick snake with a blotchy, gray-brown body. Its head is a thick diamond with dark stripes extending back from the eyes. The Massasauga's tail ends in a stubby rattle; juveniles' tails are yellowish. Like other venomous snakes, Massasaugas have sensory pits on the sides of their heads, and the pupils of their eyes are catlike instead of round.

Invertebrates Mosquitoes can be a nuisance, especially during the spring. Midge larvae (also called bloodworms), various snails, and scuds can be found on the refuge. Crayfish provide an important food item for herons, egrets, and raccoons.

ACTIVITIES

■ **CAMPING:** Camping is not allowed at Quivira.

■ **WILDLIFE OBSERVATION:** Big Salt Marsh is the best area for viewing concentrations of shorebirds, ducks, and pelicans. The west edge is a favorite area for visiting sandhill and whooping cranes. Little Salt Marsh is also a good place to observe birdlife; the road on the east side of the marsh can provide good viewing of shorebirds and geese when water levels are right. Along the drive between the two salt marshes are pastures, fields, and croplands. These are good places to observe wild turkeys, ring-necked pheasants, eastern and western meadowlarks, and kingbirds as well as migratory birds.

When the reservoir becomes low, small wetland areas ranging from marsh to mudflats appear at the water's edge. In some years brush grows up quickly. When the lake again fills, the flooded brush provides outstanding habitat and food for fish.

■ **PHOTOGRAPHY:** Because of the large number of migrating shorebirds and good accessibility, Quivira is a great place for photographing wildlife. Two blinds are available on a first-come, first-served basis. One is found near the head-quarters building on Little Salt Marsh. The other is found on a small pond near the Environmental Education Classroom from a branch of the Migrant Mile Nature Trail. Both are large and comfortable, with several ports for lenses to poke through. A sign at the head of the trail that leads to the blind tells whether it is occupied or not. Portable blinds are also allowed.

Excellent photography opportunities are also found at Big Salt Marsh. Take your time and use the car as a blind to get spectacular photos of ducks, pelicans, sandpipers, and possibly the interior least tern.

HUNTING AND FISHING
Refuge is closed to all hunting from March through Aug. In addition, it may be closed without notice when whooping cranes are present. Hunting for **duck**, **light geese**, **dark geese**, **squirrel**, **pheasants**, **quail**, **dove**, **rabbit**, **snipe**, and **rails** is allowed at varying seasons of the year. A handicapped-accessible water-fowl hunting blind is available by reservation. Because the dates and the seasons for hunting change each year, you should call the refuge for current regulations.

Fishing is permitted in all refuge waters year-round.

■ **HIKES AND WALKS:** Birdhouse Boulevard is a 1,000-foot-long concrete trail, handicapped accessible, through mature cedar trees. It showcases various types of bird feeders and houses. The Migrant Mile Trail is a 1.2-mile handicapped-accessible interpretive trail that loops through groves of locusts, mulberries, cottonwood trees, and grasslands, then takes you across a wetland on a boardwalk. Along the way, house wrens chatter, while families of flashy orange-and-black Baltimore orioles fly down the trail.

■ **PUBLICATIONS:** Refuge pamphlet with map; self-guided auto-tour pamphlet; refuge bird list; refuge hunting and fishing regulations.

Atchafalaya NWR
Krotz Springs, Louisiana

Scenic bayou, Atchafalaya NWR

The unmistakable gobble of a wild male turkey shatters the early morning stillness on a late-March day. In the dense bottomland forest a hunter, dressed in camouflage, rests motionless against a large overcup oak. He uses his mouth call to make the sound of a hen turkey. The male turkey gobbles again and seems to come closer. Again the hunter calls and the turkey answers.

Gobblers are extremely wary birds, with eyesight that can detect the blink of an eye. This gobbler is old and wise and decides something is wrong with the call, or perhaps he spied a slight movement. He moves away. The hunter never sees the bird through the thick foliage.

The terrain throughout Atchafalaya NWR is flat and wet, consisting of a complex of bottomland forests (the largest remaining bottomland forest in America), swamps, sloughs, bayous, and oxbow lakes. Biologists rank this basin as one of the most productive wildlife areas in North America. Much of the land here has never been drained. The old gobbler is but one of the many species of wildlife here in abundance.

HISTORY

Atchafalaya NWR is located in the Atchafalaya River Basin, one of five large basins that make up the Mississippi Alluvial Plain. The 800,000-acre basin stretches for 140 miles between the Atchafalaya and Mississippi rivers.

Parts of the Atchafalaya Basin are lower than the Mississippi River. In 1985 the basin was established by Congress as a floodway to receive excess waters from the Mississippi and protect downriver towns. In 1986 Congress authorized additional uses for the basin. A portion of the basin, 15,200 acres, was established as a national wildlife refuge and another area just to the north was established as the Sherburne Wildlife Management Area. The U.S. Army Corps of Engineers is acquiring an additional 50,000 acres in the vicinity to add to its holdings. The

Atchafalaya Basin project is considered a win-win situation for all involved. Human property is protected, an ecosystem is preserved, and people benefit from the added recreational possibilities.

Three public agencies (the U.S. Fish & Wildlife Service, U.S. Corps of Engineers, and the Louisiana Department of Wildlife and Fisheries) own land in the basin, but the day-to-day management is by the Louisiana Department of Wildlife and Fisheries. For most visitors, the boundaries between the various land holdings are transparent and the same rules apply.

GETTING THERE

The refuge is located in south-central Louisiana about 30 mi. west of Baton Rouge and 1 mi. east of Krotz Springs. LA 975, a gravel road running parallel to the levee on the east side of the Atchafalaya River, provides the main access to the refuge. To reach this road from Krotz Springs or Baton Rouge, take US 190 West to LA 975 and then turn south.

- **SEASON:** Refuge and state lands open year-round.
- **HOURS:** Sunrise to sunset.
- **FEES:** LA hunting or fishing license, or Wild LA stamp required.
- **ADDRESS:** Sherburne WMA, P.O. Box 127, Krotz Springs, LA 70750 (Sherburne or Atchafalaya information); Atchafalaya NWR, c/o Southeast Louisiana Refuges, 1010 Gause Boulevard, Bldg. 936, Slidell, LA 70458
- **TELEPHONE:** 318/566-2251 (Sherburne): 504/646-7555 (USFWS)

TOURING ATCHAFALAYA

- **BY AUTOMOBILE:** LA 975 provides access to the refuge and offers glimpses of the Atchafalaya River and the bottomland forest. Several gravel roads (totaling about 21 miles) lead from LA 975 into the refuge. These are secondary roads, and conditions may be poor. There are 16 miles of ATV trails for hunter access. These trails pass through wet and muddy areas and may be blocked by deadfalls and snags.

- **BY FOOT:** There is only one maintained trail near the refuge headquarters, but you can walk the secondary gravel roads. Hiking is also possible on the ATV trails, but ruts, mud, and tall weeds may make walking difficult in spots. Some bushwhacking may be attempted on the higher ridges of the refuge, but bayous and other water barriers make this difficult.

- **BY BICYCLE:** Visitors may bicycle on any of the roads open to automobiles.

The dense wetlands of Atchafalaya

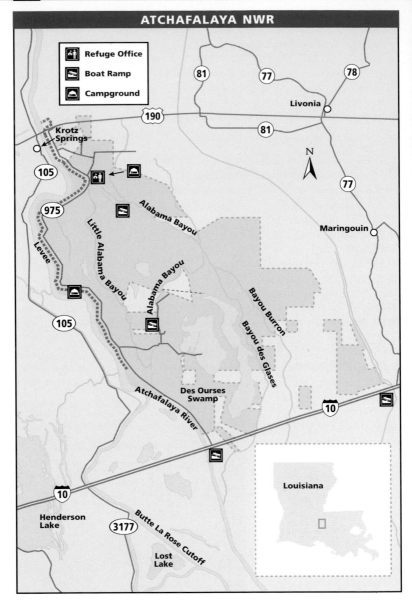

ATCHAFALAYA NWR

BY CANOE, KAYAK, OR BOAT: The ideal way to get into the refuge's interior is by shallow-draft boat (canoes or johnboats with small motors). You can follow one of several boat trails or bayous. The Little Alabama Bayou Trail is 7 miles one-way. The 8-mile Alabama Bayou Trail has boat landings at each end, making it possible to shuttle a canoe. Bayou des Glaises is a scenic bayou for the more experienced boater. Several local tour companies will take visitors into the swamp on barges.

WHAT TO SEE

LANDSCAPE AND CLIMATE As in most of the Atchafalaya Basin, much of the refuge consists of a vast, primeval-looking bottomland hardwood forest interspersed with bayous, cypress-tupelo swamps, and agricultural fields. Some of the forest has been logged or farmed, and efforts are under way to construct and restore greentree reservoirs in these areas.

The climate is mild with subtropical weather throughout the year. Average rainfall reaches 54 inches. Freezes are unusual.

■ PLANT LIFE

Forests Tree species found in the forested bottomlands include cottonwood, sweet gum, American sycamore, green ash, and water hickory, tallest of the hickories. The slow-growing, water-loving overcup oak is also common here.

Croplands Some of the original forests were cleared for cropland. Progress is being made to restore these areas to their native habitat.

Wetlands Cypress-tupelo swamps occur along the bayous. Many of the cypress trees are amply festooned with Spanish moss. Spanish moss is an epiphyte, not a parasite. It uses the trees only for support, not nourishment. Spanish moss is related to the pineapple and is used as a nest material by squirrels, rabbits, mice, and birds.

Open waters Standing water is found throughout the year in the Atchafalaya River and the many bayous that meander through the refuge. In wet times, standing water can be found in the forest as well. Aquatic plants growing in shallow waters include water hyacinth, alligatorweed, cattail, smartweed, and duckweed, which forms green carpets over the surfaces of quiet waters. Smartweeds (there are more than 30 species) are members of the buckwheat family and one of the favorite food sources of waterfowl and seed-eating songbirds. Most have attractive pinkish flowers.

■ ANIMAL LIFE

Birds Neotropical migrants that cross the Gulf of Mexico are often faced with two circumstances as they approach land. Sometimes, they have to fight strong head winds. When this happens, they look for the first landing place they can

Hooded merganser

TIMBER DOODLE American woodcocks require four specialized habitats to be successful. First, since they feed mostly on earthworms, they need rich, moist soil. Second, they must have clearings for their courtship displays. Third, they require dense second-growth hardwood forests to build their nests. Fourth, they need large fields in which to roost at night.

The woodcock's courtship displays are quite spectacular and have earned the bird the nickname "timber doodle." These displays occur at dusk and dawn in early spring. The male arrives at the courtship site, called a "singing ground." He does a few *"peent"* calls to warm up. Then he starts his aerial acrobatics. First, he takes off in an ascending spiral, spreading his flight feathers to create a twittering sound as air flows through them. He rises several hundred feet, out of sight to the naked eye. Then, he rapidly descends like a falling leaf, making a chirping call. At about 50 feet from the ground, he stops his call and lands where he took off. He repeats the process over and over, often for an hour.

find, often islands of trees in otherwise barren landscapes. When the migrants arrive in fair weather, however, they can take the time to search for prime habitat. Atchafalaya is one such place.

Located at the southern end of the Mississippi Flyway, the refuge is an important staging area for neotropical migrants and a wintering place for a large assortment of waterfowl and wading birds. A large population of canvasback ducks in Louisiana can be found in the southern part of the Atchafalaya Basin. Students from local schools are involved in projects to build nesting boxes, helping to make wood ducks and hooded mergansers more plentiful.

Wading birds commonly seen in the refuge include egrets, herons, ibises, and anhingas. Raptors, too, find Atchafalaya to their liking, including bald eagles,

Woodcock

ospreys, swallow-tailed kites, and Mississippi kites (in summer). Among the refuge's many full-time residents are the wild turkey and the American wood duck. Atchafalaya also supports a large wintering concentration of the chunky, acrobatic woodcock (see sidebar, above).

Mammals White-tailed deer, gray and fox squirrels, eastern cottontails, gray and red foxes, coyotes, striped skunks, opossum, raccoons, minks, bobcats, nutria, muskrat, river, otter, and beaver all find a home in Atchafalaya. A small remnant population of Louisiana black bears forages in the woods.

The refuge is a good place to observe the cottontail's cousin, the swamp rabbit. The swamp rabbit's ears are larger in proportion to its body than its cousin's, and its feet are rusty, not white. As you might expect, the swamp rabbit is a good swimmer.

Reptiles and amphibians Water snakes and cottonmouth water moccasins glide through refuge waters looking for prey. Gigantic alligator snapping turtles also hunt these waters and sometimes sun themselves on logs on cool but sunny days. Alligators can be seen in swamps and bayous.

Invertebrates Red swamp and white river crayfish are common in wet, muddy areas throughout the entire basin. These crustaceans are relished by a host of wading birds and other wildlife as well as Louisiana residents, who use them in such classic Cajun dishes as crayfish étouffée.

HUNTING AND FISHING Seasons have traditionally been a handicapped and youth **deer** hunt the first week in Nov., a gun deer hunt in mid-Dec., and a muzzle-loader deer hunt in Jan. **Rabbit**, **squirrel**, **woodcock**, and **waterfowl** hunting are allowed in the fall, and **raccoon** hunting is usually in Jan. There is a spring **turkey** season. Contact the refuge or the Louisiana Wildlife and Fisheries for exact dates.

More than 85 species of fish live in the basin, and their populations frequently exceed 1,000 pounds per acre. Fishing (**largemouth bass**, **white crappie**, **black crappie**, **warmouth**, **bluegill**, **redear sunfish**, **channel catfish**) is allowed year-round. **Crayfish** harvesting is allowed March through July.

ACTIVITIES

■ **CAMPING:** There is no camping at Atchafalaya; there are two primitive camping areas at Sherburne.

■ **WILDLIFE OBSERVATION:** Although you can see some wildlife from the refuge roads, the best places to view wildlife are within the interior of the refuge. To get to these places, you need an ATV or boat.

■ **HIKES AND WALKS:** A short, self-guided nature tour near the headquarters building loops through bottomland forest.

■ **PUBLICATIONS:** Refuge fact sheet; refuge map.

Bayou Cocodrie NWR
Ferriday, Louisiana

Northern shoveler

Located in east-central Louisiana near the Mississippi River town of Ferriday, Bayou Cocodrie NWR was named for the bayou meandering through it. Cocodrie is a French derivation of a Choctaw word meaning "river of crocodiles." The French called the American alligator commonly found here "crocodile."

HISTORY

This forested wetland did indeed at one time contain an abundance of alligators, but like everywhere else in the lower Mississippi Alluvial Plain, they were trapped and hunted to the verge of extinction. And, although a few alligators remain, this refuge is now better known for its bottomland forest habitat.

Bayou Cocodrie was established as a national wildlife refuge in 1992, with 11,255 acres purchased from The Nature Conservancy. Additional acquisitions over a span of five years brought its acreage to 13,168 with another 9,000 acres proposed for acquisition. Because it remains in a relative natural state, the Bayou Cocodrie has been designated a Louisiana Natural and Scenic River.

GETTING THERE

The refuge is 50 mi. northeast of Alexandria. From Ferriday, take LA 15 South about 3 mi. to Poole Road, then go southwest 3.5 mi. to the refuge. (Caution: Loose railroad spikes from this graveled-over tramway can cause flats.)

■ **SEASON:** Open year-round.
■ **HOURS:** Refuge: open daylight hours. Office open weekdays, 7:30 a.m.–4 p.m.
■ **FEES:** Entrance pass is required for all visits; $5 daily and $12 annually.
■ **ADDRESS:** Bayou Cocodrie NWR, P.O. Box 1772, Ferriday, LA 71334
■ **TELEPHONE:** 318/336-7119

TOURING BAYOU COCODRIE

While there are no improved roads into interior sections, most of the refuge is accessible either by foot, boat, or ATV. There are several miles of foot trails and about 10 miles of ATV trails that are also suitable for hiking. These trails are only accessible to ATVs during the hunting seasons. Parking areas and trails may be closed periodically due to flooding. Canoeing, a great way to experience the refuge, is sometimes possible on Bayou Cocodrie. Because water levels may be too low for canoeing, however, check at headquarters for current water conditions.

WHAT TO SEE

The land in this part of the lower Mississippi River Valley is basically flat. Where bayous cut through rich alluvial soil, years of periodic flooding have created a "ridge and swale" topography. This corduroy-like landscape has ridges 1 to 3 feet high and 120 to 350 feet wide and swales, or depressions, 50 to 350 feet wide. Under natural conditions, the ridges tend to be heavily forested while seasonal rains fill the depressions—creating ideal habitat for waterfowl and other wildlife.

Numerous beaver ponds and two lakes provide permanent water in dry periods. These lakes are of vital importance to nesting wood ducks. The remaining land is wetlands or agricultural fields. Some of the croplands are being reforested; others are planted in millet and buckwheat to provide food for wildlife.

■ **PLANT LIFE** Cypress swamps and bottomland hardwood forests of oak, gum, elm, and ash make up 75 percent of the refuge. A 1,000-acre tract of bottomland forest has been designated a Natural Resource Area because it contains some of the finest 200-year old trees in the state.

■ **ANIMAL LIFE**

Birds During spring migration, Bayou Cocodrie attracts large numbers of neotropicals and other migratory birds. Flashes of yellow, rapidly flitting from tree branch to tree branch, may be Kentucky, hooded, or prothonotary warblers. Mallards, northern shovelers, northern pintail, and blue- and green-winged teal roost and feed here. Long-legged wading birds, mostly great blue herons and egrets, are abundant and can be seen stalking small fish at the edge of sloughs and small lakes. Osprey, wood storks, bald eagles, peregrine falcons, and swallow-tailed kites are occasionally reported.

> **HUNTING AND FISHING**
> Hunting is the most popular refuge activity, particularly for **squirrels** and **white-tailed deer**. Fishing is permitted year-round.

Mammals White-tailed deer find plenty to forage on in the dense forests. Gray squirrels out number fox squirrels. Turkeys, reintroduced into the refuge, are now doing well. Gnawed trees indicate that beavers are here in good numbers. The refuge is part of a long corridor through the Mississippi River Valley where the secretive Louisiana black bear survives on tree bark, grubs, beetles, crickets, ants, fish, and the occasional bite of honeycomb.

Reptiles and amphibians The wet habitat of the refuge hosts its fair share of alligators, cottonmouths, and aquatic turtles.

ACTIVITIES

■ **WILDLIFE OBSERVATION:** Bayou Cocodrie offers a glimpse into what the presettlement bottomland hardwood forests must have looked like. Wildlife is best seen along trails or roads in the early morning or late evening.
■ **PUBLICATIONS:** Brochure with map; wildlife fact sheet.

Bayou Sauvage NWR
New Orleans, Louisiana

Egrets

It is a late spring day at Bayou Sauvage NWR. An interpreter from the U.S. Fish & Wildlife Service guides a group of nine-year-old students from New Orleans along the nature trail. The interpreter points to what appears to be a knob on a high dead branch. The fourth-graders raise their school-grade binoculars to look and gasp with delight as they discover an immature barred owl. The educator explains that many young owls walk out on tree limbs, or "branch," at this stage of their life. The naturalist leads the students to an overlook and focuses their attention on a wetland. She identifies some of the waterfowl—only coots, teal, and mallards this day. She points to the bald cypresses standing in the water and explains how their knobby knees provide them with oxygen. At the end of the program, the students receive badges and become Junior Refuge Managers. This is hands-on learning—the kind of unique education that is the speciality of the national wildlife refuges.

HISTORY

Bayou Sauvage NWR lies within the city limits of New Orleans on a strip of land separating lakes Pontchartrain and Borgne. It is only fifteen minutes from New Orleans' famous French Quarter. Consisting of 23,000 acres of marshes, swamps, bayous, and bottomland forests, it is the nation's largest urban wildlife refuge.

At one time there were plans for residential, commercial, and industrial development for the entire area. However, in 1990 President George Bush authorized the refuge under the Emergency Wetland Act of 1986. The refuge's main objectives are to preserve habitat and protect migratory birds and other wildlife.

GETTING THERE

From downtown New Orleans, take I-10 East to Exit 246 (Chalmette, I-510); go about 2 mi. on I-510 to US 90 East exit; turn left and go approximately 4 mi. From

Slidell, take I-10 West to the Irish Bayou exit (#254); turn left on US 11 and go 6 mi. to LA 90; turn right and go about 2 mi. The refuge is shown on most city maps, and some commercial tours of the city explore it.

■ **SEASON:** Open year-round.

■ **HOURS:** Open daylight hours only.

■ **FEES:** None.

■ **ADDRESS:** Southeast Louisiana Refuges, 1010 Gause Blvd. #936, Slidell, LA 70458

■ **TELEPHONE:** 504/646-7555

TOURING BAYOU SAUVAGE

■ **BY AUTOMOBILE:** A high-speed interstate and several busy city roads pass through the refuge, but these roads are not suitable for touring. The best ways to tour the refuge are by foot, bicycle, or boat.

■ **BY FOOT:** Two outstanding nature trails provide access to the refuge's interior. Visitors may also walk the levees and service roads. Two trails through the higher ground offer a chance to see some of the birds and other wildlife of the refuge.

■ **BY BICYCLE:** A newly constructed bikeway parallels the shore of Lake Pontchartrain on the north side of the refuge between I 10 and the lake.

■ **BY CANOE, KAYAK, OR BOAT:** Boating is permitted on several lakes and bayous. Inside the hurricane protection levee that rings a good portion of the refuge, outboards are restricted to 25 hp or less and airboats are prohibited.

The refuge sponsors weekend canoe trips on beautiful Bayou Thomas. The tours are free and available on a first-come, first-served basis, but you must make reservations by calling 504/646-7544. The refuge provides canoes, paddles, life vests, and an interpreter to help identify animals and plants.

Aerial view of Bayou Sauvage NWR

WHAT TO SEE

■ **LANDSCAPE AND CLIMATE** Bayou Sauvage and all of metropolitan New Orleans lie in the huge Mississippi Delta where the Mississippi River empties into the Gulf of Mexico. This is some of the flattest, lowest, and geologically youngest land in the United States. Silt deposited by the Mississippi only 200 to 500 years ago formed the land. Some of the land is slightly below sea level.

The refuge occupies a strip of deltaic land between two large lakes, Pontchartrain to the north and Borgne to the south. Chef Pass, a waterway that connects the

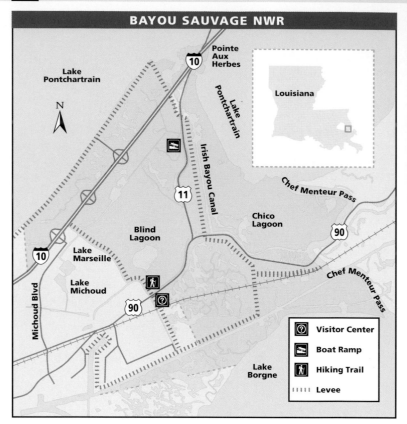

BAYOU SAUVAGE NWR

two lakes, forms the eastern boundary of the refuge. The Intracoastal Waterway, a man-made canal for barge traffic, cuts across the southern part of the refuge.

Although outside of the refuge boundary, Lake Pontchartrain, a large freshwater lake, is extremely important to refuge birds and other wildlife. Lake Borgne, an inlet of the Mississippi Sound, connects Lake Pontchartrain with the Gulf of Mexico.

The system of massive levees inside the refuge were built to hold back storm surges and maintain water levels in low-lying New Orleans. These hurricane levees interrupt natural water-flow patterns and are a challenge to refuge managers who are trying to maintain Bayou Sauvage in a natural state.

The climate is hot, humid, and rainy most of the year. Annual rainfall averages about 60 inches per year. Hurricanes sometimes occur in late summer and fall.

■ PLANT LIFE

Forest About 400 acres of the refuge is bottomland hardwood forests dominated by bald cypress trees. A program is under way to reforest additional lands with cypress and other native species in areas that were lost to development. Two exotics, the Chinese tallow tree and the tamarisk, an ornamental shrub or small tree, are invading higher parts of the refuge.

Wetlands Most of Bayou Sauvage consists of freshwater (13,000 acres) and brackish (9,000 acres) marshes. A brackish marsh is one that is irregularly flooded with tidewater and dominated by salt-tolerant plants.

An introduced species, nutria feed on plants that grow along the water.

Along Lake Borgne a large freshwater marsh extends northward to the higher ground on which I 10 and US 90 are built. Cattail is perhaps the most recognized freshwater marsh plant here. Its stiff leaves and "hot dog on a stick" fruit make it easy to identify. Where found, the plant grows very densely, providing good habitat for red-winged blackbirds and common yellowthroat. The plant is also a veritable grocery store for humans. The rootstalk can be eaten as a potato or dried and ground into flour. The flower spikes can be boiled and eaten like corn-on-the-cob, and the sprouts can be served in salads or boiled and eaten as spinach. The pollen can be added to pancakes or muffins, giving them flavor and wonderful color. Other plants of the freshwater marsh include panic grass and alligator.

Much of the freshwater marsh at Bayou Sauvage was cypress swamp until the 1958 Protection Levee System was completed. A few cypress and willow trees still line the areas's many sloughs and bayous.

The brackish marsh lies outside the hurricane levees and is interspersed with small canals and bayous. Wiregrass, a low-growing, salt-tolerant grass, is the dominant plant in this marsh. Other plants include widgeon grass, marsh-hay cordgrass, saltgrass, three-cornered grass, and salt marsh bulrush. Salt marsh, or three-square, bulrush, is a tall, sturdy grass with long, sharp leaves. This plant can grow to 3 feet tall and is a member of the sedge family. Sedges resemble grasses but have solid, three-sided(triangular) stems and small, often spiky flowers. The salt-marsh bulrush produces small, lustrous dark seeds that are relished by ducks and other marsh birds. Muskrats prefer the stems.

Spartina is a family of grasses widely distributed in salt, brackish, and freshwater marshes. Their stems are generally erect, thin, and wiry while their leaf blades are long and coarse. They produce inflorescences with bristled individual flowers. Marsh-hay cordgrass (*Spartina alterniflora*), also called salt-meadow grass, grows in both fresh and brackish waters throughout coastal Louisiana.

Open waters Several lakes and ponds within the refuge have relative open

Louisiana heron

water and attract migrating waterfowl. Several bayous discharge their water to Lake Pontchartrain.

■ ANIMAL LIFE

Birds During fall, winter, and early spring the skies and waters of Bayou Sauvage are filled with the sights and sounds of wintering shorebirds and waterfowl. Nearly every shorebird that uses the Mississippi Flyway passes through the refuge. Neotropical migrants abound during fall and spring migrations. Thirty-four species of warblers have been counted on the refuge. Northern parula, yellow-throated, prothonotary, and hooded warblers are known to nest on the refuge. The remainder are spring and fall migrants.

The state's namesake, the Louisiana heron, is common throughout the refuge, as are a host of gulls and terns. Other common nesting birds include both the clapper and king rail, glossy and white-faced ibis, and the purple gallinule, a beautifully colored chicken-sized marsh bird. The endangered wood stork is sometimes seen. These spectacular wading birds with white body and massive black beak and head retreat to remote parts of the refuge where they stalk slowly and deliberately through shallow waters for food.

Brown pelicans fly low over the waves, their wingtips just barely skimming the surface of the water. When feeding, these endangered birds sometimes make spectacular headfirst dives from as high as 60 feet into the water for fish. Brown pelicans were once on the verge of extinction, having been hunted for their plumes at the turn of the 20th century and later exposed to high levels of DDT. The DDT concentrations caused the pelican's eggs to develop improperly and break before incubation was complete. After the use of DDT was halted (thanks largely to Rachael Carson's book *Silent Spring)*, the birds began to make a remarkable comeback.

Peregrine falcons, a winter resident, were also affected by DDT, but populations of peregrines have recovered. Peregrines are spectacular hunters. They begin by flying very high to spot their prey and then drop into a dive at speeds of up to 200 miles per hour before striking their prey with talons outstretched. They usually take a duck or other bird in the air but can also take animals on the ground.

Other raptors that hunt the refuge include northern harriers and Cooper's hawks. Bald eagles, Mississippi kites, red-shouldered hawks, and great horned owls nest on the refuge. A total of 268 species of birds have been recorded at Bayou Sauvage.

Mammals White-tailed deer and cottontail rabbits are common throughout the refuge, emerging from the woods at dusk to feed on tender grasses and shrubs. Feral hogs dig for roots everywhere. The nocturnal raccoon ventures forth in the evening in search of picnic scraps, frogs, and crayfish, while the opossum looks for carrion or fruits and berries. Nutria feed on plants that grow along the waterways. These large South American rodents were introduced to the southern marshes in 1899. At that time, beaver had been trapped out, and it was hoped that nutria fur would replace it in popularity. Nutria trapping did not catch on, and now the rodents are the most common mammal in many southern refuges.

Invertebrates The grassy marshes of Bayou Sauvage provide critical spawning and nursery habitat for many fresh and saltwater species, including crabs and shrimp. These crustaceans feed on small animals, carrion, each other, and detritus in the waterways. These animals are in turn preyed on by herons and other wading birds, raccoons, mink, otter, and fish. Unfortunately, marshes are fast disappearing throughout much of the Gulf coastal area, taking with them critical breeding grounds for invertebrates and fish.

Alligator gar

Fish Freshwater lagoons, bayous, and ponds produce bass, crappie, bluegill, and catfish. One unusual fish that haunts the canals and bayous of Bayou Sauvage is the alligator gar. This is a primitive behemoth of a fish; the Louisiana state record is 179 pounds (10-foot-long, 300-pound fish have been reported). The fish is long and skinny with a broad snout and needle-sharp teeth protruding from its mouth. It is covered by bony armorlike scales. The eggs of the fish are poisonous, but locals prepare the fish as a delicacy. This alligator gar wreaks havoc on commercial fishermen's nets and may be responsible for many alleged "alligator attacks." Fishermen who hook into one of these using light tackle for crappie and bluegill hook have the fishing story of a lifetime to tell.

ACTIVITIES

■ **WILDLIFE OBSERVATION:** It is possible to tour the refuge on your own. Many people enjoy walking the trails or pulling off US 90 or 11 to watch great blue and green herons stalking fish. But the best way to see wildlife at Bayou Sauvage is to take one of the tours offered by the refuge staff. Bayou Sauvage has an excellent interpretive staff who know where the wildlife will be. They offer canoe tours, hikes, bike trips, and bird-watching trips and will make special arrangements for groups. Call the refuge headquarters to make a reservation.

■ **PHOTOGRAPHY:** The refuge makes an ideal day trip for nature photographers. It is not uncommon to meet an entire camera club from New Orleans on an outing at Bayou Sauvage. The trails and even the parking lots offer many opportunities to photograph small mammals and birds.

HUNTING AND FISHING
Hunting is not permitted at Bayou Sauvage, but **crabbing** and **crayfishing** are allowed year-round. Nets and traps must be tended at all times. Fishing (for **warm-water species, redfish, speckled trout**) south of the Intracoastal Waterway and US 11 is allowed year-round. Fishing in the remainder of the refuge is permitted March through Oct.

■ **HIKES AND WALKS:** Edge Trail is a 0.5-mile trail through bottomland hardwood forest. The trailhead is located on US 90, about 2 miles east of its junction with US 11. There is ample off-highway parking, restrooms, and a pavilion that can be reserved. The trail is well maintained and features an elevated boardwalk through the wetter portions of the forest. Ridge Trail (3 miles one-way) starts at the same place Edge Trail does. This trail leads to the north along a road and passes between a canal on the west and a lake on the right.

■ **SEASONAL EVENTS:** March: Earth Day. Natural-history programs and opportunities for students to learn about wetlands. April: Bike Fest—test your bike and your endurance on some of the refuge's bike trails; Gatorfest—the "world's fair" of alligator events. A wonderful opportunity to learn everything you ever wanted to know about Louisiana's official state reptile. Several tasty alligator dishes are served, and the event is free; Great Louisiana Birdfest—features field trips to the refuge. May: Migratory Bird Day: a opportunity to see exactly how important places like Bayou Sauvage are to neotropical migrants.

For monthly schedules of outings, contact the Slidell headquarters.

■ **PUBLICATIONS:** Refuge fishing regulations; refuge bird list; refuge fact sheet; Bayou Sauvage/Big Branch Marsh NWRs Calendar of Events; Southeast Louisiana NWRs brochure.

Big Branch Marsh NWR
Slidell, Louisiana

Big Branch Marsh bayou

On a windy, rainy spring day, several people have gathered at a concrete bridge that crosses a small canal at the tip of Goose Point in Big Branch Marsh NWR. Despite the wind and the rain they can see across the lake into the heart of New Orleans.

An elderly woman has come to crab. She is using a metal hoop with a shallow net attached to it. In the center of the net she has tied a piece of raw chicken. Three stout cords are attached equal distance around the metal hoop. The cords are joined to a hand line about 30 feet long. She tosses the hoop out and waits for crabs to find the chicken. When the time feels right, in five minutes or so, she pulls in the net. Several gluttonous blue crabs remain attached to the chicken. She shakes the 10-legged bluish crabs into her cooler and rebaits the net. The woman is using four nets, two on each side of the bridge. She spends her time jumping over the rail and checking each net. Within two hours her cooler is filled with enough crabs to make a glorious gumbo. Nearby a couple have been fishing. When asked about their luck, they proudly show their catch of *barbu* (channel catfish), *sac á lait* (white crappie), and Chinquepin (redear sunfish). Such is life on Big Branch National Wildlife Refuge, the Mississippi Delta region where the locals retain a deep understanding of their natural surroundings and the resources it has to offer.

HISTORY

Big Branch Marsh NWR is relatively new. It was established in 1994 to preserve a portion of the unique habitat and wildlife that surround Lake Pontchartrain. Big Branch Marsh is also helping to preserve the cultures of groups who have depended on its natural resources for hundreds of years.

The refuge got its start with funding from the Richard King Mellon Foundation and The Conservation Fund. Currently it consists of 14,000 acres, with more being added as lands and funds become available.

Big Branch Marsh is one of the last large natural areas remaining in the rapidly developing New Orleans metropolitan area. Because the refuge is so new, its facilities are under development. Future plans call for boat launches, parking areas, nature trails, and a Visitor Center and administrative facility in the Lacombe area.

GETTING THERE

The refuge is on the north shore of Lake Pontchartrain between Slidell and Mandeville. It can be reached by taking Exit 74 (LA 434) off US 112. Several roads off LA 434 lead into the refuge. The refuge can also be reached by boat through Lake Pontchartrain or one of several bayous.

■ **SEASON:** Open year-round.
■ **HOURS:** Open daylight hours.
■ **FEES:** None.
■ **ADDRESS:** Southeast Louisiana Refuges, 1010 Gause Blvd., #936, Slidell, LA 70458
■ **TELEPHONE:** 504/646-7555

TOURING BIG BRANCH MARSH

■ **BY AUTOMOBILE:** A number of public roads lead to or through the refuge. For the best view of the refuge by car, follow LA 434 South to its end at Goose Point. From here there is a good view of the Lake Pontchartrain shoreline and on a clear day, New Orleans in the distance.
■ **BY FOOT:** Trails are still being developed at Big Branch Marsh. A hiking trail and a nature boardwalk pass through small portions of the refuge. The Boy Scout Road and Nature Trail has a self-guided tour through the refuge.
■ **BY BICYCLE:** Bicyclists can access the refuge from the Tammany Trace Bike Trail. Biking is also possible on LA 434 to Goose Point. Staff-led bike tours (bring your bike) take visitors through

CREOLE DICTIONARY When visiting Big Branch NWR, it is possible to hear Creole, a dialect spoken by the Creoles of southern Louisiana, people of French and African descent. Here are some of the Creole names for fish and other wildlife of the Big Branch Marsh area. Listen for these words when you overhear local Creoles talking.

fish
channel catfish: *barbu*
crawfish: *écrivisse*
crappie: *sac à lait*
garfish: *poisson armé*

reptiles
alligator: *cocodril*
alligator snapping turtle: *tortue cocodrie*
lizard: *lézard*
rattlesnake: *serpent sonnette*
snake: *serpent*
soft shell turtle: *tortue écale molle*
toad: *crapeau*
water moccasin: *congo*

insects
bumble bee: *bourdon*
firefly: *mouche à feu*
mosquito: *moustique, maringouin*

birds
hummingbird: *suce fleur*
mallard: *canard Françis*
owl: *hibou, coucou-ois*
wood duck: *canard du bois*
yellow-crowned night-heron: *gros bec*
coot: *poulle d'eau*

mammals
deer: *chevreuil*
mink: *fuine*
squirrel: *éureuil*

the diverse habitats of Big Branch Marsh. Contact the headquarters in Slidell for details. Biking is allowed on the Boy Scout Road Nature Trail (2.2 miles one-way).

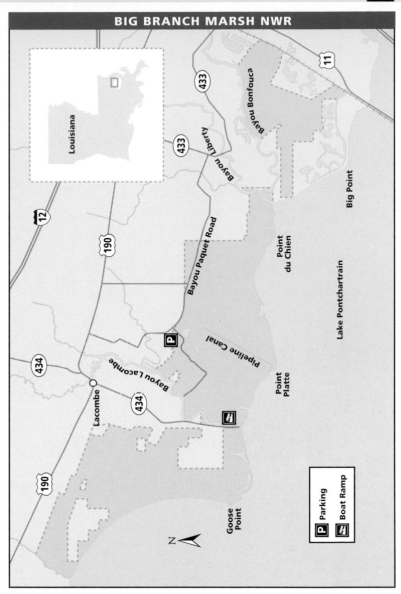

BIG BRANCH MARSH NWR

Louisiana

11

433

433

Bayou Bonfouca

Bayou Liberty

Big Point

12

190

Bayou Paquet Road

Point du Chien

Lake Pontchartrain

P

Pipeline Canal

434

Bayou Lacombe

Lacombe

434

Point Platte

190

Goose Point

N

Parking

Boat Ramp

■ BY CANOE, KAYAK, OR BOAT: The ideal way to explore Big Branch Marsh is from the seat of a canoe traveling down Bayou Cane. There is little current as you pass beneath giant bald cypress trees festooned with Spanish moss. The refuge offers a staff-led weekend canoe tour and provides canoes, paddles, and life vests. An interpreter will help identify the animals and plants. For reservations or more information, contact the headquarters at Slidell. Lacombe, Liberty, and Bonfouca bayous can be explored by canoe or motorized boat. Boat ramps, suitable for canoes and motorized boats, provide access to all of the bayous.

If you plan to boat the refuge from the Lake Pontchartrain side, be alert for changing weather conditions. Lake Pontchartrain is large, and winds can create high waves not safe for small outboard boats.

Brown pelican

WHAT TO SEE

■ **LANDSCAPE AND CLIMATE** The refuge lies at the eastern edge of the Mississippi Delta in coastal Louisiana. The large brackish Lake Pontchartrain forms its southern boundary, although some of the lakefront is actually the St. Tammany State Wildlife Refuge. Big Branch Marsh is bounded on the west by the Fontainebleau State Park.

The refuge encompasses several vegetation zones running south to north from the lake. First a band of grassbeds lies offshore. Next, fringing the lakeshore is a strip of sandy beaches dominated by wax myrtle shrubs. Moving inland is brackish marsh. Farthest inland is a zone consisting of pine ridges with an understory dominated by wiregrass. Throughout the pine forest are hardwood zones and freshwater marshes. Sloughs and meandering bayous cut across all the zones. A drive along LA 434 from I-12 or US 190 to Goose Point gives an idea how quickly the plant communities change from north to south.

Like the rest of coastal Louisiana, the climate is hot, humid, and rainy. Hurricanes are possible in late summer and fall.

■ PLANT LIFE

Forests The pine forests of the refuge are dominated by slash and some loblolly pines mixed with a few hardwoods such as water oak, sweetbay, and red maple. The midstory and understory include dwarf palmetto, and grasses accented with a variety of berries. Chinese tallow tree has invaded some regions. The hardwood hammocks consist mainly of large live and water oaks, red maple, sweet gum, and bald cypress.

The water oaks are fast growing and can reach heights of 100 feet. These handsome trees, with fine-textured foliage and furrowed bark, produce small, round acorns with shallow, saucer-shaped cups, favored foods of squirrels, deer, and other woodland creatures.

Wetlands Most of the marshes on the refuge are brackish. Here the dominant plant is marsh-hay cordgrass mixed with other salt-tolerant plants including switch grass, bulltongue, spikerush water millet, coastal water hyssop, deer pea, and black rush. Several freshwater sloughs dominated by bulltongue are found throughout the refuge.

In shallow freshwater pockets, cattails form dense stands. Bald cypress and willow line the area's many sloughs and bayous.

Open waters Several bayous discharge their water to Lake Pontchartrain. These cypress-lined slow-moving waterways wind beneath the pines and then through the marshes as they empty into the lake. Although outside of the refuge boundary, Lake Pontchartrain is extremely important to the freshwater and marine wildlife inhabiting the refuge.

■ ANIMAL LIFE

Birds Big Branch Marsh attracts large concentrations of migratory waterfowl, shorebirds, songbirds, and neotropical migrants. In winter the shoreline is filled with wintering loons, grebes, ducks, gulls, and other waterbirds. Sandpipers, willets, and yellowlegs probe the sand at the lakeshore edge. Snipe feed in the muck at the edges of marsh and ponds. Year-round brown pelicans, wings spread wide, cruise slowly over the lake searching for fish and then dive head-first to grab them in their large pouchlike bills.

Raptors include the fish-eating osprey and bald eagle, who perch in trees and poletops waiting for prey. When they sight the prey, they swoop down and catch it with their powerful talons. However, when osprey and bald eagles work the same area, the eagle will sometimes let the osprey do the hard work of catching the fish. Then the eagle chases the osprey until it drops its catch.

In the pine forests several clusters of the endangered red-cockaded woodpeckers raise their young in cavities dug out of pine trees. Woodcock probe woodland soil for earthworms. Wood ducks nest among the cypresses that flank the bayous. Northern bobwhite quail are commonly seen. Their whistles can often be heard throughout the day in spring.

Mammals A variety of mammals find a home at Big Branch Marsh. Game animals include white-tailed deer, squirrels, rabbits, and feral hogs. Furbearers such as mink, otter, raccoon, muskrat, nutria, and many other nongame species are found here in abundance.

One mammal that is doing well at Big Branch Marsh is the river otter. These are sociable (you often see them in pairs or small groups), fun-loving mammals that grow to 5 feet long and 30 pounds. They often gather to eat on small hummocks along the bayous.

Fish The grassy marshes of Lake Pontchartrain provide critical spawning and nursery habitat for

Snipe

many freshwater and saltwater species. Redfish, speckled trout, largemouth bass, catfish, bream, and other species can all be found within the refuge at some time.

Invertebrates The blue crab is sought by wildlife and humans alike. These arthropods with hard shells and 10 legs are a noted delicacy. They are found all along the Atlantic and Gulf coasts and prefer sandy bottoms in inlets and channels. Shrimp and crayfish are also abundant here.

ACTIVITIES

■ **CAMPING:** Camping is not permitted at Big Branch Marsh, but campsites are located in nearby Fontainebleau State Park.

■ **WILDLIFE OBSERVATION AND PHOTOGRAPHY:** The best opportunity for observing and photographing wildlife is from a boat in the small bayous and canals. Travel slowly, without talking or banging the bottom of the boat, and you will slip up on numerous refuge animals. As you move down these bayous keep a lookout for the hummocks where otters often feed.

■ **HIKES AND WALKS:** A 2.2-mile hiking trail begins at a parking lot off Bayou Paquet Road and leads through the refuge's major habitats — marsh, hardwood forests, and piney woods. Red-cockaded woodpeckers nest in the trees of the piney woods. A nature boardwalk leads off the trail. Park at the Boy Scout Road.

HUNTING AND FISHING Deer hunting (archery) is allowed Oct. through Jan. Also hunted here are **squirrel**, **rabbit**, and **snipe**; seasons vary year by year, so call the refuge for the latest dates and regulations. The season for waterfowl is set annually. **Hogs** may be taken during deer season.

Fishing (**warm-water species, redfish, speckled trout**) is permitted year-round.

■ **SEASONAL EVENTS:** April: Great Louisiana Bird Festival; May: International Migratory Bird Day; August: Louisiana Youth Environmental Summit, International Hummingbird Day; October: National Wildlife Refuge Week.

■ **PUBLICATIONS:** Refuge fact sheet; refuge hunting and fishing regulations with map; Bayou Sauvage/Big Branch Marsh NWRs Calendar of Events; Southeast Louisiana NWRs brochure.

Black Bayou NWR
Monroe, Louisiana

A double-crested cormorant dries its wings in the sun.

Black Bayou Lake has always been a popular destination for fishermen and duck hunters. Many a tale has been passed from generation to generation about the big gators that inhabit the lake. Today, Black Bayou Lake NWR is a quiet place where boats carry fishermen to secret fishing spots. In the future, the refuge will be a place where children study wetland ecosystems, and guided tours carry visitors into more remote portions of the refuge.

HISTORY

Through a partnership between the U.S. Fish & Wildlife Service and the city of Monroe, Black Bayou Lake NWR was established in 1997 to protect the water quality of this 2,000-acre wetland. The lake serves as the secondary water supply for the city of Monroe in north-central Louisiana. It also provides food and habitat for wildlife.

Forty acres of the refuge will be developed specifically for environmental education. Volunteers have already begun to restore a historic plantation home located on refuge land as an environmental education center. Plans also call for the development of an arboretum for native plants here.

Friends of Black Bayou, Inc., is an active citizens group that supports the goals of the refuge and participates in planning, fundraising, and carrying out numerous educational and conservation projects. Prospective new members are welcome and should contact the refuge for information.

The refuge is administered by the North Louisiana refuges staff.

GETTING THERE

From Monroe, take US 165 North about 4 mi. and turn right at the refuge sign.
- **SEASON:** Open year-round.
- **HOURS:** Open daylight hours for permitted uses.

■ **FEES:** No entrance fee, but a $2 fee required to launch a boat (1$ for Golden Age Passport holders).

■ **ADDRESS:** Black Bayou Lake NWR, c/o North Louisiana Refuges, 11372 Hwy. 143, Farmerville, LA 71241

■ **TELEPHONE:** 318/726-4222

TOURING BLACK BAYOU LAKE

The best way to see the refuge is by boat. After entering the refuge, a gravel road leads to a boat launch ramp and a parking lot. Canoes and boats with motors of 50 hp or less are allowed on the lake. Water trails have not been officially established, but there are obvious canals through the vegetation.

For landlubbers, a short hiking trail begins at the boat launch parking lot and then leads to a handicapped-accessible boardwalk that juts into the lake.

WHAT TO SEE

Most of the current refuge is occupied by Black Bayou Lake. Bald cypress trees draped with Spanish moss rise in random beauty from the surface of this beautiful lake. Bottomland hardwoods line its shore. A 40-acre field lies near the boat launch and boardwalk. Part of this field is being restored as native prairie.

The climate in this part of Louisiana is relatively mild and allows access to the lake year-round.

Though small, the watery refuge provides excellent habitat for waterfowl, wading birds, neotropical migrants, and game fish. Prehistoric-looking double-crested cormorants with wings outstretched often perch in cypress trees throughout the lake. The cormorant's feathers are not as water resistant as those of ducks and geese. After feeding forays, where they dive underwater to spear fish, they must spread their wings in the sun to dry.

Near the shoreline, carefully perched on cypress knees, green-backed herons often pose frozen in an inverted position waiting for a small fish to swim within striking distance. Great blue herons, egrets, and little blue herons also use these trees.

Just beyond the shoreline, the songs of prothonotary warblers, vireos, orioles, and tanagers often drift from the woods surrounding the lake. Red-shouldered hawks zoom through the forest or circle high over the lake searching for prey. Deep within the refuge, colonies of endangered red-cockaded woodpeckers raise their families in cavities dug out of pine trees.

Throughout the refuge the ubiquitous alligator slowly plies waters looking for food, often stopping along the lake's banks to sun itself.

ACTIVITIES

Although a boat is helpful for seeing most of the refuge, nature lovers should be able to see plenty of wildlife from the parking lot, nature trail, or boardwalk. The boardwalk is also a good place to fish.

HUNTING AND FISHING
Fishing for **bass** and **crappie** is the most popular activity at the refuge. Hunting is not allowed at the refuge.

Bogue Chitto NWR
Slidell, Louisiana

Along the waterways of Bogue Chitto NWR

Letting the current do the work, two canoeists move slowly along the tree-lined Bogue Chitto River. Within a short time they have entered a world not much different than it was hundreds of years ago. A swallow-tailed kite swoops overhead, rolls, and then zooms high into the air to snatch an insect. A prothonotary warbler hops onto a willow branch overhanging the water, tilts back its head, and begins a joyous song. A family of wood ducks slips quietly under brush at the water's edge.

HISTORY

Bogue Chitto (pronounced "Boga Chitta") NWR is a 36,000-acre area of relatively pristine bottomland hardwood forest. The refuge was established in 1980 to preserve this unique wetland and to protect wildlife and migratory birds. Three of the refuge's waterways have been designated as Natural and Scenic Streams by the state of Louisiana.

GETTING THERE

The refuge is located 9 mi. north of Slidell. Most of the refuge is accessible only by watercraft. Put in at Walkiah Bluff Water Park northwest of Picayune, MS, or at the U.S. Army Corps of Engineers boat ramps at Lock 1 (north of Slidell) or Lock 3 (south of Bogalusa).

■ **SEASON:** Open year-round.
■ **HOURS:** Refuge: daylight hours. Office open weekdays, 7:30a.m.–4 p.m.
■ **FEES:** None.
■ **ADDRESS:** Southeast Louisiana Refuges, 1010 Gause Blvd., #936, Slidell, LA 70814
■ **TELEPHONE:** 504/646-7555

TOURING BOGUE CHITTO

Only a small portion of the refuge is accessible by car. There are no maintained hiking trails. Although hunters manage to hike the dense woodlands, the best way to tour the refuge is by boat.

A canoe trail begins at Lock 3 south of Bogalusa on the north end of the refuge and ends at Walkiah Bluff Water Park northwest of Picayune, MS. The trail is open only when the Pearl River reaches a level of 12 feet or higher, generally from January through June. Guided canoe trips and canoe rentals are available from a refuge concessionaire.

WHAT TO SEE

Bogue Chitto lies totally in the floodplain of the Pearl River. The low-lying terrain is flat and wet and densely forested. More than 50 miles of bayous, sloughs, creeks, and rivers form a maze of waterways through Bogue Chitto.

The bottomland forest is divided between mixed bottomland hardwoods and cypress-tupelo brakes, or thickets. The cypress-tupelo brakes occur in the wettest sites near waterways and support stands of bald cypress, tupelo gum, swamp black gum, and ash. The mixed bottomland hardwood forests occur in the slightly higher areas between the rivers and consist of oaks, hickories, American elm, sweetgum, sycamore, and black willow. There are also small upland areas (860 acres) of loblolly and slash pine.

The dense forest and swamp attract a host of birds, including pileated woodpeckers, great horned, barred, and screech owls, wild turkeys, wood ducks, and hooded merganser. These birds nest at Bogue Chitto and live there full time.

Summer visitors include migratory wading birds, waterfowl, and neotropical migrants. Egrets and herons commonly hunt in shallow waters.

More than 40 species of mammals find homes in the refuge. White-tailed deer feed in open areas in the evening. Gray squirrels scoot across trees and rummage the forest floor for nuts. Bobcat and coyotes patrol the refuge at night for prey.

Gopher tortoise

BOGUE CHITTO HUNTING AND FISHING SEASONS

Hunting (Seasons may vary)	Jan	Feb	Mar	Apr	May	Jun	Jul	Aug	Sep	Oct	Nov	Dec
deer (gun)											■	■
deer (bow)	■									■	■	■
swamp rabbit	■	■								■	■	■
gray squirrel	■	■								■	■	■
feral hog	■	■								■	■	■
waterfowl	■										■	■
woodcock	■											■
turkey			■	■								

Fishing	Jan	Feb	Mar	Apr	May	Jun	Jul	Aug	Sep	Oct	Nov	Dec
largemouth bass	■	■	■	■	■	■	■	■	■	■	■	■
spotted bass	■	■	■	■	■	■	■	■	■	■	■	■
crappie	■	■	■	■	■	■	■	■	■	■	■	■
bluegill	■	■	■	■	■	■	■	■	■	■	■	■
catfish	■	■	■	■	■	■	■	■	■	■	■	■

Contact the refuge for current regulations and seasons.

River otter, mink, and beaver find food along the waterways. Raccoons and swamp rabbits come out in the evenings to search for food. Feral hogs root throughout the refuge.

Among the refuge's 131 species of reptiles and amphibians are two threatened turtles. The gopher tortoise prefers upland areas and, true to its name, digs extensive tunnels up to 35 feet long and wide enough for making U-turns. Burrowing owls and other animals often take advantage of the turtle's excavations.

The colorful ringed sawback turtle lives along refuge waterways. With yellow and black stripes and spots on its head and neck, this turtle is easy to identify.

ACTIVITIES

■ **CAMPING:** Primitive camping is allowed in designated areas. Camp sites must be within 100 feet of designated streams. Camping is not allowed when the Pearl River reaches 15.5 feet or more.

■ **WILDLIFE OBSERVATION AND PHOTOGRAPHY:** The refuge is an excellent place to observe and photograph wildlife. Take your camera and binoculars on the canoe trail and you are sure to see plenty of animals. Though rare, ringed sawbacks may be seen sunning themselves on logs along the way. Otters sometimes frolic along the riverbanks. The sandbars provide clearings where lucky visitors may get glimpses of wild turkeys.

■ **SEASONAL EVENTS:** April: Earth Day; May: Migratory Bird Day; June: Youth Fishing Rodeo; October: National Wildlife Refuge Week.

■ **PUBLICATIONS:** Refuge brochure; refuge fact sheet; refuge hunting and fishing regulations; bird list; Southeast Louisiana NWRs brochure.

Breton NWR
Gulf of Mexico, Louisiana

Aerial view of Breton NWR

Only 25 miles off the east coast of Louisiana, Breton and the other Chandeleur Islands sparkle in the Gulf of Mexico, like shiny pearls on a string. This chain of barrier islands—long, narrow islands parallel to the shore—makes up Breton NWR.

HISTORY

President Theodore Roosevelt, in his passion to preserve the nation's natural heritage, declared Breton a refuge for nesting and wintering seabirds in 1904. Only one refuge is older, Florida's Pelican Island. The refuge consists of 7,000 acres, 5,000 of which are designated wilderness. About 20,000 people conquer the logistical challenge of visiting Breton every year.

Like most barrier islands, the Chandeleurs are constantly battered by storms and hurricanes. Once there was a small fishing community on Breton Island, but it was destroyed by a hurricane and never rebuilt. The Chandeleur Lighthouse on Breton Island was constructed in 1899 to replace one constructed in the early 1800s. It is listed on the National Register of Historic Structures.

Hurricane Georges, in September 1998, hit Breton hard. Most of the refuge infrastructure—a small office, a boathouse, and a boat dock located in Venice—was destroyed. Wind and water currents from the storm also washed away about 40 percent of the islands. Now, the natural processes that built the islands in the first place—water currents and wind—are rebuilding those islands, and biologists are studying the processes.

GETTING THERE

The only way to visit the refuge is by boat or seaplane. Boats are available in Venice, LA (about 15 mi. to the southern most islands) or Gulfport and other places on the Mississippi coast (about 15 mi. to the northern most islands). Most boats that go to the islands are fishing boats that welcome nonfishermen. Visitors with seaworthy boats and who are experienced at boating in Gulf waters may go on their own. There are no facilities.

- **SEASON:** Year-round, but visitors must not interfere with nesting wildlife.
- **HOURS:** Open daylight hours, except for campers.
- **FEES:** None.
- **ADDRESS:** Southeast Louisiana Refuges, 1010 Gause Blvd., #936, Slidell, LA 70458
- **TELEPHONE:** 504/646-7555

WHAT TO SEE

The islands of Breton NWR stretch for about 100 miles in a shallow arc. Most are arranged in clusters. These islands are generally flat and narrow with sandy beaches and low dunes. Thickets of wax myrtle and groundsel bush, a shrub whose seeds produce a cottony pappus, grow on the higher ground in the center of the islands.

Breton is hot, humid, and wet, with an annual rainfall of 60 inches. Hurricanes sometimes occur in late summer and fall.

> **HUNTING AND FISHING**
> Most fishers who come to Breton seldom get onto the islands. They fish from boats for **spotted weakfish** and **red drum**.
>
> Hunting has been banned since President Roosevelt visited nearly a century ago.

- **PLANT LIFE** Black mangrove grows in shallow waters at the islands' edges. These massive coastal trees have leathery breathing roots that stick up around them like little cypress-tree knees and provide oxygen and support. Manatee grass, turtle grass, and widgeon grass, all named for animals that feed on them, grow in the shallow bays around the islands. These bays teem with aquatic life. Shrimp burrow in the muck, and small fish feed and hide in the grasses.

■ ANIMAL LIFE

Birds From March through August, the islands draw large colonies of nesting seabirds. Here are more brown pelicans than are found anywhere else in Louisiana; up to 20,000 royal, Caspian, and sandwich terns; and an abundance of reddish egret rookeries. Magnificent frigatebirds stage here. These spectacular black birds are also called man-o'-war birds. They are extremely agile and can easily pick a fish out of the water or out of the mouth of another bird. After the nesting birds have dispersed, the area becomes a major wintering ground for water and shorebirds. Tens of thousands of redhead ducks may spend their winter at Breton. These diver ducks can plunge as deep as 12 feet in search of aquatic plants. Threatened piping plovers run nimbly along the beaches foraging for food.

Mammals Few mammals have made it across the Gulf of Mexico to Breton, but some that have include nutria, rabbits, and raccoons.

Reptiles Loggerhead sea turtles, large turtles with limbs modified into flippers, may be seen in the nearby waters of the Gulf of Mexico. Their numbers are dwindling from overhunting and nest destruction. Loggerheads are protected by law during egg laying, and their eggs and nests are protected after the adults have left.

ACTIVITIES

- **CAMPING:** Primitive camping is allowed, however, campers are prohibited from areas where birds and turtles are nesting.
- **PUBLICATIONS:** Refuge fact sheet; Southeast Louisiana NWRs brochure.

Cameron Prairie NWR
Bell City, Louisiana

The Louisiana iris grows on Cameron Prairie NWR.

It is truly serendipitous to discover Cameron Prairie, a national wildlife refuge tucked amid the coastal marshes of southern Louisiana. Pintail Wildlife Drive, a three-mile loop through the heart of the refuge, reveals the refuge's natural bounty. Here, the azure-blue flowers of the Louisiana iris blow gently in the wind in wet places along the drive. Beyond the iris are marshes and coastal prairies where roseate spoonbills feed in the shallow water. Partially hidden in the tall grass, they appear and then disappear, revealing their salmonlike color. White-faced ibises, snowy egrets, great blue herons, and other wading birds also feed in the marsh and prairie grasses.

On ditch banks beside the road, 8-foot alligators rest with heads toward the water. The gators watch the cars and their occupants approach and then, without warning, slip into the water, barely disturbing the surface. They reappear with only their eyes and nostrils showing.

HISTORY

Cameron Prairie, acquired in 1988 with $5.1 million from the Migratory Birds Conservation Fund, was the first national wildlife refuge formed under the North American Waterfowl Management Plan. Although relatively new and largely undiscovered, this 24,548-acre refuge is an important sanctuary for migrating waterfowl and other water birds.

The refuge consists of two units. The 14,927-acre East Cove Unit, which borders the southeast sector of Calcasieu Lake, consists largely of brackish and intermediate salt marsh. It is accessible only by boat. It was originally a part of nearby Sabine NWR. The more accessible 9,621-acre Gibbstown Unit, some 10 miles northeast, consists mainly of freshwater marsh, old rice fields, and a small tract of coastal prairie. It is managed to provide natural foods for wintering waterfowl and other birds.

Cameron Prairie, and its sister refuges, Lacassine and Sabine, are on the Creole Nature Trail National Scenic Byway. This outstanding auto tour was named as one of the top 40 birding spots in America by *Wildbird Magazine*. For more information about this trail, call the Southwest Louisiana Convention and Visitors Bureau. 800-456-SWLA.

GETTING THERE

The Gibbstown Unit is about 25 mi. southeast of Lake Charles. From Lake Charles, take LA 14 East to Holmwood, then follow LA 27 South about 11 mi. to the Visitor Center. The East Cove Unit is accessible by boat from Calcasieu Lake.

■ **SEASON:** Gibbstown Unit open year-round. East Cove Unit closed to all public use during the waterfowl hunting season and when the Grand Bayou Boat Bay is closed; otherwise open year-round.

■ **HOURS:** General refuge: sunrise to sunset. Visitor Center open weekdays, 7:30 a.m.–4 p.m.; Sat., 10 a.m.–4 p.m.

■ **FEES:** None.

■ **ADDRESS:** Cameron Prairie NWR, 1428 Hwy. 27, Bell City, LA 70630

■ **TELEPHONE:** 318/598-2216

■ **VISITOR CENTER:** Features Cajun Woman, an automated mannequin who greets you as you enter the building. Fishing from a small pirogue, she speaks in authentic "cajunese" about the refuge and its wildlife.

TOURING CAMERON PRAIRIE

■ **BY AUTOMOBILE:** Cars are permitted on the main road leading through the Gibbstown Unit of the refuge, the Bank Fishing Road, West Cameron Road, and the three-mile long Pintail Wildlife Drive, which starts about two miles south of the Visitor Center on the east side of LA 27.

PLANTS OF MARSHES Despite a seeming uniformity, marshes support a wide variety of plants. These plants can be divided into three broad categories: emergent, submergent, and floating plants.

Emergent plants grow partly in and partly out of water. Their leaves can be narrow or broad. Some have showy flowers while the flowers of others are inconspicuous. Typical narrow-leaved emergents include grasses, sedges, and rushes (maidencane, cordgrass, spike rushes, common reed). These persist throughout winter. Broad-leaved emergents include bladderworts, bulltongue, smartweed, and pickerelweed. They die back at the end of the growing season.

Submergent plants, such as pondweed, grow underwater while floating plants grow on top of water. Floaters include both those that float freely on the water's surface, such as duckweed and water hyacinth, and those that, like water lilies, floating hearts, and alligatorweed, are rooted in the marsh muck and only extend their leaves to the water'suface.

In many marshes the occurrence of plants is zonal. Emergent plants live in the shallower waters, floaters grow beyond, and submergents grow in the deepest waters. However, in some marshes the various plant types occur together mixed with shrubs and trees. The intermingling of plant types is called interspersion and forms a habitat very beneficial to waterfowl.

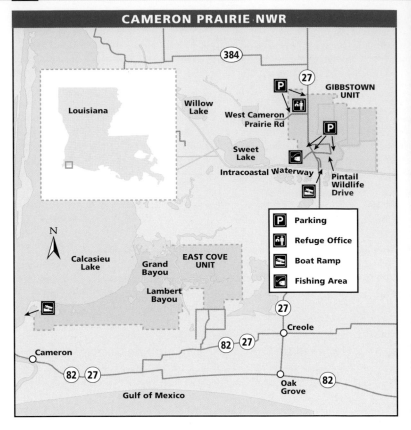

■ **BY FOOT:** No hiking trails have been developed, but you can walk along the levees that crisscross old rice fields at the Gibbstown Unit.

■ **BY BICYCLE:** Bikes are permitted on the main refuge roads as well as the three-mile Pintail Wildlife Drive in the Gibbstown Unit.

■ **BY CANOE, KAYAK, OR BOAT:** Canals and ditches border the network of levees in the refuge. Boats with motors no greater than 25 hp are allowed only in the outfall canal from mid-March through mid-October. Nonmotorized boats are permitted in the bank fishing area.

In the East Cove Unit motorized boats may be operated in refuge canals, bayous, and lakes. Horsepower is not restricted. Only electric trolling motors may be used in refuge marshes.

WHAT TO SEE

■ **LANDSCAPE AND CLIMATE** Cameron Prairie NWR lies in the Gulf Coastal Plain of southern Louisiana. Virtually every inch of land in Cameron Prairie NWR has been cut, recut, dug up, dammed, grazed, hunted, or otherwise manipulated by man. Essentially no area remains pristine. Yet through various restorative efforts, Cameron Prairie has become a premier habitat for wildlife.

The Gibbstown Unit, a generally flat area sporadically dotted by trees, straddles a zone where former coastal prairie, rice fields, pastures, and fields meet deep freshwater marshes. The slight differences in elevation here create a varied habitat perfect for waterfowl. The old rice fields are crisscrossed by earthen levees bordered by canals. Water collects in the fields in winter and drains or is drawn off in summer.

The brackish and intermediate salt marshes of the East Cove Unit serve as an important nursery for a host of estuarine creatures and attract a multitude of waterfowl and other waterbirds.

Cameron Prairie has a hot, humid, subtropical climate characterized by frequent heavy rainfall, a long growing season, and mild, sunny winters. The region is subject to hurricanes in late summer and early fall.

■ PLANT LIFE

Forests Although the refuge is virtually treeless, a few scattered cypress, hackberries, black willows, and invading tallows can be found on levees and higher ground within the Gibbstown Unit.

Croplands The former rice patties in the Gibbstown Unit are managed as moist-soil units to encourage the growth of native plants. Earthen levees have been repaired and water-control structures installed to maximize water management. Spangletop, millet, and smartweed are among the desirable wildlife food plants now found in these fields.

Wetlands Coastal prairies once covered more than two million acres of southwestern Louisiana. These prairies occupied a zone between the freshwater marshes to the south and pine savannahs and flatwoods to the north. Now only remnant parcels remain, most along old railroad tracks. One small parcel is located in Cameron Prairie's Gibbstown Unit. Coastal prairies are intermittently flooded wetlands generally supporting a diversity of plants associated with freshwater marshes and pine savannahs.

The dominant plants of the coastal prairie are grasses, but forbs, sedges, and some trees and woody species may also be present. Common grasses include brownseed paspalum, grama grass, little and big bluestem, three-awn grass, love grass, marsh-hay cordgrass, switch grass, panic grass, and Indian grass. Common

Grassy wetlands, Cameron Prairie NWR

sedges of Louisiana's coastal prairie include caric sedges, umbrella sedges, beaked sedges, and nutrushes.

In the deep freshwater marshes of the Gibbstown Unit grows the usual assortment of Gulf coastal marsh grasses and plants—Indian ricegrass, cattail, California bulrush, smartweed, bulltongue, spike rush, marsh-hay cordgrass, and maidencane, to name a few. Some marshes are drained or burned periodically in the fall to promote the growth of natural grasses.

The brackish and intermediate salt marshes of the East Cove Unit are managed in a cooperative effort among local, state, and federal agencies and private businesses to restore 64,000 acres of marsh in Cameron Parish that have been destroyed by the invasion of saltwater from ship channel dredging in Lake Calcasieu. So far, 19 miles of levee have been built on the edge of the lake to restore natural salinity levels. Among the methods being used are recycling Christmas trees to reduce wave action and planting bulrushes to build new land. The revitalized marshes now support varieties of cordgrass, salt grass, leafy three-square, and other salt-tolerant plants.

A wide array of wildflowers often provide splashes of bright color to the otherwise muted greens and browns of the coastal prairies and marshes, among them blue flag iris and the cheery swamp sunflower, brown-eyed Susan, and fringy seaside goldenrod.

Swamp rose mallow with pink flowers up to 7 inches in diameter, wooly rose mallow (hibiscus) with 8-inch white flowers with a crimson center, and salt-

marsh mallow with 2-inch pink flowers are other flowering plants that enliven both freshwater and brackish marshes. All are wild members of the hibiscus family. The swamp milkweed looks similar to other members of the milkweed family. Its deep pink flower and lancelike leaves brighten coastal areas in summer; later, their hairy pods burst open, releasing seeds with tufts of white hair.

■ ANIMAL LIFE

Birds Though its bird list is in its infancy, more than 200 species have been recorded at Cameron Prairie since its opening in 1988. Literally thousands upon thousands of geese and ducks flock to Cameron Prairie each winter, including snow, Canada, and white-fronted geese, green-winged teal, ring-necked ducks, mallards, shovelers, gadwalls, and pintails.

White-faced ibis

Other winter residents include common snipe, woodcock, and peregrine falcons.

Spring and summer bring great waves of songbirds, wading birds, and shorebirds. The shorebird migration in particular is often spectacular and includes an abundance of black-necked stilts and lesser yellowlegs. Waders include white-faced ibises, snowy egrets, common moorhens (a ducklike swimming bird), a variety of herons, and the spectacular roseate spoonbill.

Roseate spoonbills in shallow water

The roseate spoonbill was nearly eliminated by the turn of the century, their wings being in much demand for ladies' fans (because feathers from spoonbills faded, they were not as suitable for hats as the feathers from American and snowy egrets). By 1900, the total breeding population in the United States had dwindled to 20 to 30 pairs in Florida. Today spoonbills have recovered and are a common sight in southwest Louisiana. The birds forage for food day and night by dipping their long, spoonlike bills into the water and swivelling from side.

Cameron Prairie can also boast a number of full-time residents, including colonies of egrets, herons, cormorants, ibises, anhingas, king rails, mottled and fulvous whistling ducks, assorted songbirds, northern bobwhites, and mourning doves. The fulvous whistling ducks are named for their rich tawny color and whistling calls. Although they are ducks, their long necks and legs give them a gooselike appearance. These ducks often nest on the ground atop levees.

Glimpses of the black rail are a rare treat for birders. This black bird, no bigger than the common house sparrow, is perhaps the most secretive bird in America. The black rail lives in marshes, where it runs along mouse trails through dense cover; it seldom flies. Although rarely seen, its distinctive *"kik—kee—do"* gives away the bird's presence.

Mammals Nutria are the most common mammal. They have become a popular food of resident alligators. White-tailed deer are also ubiquitous. Other easily observed mammals include raccoon, skunk, cottontail and swamp rabbit, armadillo, and opossum. More elusive inhabitants include coyote, bobcat, river otter, and muskrat.

Reptiles and amphibians Cameron Prairie supports a variety of reptiles and amphibians, the most noteworthy of which are alligators, which can reach lengths of 12 feet. Alligators can be dangerous, so visitors are cautioned to keep a safe distance, to avoid feeding them, and to keep all pets in the car.

Other cold-blooded inhabitants of the refuge include a variety of salamanders, frogs, toads, lizards, turtles, and snakes, including water moccasins, speckled king snakes, and numerous nonpoisonous water snakes.

Invertebrates The brackish waters of the East Cove Unit team with invertebrate life such as brown and white shrimp and blue crabs. The freshwater marshes support a healthy population of crayfish. A wide array of insects inhabit the entire region. Nuisance insects include biting deer flies and ravenous mosquitoes in summer.

ACTIVITIES

■ **CAMPING:** Camping is not allowed on Cameron Prairie NWR, but there are a number of private campgrounds in the nearby area.

■ **WILDLIFE OBSERVATION:** The Pintail Wildlife Drive is a great place to observe wildlife throughout the year. Here you can see roseate spoonbills wading in the shallow waters from late summer to early winter. Young spoonbills are pale pink, almost white. As they get older, the pink becomes more vibrant. Watch for spoonbills as they fly overhead with necks and legs outstretched. They are especially spectacular when seen at night, silhouetted in the moonlight.

Look in the rice fields, marshes, and shallow waters for fulvous whistling ducks. Look also in fields along the roads for other ducks and geese.

A boardwalk crosses a small reconstructed marsh in front of the Visitor Center. This is a good place to spot animals at close range. Alligators bask in the sun and turtles swim in the clear water. Snowy egrets stalk for minnows in the shallow water. Common yellowthroats make their *"wichity, wichity, wichity"* calls from the cattails. A second short trail leads from the Visitor Center to a platform that overlooks a moist-soil management area and provides opportunities to see an assortment of birds. White-tailed deer can be seen in the morning hours from the observation deck located behind the Visitor Center.

■ **PHOTOGRAPHY:** The platform overlooking the moist-soil management area is a good place to photograph shorebirds and wading birds. Mornings provide good backlight and evenings often present spectacular sunsets.

■ **HIKES AND WALKS:** While there are no maintained trails through the refuge, visitors may walk the dikes and levees. Remember to bring insect repellent to ward off pesky mosquitoes and biting flies and keep an eye open for poisonous snakes.

■ **SEASONAL EVENTS:** None.

■ **PUBLICATIONS:** Refuge brochure with map; refuge fact sheet; refuge fishing regulations; refuge hunting regulations; bird list.

SATELITTE REFUGE

■ **Mandalay NWR** Mandalay NWR is a satellite refuge managed by the Cameron Prairie staff. The refuge is approximately five miles west of Houma. It straddles the Gulf Intracoastal Waterway and is accessible only by boat.

Mandalay was established to protect wetland habitat and contains 4,212 acres of freshwater marsh and cypress-tupelo swamp intersected by canals used by the petroleum industry. The refuge contains Lake Hatch (about 200 acres) and several marsh pond areas and canals that contain viable populations of sport fish including largemouth bass, bluegill, redear sunfish, and channel catfish. Fishing is allowed on the refuge, but hunting is not.

■ **ADDRESS:** Mandalay NWR, 3599 Bayou Black Drive, Houma, LA

■ **TELEPHONE:** 504/853-1078

Catahoula NWR
Rhinehart, Louisiana

Boardwalk and observation tower, Duck Lake, Catahoula NWR

The huge concentrations of colorful ducks and geese are reason enough for a visit to this east-central Louisiana refuge. Indeed, Catahoula Lake is one of the most important wintering areas for waterfowl in North America. But Catahoula NWR is also home to many other fascinating creatures. One such resident, the green anole, can be found all along the boardwalk, on trees, bushes, even the boardwalk railings. These small lizards, some green, others brown, mottled, streaked, or spotted, sun themselves in the morning light. In a confrontation between two males, one spreads its pink throat patch wide, bobs its head, and does reptilian push-ups on tiny legs to signal the other to stay out of its territory. The display works; the intruder scurries off.

HISTORY

The name Catahoula is thought to have come from an Indian word meaning clear or beautiful water. Catahoula NWR is a relatively small (6,535 acres) refuge in east-central Louisiana consisting mainly of bottomland hardwood forest. But its proximity to 26,000-acre Catahoula Lake, which borders it for 9 miles to the west, makes it a natural area of great significance. Catahoula refuge was established in 1958 to provide wintering habitat for migrating waterfowl. At that time the forest had been badly logged and grazed over. Today, innovative management practices have restored it to a natural state. Most of the refuge visitors come to Catahoula to hunt or observe waterfowl.

Although none of Catahoula Lake belongs to the refuge, the refuge staff manages its water level, drawing it down to 5,000 acres in the summer. This encourages the growth of chufa—a sedge greatly favored by waterfowl—and other vegetation that will feed the tens of thousands of birds that come to the region each fall.

GETTING THERE

The refuge lies northeast of Alexandria and east of Jena. From Alexandria, take LA 28 North for 20 mi to US 84, then left 1 mi. to the refuge. From Jena take US 84 east 12 mi. and then look for the refuge sign on the right.

- **SEASON:** Open year-round, but closed at times due to high water.
- **HOURS:** Refuge: daylight hours. Office open weekdays, 7 a.m.–3:30 p.m.
- **FEES:** None.
- **ADDRESS:** Catahoula NWR, P.O. Drawer Z, Rhinehart, LA 71363
- **TELEPHONE:** 318/992-5261

TOURING CATAHOULA

- **BY AUTOMOBILE:** A 9-mile auto tour circles Duck Lake, a crescent-shaped impoundment in the center of the refuge, and provides places to stop and fish or to view wildlife. Two other roads off LA 28 provide access to the southern section of the refuge. One skirts French Fork Little River and leads to a boat ramp on Catahoula Lake. The other skirts Muddy Bayou.
- **BY FOOT:** Hiking is permitted throughout the refuge. Four miles of foot trails give visitors opportunities to observe wildlife and learn about the flora.
- **BY BICYCLE:** Visitors may bicycle on any roads open to automobiles.
- **BY CANOE, KAYAK, OR BOAT:** Boating is allowed on Duck Lake from early March to late October. Cowpen Bayou is open to boating all year. Three boat-launching ramps provide easy access. Only nonmotorized boats or boats with motors of 10 hp or less are permitted on refuge waters.

WHAT TO SEE

- **LANDSCAPE AND CLIMATE** Catahoula lies at the western edge of the Mississippi Alluvial Plain in the sluggish backwaters of the confluence of the Red and Ouachita rivers. This is a flat, low-lying, and frequently flooded area (only about 50 feet above sea level).

The refuge is bounded on the west by Catahoula Lake and on the east by the French Fork Little River. Most of the land in between (4,435 acres) is occupied by bottomland hardwood forest. At the heart of this dense forest lies Duck Lake. In between Duck Lake and Catahoula Lake lies the Cowpen Bayou, a cypress and willow lined impoundment. Other small bayous cut through the forest at the southern end of the refuge.

Little blue heron

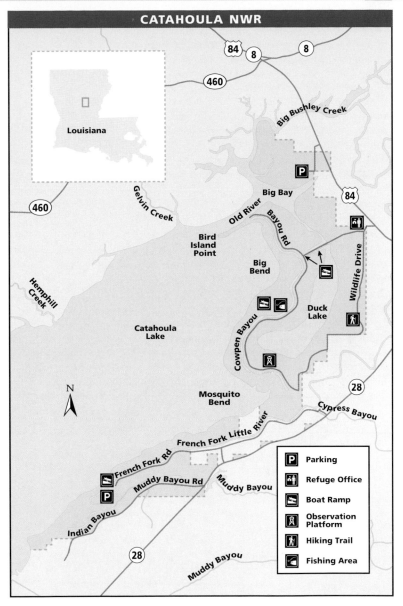

Old fields and shrubby lands occupy slightly elevated areas of the refuge. Surprisingly, because the refuge sits on sizable oil deposits, active oil wells are scattered throughout Catahoula.

The climate is hot and humid, with 60 inches of rain annually. Fall, winter, and spring can be delightful.

■ PLANT LIFE

Forest Tree species living in this bottomland hardwood forest must tolerate flooding for up to six months a year. The dominant trees are water oak and pecan. The water oaks retain their leaves longer in the fall than most other hardwoods and provide valuable cover for wildlife. Other trees here include sweetgum, overcup oak, willow oak, and water hickory.

The tall, narrow-crowned water hickory makes an excellent den tree. It also produces an abundance of thin-shelled nuts. However, because the nuts have a strong, bitter taste animals eat them as a last choice—preferring the acorns of the water, overcup, and willow oak.

Green hawthorns, thicket-forming trees with small red to yellow fruit and showy white flowers, grow beneath the taller trees of the bottomland forest. Mistletoe grows in the crowns of many trees, and poison ivy grows as a vine up tree trunks or as a sprout on the forest floor.

Wetlands The lowest lands at the edges of the forest and around the lakes and bayous support dense stands of swamp privet and water elm interspersed with water locust and moss-covered cypress trees. Swamp privet is a small, thicket-forming tree with long-pointed leaves. The water elm is a small elmlike tree with spreading branches.

Open water Duck Lake and Cowpen Bayou make up 1,000 acres of the refuge. Duck Lake was formed when a portion of a brush-filled sump (the low point where water collects) was dammed. Open water also occurs in the several bayous flowing through the southern part of the refuge.

■ ANIMAL LIFE

Birds Catahoula and nearby Catahoula Lake attract as many as 50,000 to 450,000 migratory waterfowl each year. Tens of thousands of ducks winter here. Most numerous are mallards, but northern pintail, blue- and green-winged teal, gad-wall, wigeon, ring-necked, canvasback, and lesser scaup also winter here. Wood ducks nest and raise their young in tree cavities along the bayous.

The waterfowl move back and forth from Catahoula Lake, where they feed and are hunted, to Duck Lake, where there is less food but no hunters. Bald eagles and ospreys disregard the No Hunting signs on Duck Lake and Cowpen Bayou and prey on weak and sick waterfowl in the winter.

When conditions are right in summer, hundreds of shorebirds and other waterbirds come to Catahoula to feed—among them are herons, egrets, ibises, and a few regal wood storks. Myriad songbirds come through in spring and fall.

Each year the trees of the bottomland hardwood forest take a pounding from the many woodpeckers residing here at Catahoula—from the little downy to the handsomely mus-tached flicker to the large, dash-ing pileated. Males drum on trees to attract a mate. Then the

Chickadee

CATAHOULA HUNTING AND FISHING SEASONS

Hunting (Seasons may vary)	Jan	Feb	Mar	Apr	May	Jun	Jul	Aug	Sep	Oct	Nov	Dec
deer (bow)	■	□	□	□	□	□	□	□	□	■	■	■
rabbit	□	□	□	□	□	□	□	□	□	■	□	□
squirrel	□	□	□	□	□	□	□	□	□	□	□	■
raccoon	□	□	□	□	□	□	□	□	□	□	■	□
feral hog	■	□	□	□	□	□	□	□	□	■	■	■
Fishing												
warm-water species	■	■	■	■	■	■	■	■	■	■	■	■

The fishing pier on Cowpen Bayou is wheelchair-accessible.

pair excavates cavities in dead trees for their nest. Abandoned cavities are used by other cavity-nesting birds who cannot make their own cavities, such as chickadees, titmice, bluebirds, and kestrels. A total of 192 species of birds have been observed on the refuge.

Mammals The refuge provides ideal habitat for a variety of forest and swamp-dwelling mammals such as swamp rabbits, white-tailed deer, nutria, beaver, river otter, and nine-banded armadillo. Bobcats, red and gray foxes, and coyotes search the forests and waterways for mice, voles, and other small prey.

Reptiles and amphibians The southern cricket frog is one of the many amphibians that inhabits the refuge's shallow waters. This small, warty frog makes a rapid, metallic clicking noise that can be heard throughout the refuge in all seasons except winter. Common reptiles include cottonmouths, water snakes, aquatic turtles, and anoles.

ACTIVITIES

■ **CAMPING:** Camping is not permitted at Catahoula, but campsites are available at nearby Dewey Willis WMA.

■ **WILDLIFE OBSERVATION:** Wildlife can be spotted from anywhere on the auto-tour route, but especially in places where the road comes close to water. The observation tower at the south end of Duck Lake provides good views of the lake and the thousands of waterfowl that visit in winter.

■ **PHOTOGRAPHY:** Photographic opportunities are good at the observation tower. The tower is located far enough into the lake that photographers can get sunrise and sunset pictures with waterfowl flying in front of the sun.

■ **HIKES AND WALKS:** The short (one-quarter-mile) trail on the south end of Duck Lake leads to a boardwalk and the observation tower. Water Hickory Wildlife Trail is a three-quarter-mile self-guided nature trail through the beautiful bottomland hardwood forest between the auto-tour road and Duck Lake. An old logging trail behind cowpen bayou provides an additional three miles of trail.

■ **SEASONAL EVENTS:** May: Migratory Bird Day; fall: Earth Fair and free fishing days; December: Christmas Bird Counts.

■ **PUBLICATIONS:** Refuge brochure with map; refuge hunting and fishing regulations; Water Hickory Wildlife Trail interpretive brochure; bird list.

D'Arbonne NWR
Farmerville, Louisiana

American wigeon

Quiet old roads meander through the stands of shortleaf and loblolly pines in the upland areas of D'Arbonne NWR. Small farms once occupied this area, but hard times caused the farmers to abandon their efforts. These days, it is not the sound of grinding tractor motors in the air but the well-meshed clicks of shifting bicycle gears and chains.

Overhead the sunlight filters through the pines. Red buckeyes bloom at eye level; the brown carpet of fallen pine needles covers the forest floor on each side of the road. The going is smooth and the terrain fairly level, and the natural wonders of the D'Arbonne refuge are ready to be explored.

HISTORY

D'Arbonne NWR, in northeast Louisiana just 23 miles from the Arkansas state line, was established in 1975 to preserve bottomland hardwood forests and provide habitat for waterfowl and other wildlife.

Cotton and corn had been grown on the uplands portion of the refuge until the late 1950s. Since then, most of the uplands have reverted to pine forest. In the mid-1950s, about 1,000 acres of bottomland were cleared and planted in bald cypress, sweetgum, and water tupelo. Only the bald cypress survived. In 1966-67 this area, plus 1,000 additional acres, were cleared and planted in soybeans, but repeated flooding doomed them to failure. Today, the 17,421-acre refuge consists mainly of open water and bottomland hardwood forests.

GETTING THERE

The refuge office is about 6 mi. north of West Monroe. From I-20, take LA 143 (also called 7th Street) north. Several parking areas along the route provide entry points to the refuge.

■ **SEASON:** Open year-round. Some areas may be inaccessible during certain seasons because of flooding.

■ **HOURS:** Refuge: open to public access 24 hours a day. Headquarters open weekdays from 7:30 a.m.–4 p.m. except holidays.
■ **FEES:** None.
■ **ADDRESS:** North Louisiana Refuges, 11372 Hwy. 143, Farmerville, LA 71241
■ **TELEPHONE:** 318/726-4222

TOURING D'ARBONNE

■ **BY AUTOMOBILE:** About 13 miles of roads are open for automobiles. Most of these are access roads to boat ramps or parking lots. Many roads are not passable during wet periods. ATVs are not allowed.
■ **BY FOOT:** About 50 miles of old farm roads, staff access roads, and fire maintenance roads through the upland pine forest can be hiked.
■ **BY BICYCLE:** Bicycling is permitted on any of the interior roads.
■ **BY CANOE, KAYAK, OR BOAT:** A canoe or small boat is an excellent way to see D'Arbonne. There are four boat ramps that provide access to Bayou D'Arbonne.

WHAT TO SEE

■ **LANDSCAPE AND CLIMATE** Bayou D'Arbonne is the refuge's main feature. While the refuge is only 8 miles long and 2 to 4 miles wide, Bayou D'Arbonne cuts a 15-mile twisted path through it. Hardwood-covered bottomlands straddle the bayou on both sides and then rise to upland pine forests on refuge perimeters. Oxbow lakes, sloughs, and bayous also intersect the refuge.

Temperatures in northern Louisiana are mild, normally ranging from 20 to 95 degrees throughout the year. Rainfall averages about 50 inches per year; the wettest months are February to April. Snow is unusual.

■ **PLANT LIFE**
Forest Upland forests comprise 3,000 acres of the refuge. Common species here are loblolly and shortleaf pine. Mayhaw, also known as a member of the hawthorn family, grows in the understory. It produces a fruit that many locals use for homemade jelly.

The 11,000 acres of bottomland forest are dominated by overcup and willow oak in slightly drier areas and bald cypress and water tupelo in wetter areas. The pointed-leaf swamp privet and the aquatic buttonbush form the understory. In fall the acorns attract mallards and other wildlife.

About 800 acres of refuge land is managed as moist-soil units. Panic grass has invaded

Pines at D'Arbonne NWR

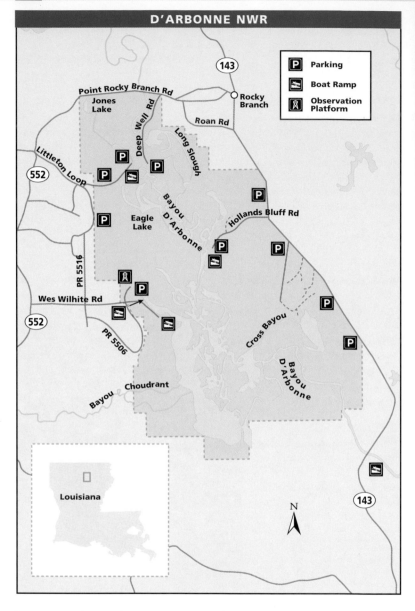

large areas where reforestation attempts failed, but slower growing and later invading species—buttonbush, willow oak, overcup oak, and persimmon—are slowly taking over. Sedges and millet produce seed that attract up to 75,000 ducks to these units.

Open waters This is a watery, often flooded refuge with some 2,121 acres of permanent water—mostly contained in the bayou, sloughs, and oxbow lakes. Trees draped in Spanish moss are common along the banks.

■ ANIMAL LIFE

Birds Birders have counted 238 species of birds on the refuge, including the endangered wood stork, bald eagle, and red-cockaded woodpecker. The wood stork retreats to the more inaccessible parts of the bottomland forest. The red-cockaded nests in the upland pine forests. The bald eagle follows the fall migration of waterfowl to the region.

Both black and turkey vultures are among D'Arbonne's permanent residents, and the refuge is a good place to learn to distinguish them. Turkey vultures have red heads (although this color is not always distinguishable at long distances), two-toned black wings with silver flight feathers, and (the best way to tell is at long distance) fly with their wings in a dihedral, or shallow, V. Black vultures have shorter wings. Their heads are black, their wings are black tipped with white, and they fly with wings held flat.

D'Arbonne's diverse habitats attract a large number of migrants. In spring the refuge is alive with the whir and sounds of warblers, sparrows, and other songbirds. In fall a host of waterfowl begin arriving. Wintering waterfowl include four species of geese—greater white-fronted, snow, Ross', and Canada—plus numerous ducks, among them canvasbacks, redheads, ring-neckeds, buffle-heads, ruddies, greater scaups, lesser scaups, mallards, gadwalls, American wigeons, northern shovelers, northern pintails, and blue- and green-winged teals. Jaunty multicolored wood ducks live here year-round and raise their young in refuge bayous.

In summer yellow-crowned night-herons search the cypress swamps and bayous for their favorite food, crayfish.

Mammals Beavers, river otters, and muskrats are among the mammals who call this watery habitat home. Coyotes and bobcats prowl the uplands. Bobcats are nocturnal, but occasionally come out in daytime or dusk to look for food. Like the domestic cat, they are curious animals and frequently stop on their rounds to sniff around. Bobcats can weigh as much as 40 pounds and sometimes kill fawn, but

Bobcat

Spotted salamander

their preferred food is rabbit. They also prey on mice, shrews, rats, opossum, squirrels, raccoons, wild turkey, and domestic cats who have wandered too far from home.

Reptiles and amphibians Reptiles and amphibians are abundant at D'Arbonne. The mass breeding of the spotted salamander is one of nature's lesser-known spectacles. These amphibians stay underground for most of their lives, but in spring congregate by the hundreds in roadside ditches or small woodland ponds (without predatory fish) after the first warm rains for courtship and egg-laying. When mating, the male and female go through a kind of nuptial dance. The male deposits his sperm in a special packet (spermatophore), and the female transfers this packet to her cloaca, or generative canal. The eggs become fertilized when she lays them. The young, or larvae, which hatch in about a month, have gills and live in water for up to two years before they transform into adults.

ACTIVITIES

■ **CAMPING:** Camping is not permitted at D'Arbonne, but campsites are located in nearby Lake D'Arbonne State Park and at both municipal and commercial campgrounds in and around Monroe.

■ **WILDLIFE OBSERVATION:** Five active red-cockaded woodpecker clans inhabit the refuge. The cavity trees are usually easy to spot because biologists have marked them with a band of white paint.

A wildlife observation tower located on the southwest side of the refuge is a good place for watching wintering waterfowl feeding in a nearby area known as the "bean field." Walking or biking the roads quietly can also be productive.

■ **HIKES AND WALKS:** The access roads and fire lanes make pleasant and easy walking. There are numerous combinations to try.

■ **SEASONAL EVENTS:** December: Christmas Bird Count.

■ **PUBLICATIONS:** Refuge fact sheet; D'Arbonne/Upper Ouchita NWRs hunting and fishing regulations; D'Arbonne/Upper Ouchita NWRs educational

D'ARBONNE HUNTING AND FISHING SEASONS

Hunting
(Seasons may vary)

	Jan	Feb	Mar	Apr	May	Jun	Jul	Aug	Sep	Oct	Nov	Dec
deer (gun)											■	
deer (bow)	■									■	■	■
rabbit	■	■								■	■	■
quail	■	■									■	■
woodcock	■											■
raccoon	■											
opossum	■											

Fishing

	Jan	Feb	Mar	Apr	May	Jun	Jul	Aug	Sep	Oct	Nov	Dec
warm-water species	■	■	■	■	■	■	■	■	■	■	■	■

Waterfowl season is set each year. Deer hunting with firearm is permitted on certain weekends in Nov. and other dates are subject to change; contact the refuge for current regulations and seasons.

opportunities; North Louisiana NWRs bird list; North Louisiana NWRs general brochure.

SATELLITE REFUGE

■ **Handy Brake NWR** Located in Bastrop in northeast Louisiana, Handy Brake NWR is a tiny (501 acres) unit operated as a satellite of D'Arbonne NWR in the north Louisiana refuges complex. Handy Brake became a refuge in 1989 when the Farmer's Home Administration transferred land to the U. S. Fish & Wildlife Service. Attempts to drain the area for agriculture failed, and the area was restored to natural wetlands. Waterfowl winter here, and nesting boxes have been placed around the refuge for resident wood ducks.

Services are limited. There are no roads or trails into the refuge; however, a parking lot and observation platform are open year-round during daylight hours only. The remainder of the refuge is closed to the public.

■ **ADDRESS:** Handy Brake NWR, % N.E. Louisiana Wildlife Refuges, 11372 Hwy. 143, Farmerville, LA 71241

■ **TELEPHONE:** 318/726-4200

Delta NWR
Venice, Louisiana

Delta NWR wetlands

Delta is aptly named—this waterfowl sanctuary lies at the mouth of the Mississippi and reflects what the giant delta may have looked like before levees and canals altered its hydrology.

HISTORY

Delta NWR comprises approximately 48,800 acres of the Mississippi Delta. It was established in 1935 to provide sanctuary and wintering habitat for waterfowl and other migratory birds.

Refuge managers work hard to preserve the refuge in its natural state. For eons the 2,000-mile-long Mississippi River periodically overflowed the delta and deposited fine silts upon it. Today narrow canals channel floodwaters directly into the Gulf. Innovative water management by the U.S. Fish & Wildlife Service at Delta diverts water from the river to capture some of its rich sediments. To date, 1,000 acres of new marsh has been created.

The refuge sits atop large oil and gas deposits and more than one-half of the refuge has some petroleum-related activity.

GETTING THERE

To get to the refuge office from New Orleans, take LA 23 about 80 mi. to Venice. When the road ends, turn left (east) and look for the Delta-Breton NWR satellite headquarters building. This is not a Visitor Center and is not usually occupied while staff are in the field. The refuge itself is located 5 mi. south of Venice near Pilot Town. It is accessible only by boat.

■ **SEASON:** Open year-round, but some areas are closed to the public during the hunting season or to protect waterfowl.
■ **HOURS:** Sunrise to sunset.
■ **FEES:** None.

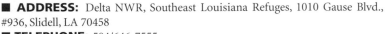

■ **ADDRESS:** Delta NWR, Southeast Louisiana Refuges, 1010 Gause Blvd., #936, Slidell, LA 70458
■ **TELEPHONE:** 504/646-7555

TOURING DELTA

There are no roads into the refuge. Charter boats are available from Venice. Boat access is also possible from the Gulf. Travel in Gulf and Mississippi waters can be hazardous because of rough water, fog, heavy traffic, and swells from ships and crew boats, so you'll need a boat that is both seaworthy and capable of navigating the refuge's shallow channels. Air-thrust boats, motorized pirogues, and go-devils are not permitted.

WHAT TO SEE

The delta is low-lying and has many channels, passes, bayous, and shallow ponds cutting through it. Although the land appears totally flat, it slopes imperceptibly away from the banks and gradually gets lower and lower until it reaches sea level. Some land is actually below sea level.

Willows, groundsel bush, and coffee bean grow at the slightly higher elevations along the river, channels, and cuts. Marsh covers the lowest regions. About 60 percent of the marsh is freshwater. The marsh areas along the Gulf are brackish.

The climate is subtropical; hot and humid in the spring and summer and mild to cold in the fall and winter. Annual rainfall is approximately 60 inches. Hurricanes are possible in late summer and fall.

■ **PLANT LIFE** The predominant plants of the freshwater marsh are low-growing and include duck potato, elephant ear, wild millet, delta three-square, and roseau cane. In the brackish marsh wiregrass, widgeon grass, marsh-hay

Greater yellowlegs

cordgrass, saltgrass, and three-cornered grass are common. Delta's marshes are extremely important nursery areas for fresh and saltwater species of fish.

■ ANIMAL LIFE

Birds Delta attracts an amazing variety of migratory birds. Tens of thousands of wintering waterfowl flock to the refuge each year including snow and blue geese and myriad species of ducks. Mottled ducks are year-round residents. These blotchy, brown and sandy birds look a lot like female mallards and are actually close relatives of the more widespread bird.

> **HUNTING AND FISHING** This region has always been popular with hunters, anglers, and trappers. At Delta there are seasons for **waterfowl**, **rabbit**, and **deer** (archery).
>
> Fishing (**spotted weakfish**, **red drum**, **flounder**, **catfish**, **largemouth bass**) is permitted year-round. Commercial fishing and sport shrimping are prohibited.

In summer large concentrations of shorebirds and wading birds collect at the refuge including endangered brown pelicans, greater and lesser yellowlegs, long-billed dowitchers, dunlins, western sandpipers, herons, egrets, willets, and Wilson's plovers. Extraordinary black skimmers, with red bills and legs, are abundant and can be seen as they "skim" the water for small fish. Brightly colored purple gallinules feed and nest in the marsh vegetation.

Huge numbers of songbirds stop at the refuge during spring and fall migrations. For some spring migrants Delta is their first landfall.

The refuge is perfect habitat for raptors. In winter northern harriers fly low back and forth over the marsh searching for prey, sometimes racking up as much as 100 miles or more of air time each day. The magnificent frigate bird and groove-bill ani (a small blackish bird with a thick parrotlike bill) are some of the more unusual birds found on the refuge.

Mammals Delta also supports a wide variety of other wildlife. White-tailed deer graze on the natural pass banks, man-made spoil banks, and the marshes. Swamp rabbits nibble on marsh grasses.

ACTIVITIES

■ **WILDLIFE OBSERVATION AND PHOTOGRAPHY:** Cruising a boat slowly through refuge canals is a good way of seeing and photographing wildlife. Visitors are allowed to bring in their own canoes.

■ **PUBLICATIONS:** Refuge fact sheet; refuge hunting and fishing regulations; Southeast Louisiana Refuges brochure.

Lacassine NWR
Lake Arthur, Louisiana

Sunrise on the coastal wetland at Lacassine NWR

The bass boat cruises slowly down the open canal at sunrise. The morning is misty and foggy as the sun begins to burn a fiery hole in the sky. The boat passes snowy and common egrets that flush, circle, and return. In a short time, the boat reaches its destination. Shutting off the motor, the fishermen prepare their tackle. In the hush of the morning the sounds of the marsh become intense. Red-winged blackbirds and great-tailed grackles squabble, defending their territories. Overhead, a red-shouldered hawk screams its *keeee-yeeer* call.

A quick snap of the wrist sends the purple plastic worm across the open canal. The worm lands just at the edge of the weeds with open water on one side. The worm begins to sink slowly when suddenly there is a boil of water and the 8-pound test line draws tight. The angler sets the hook and begins to play the fish, which swims a short way and then jumps from the water. It is a largemouth bass. The fish "tailwalks" and goes under again.

The angler deftly works the fish toward the boat and then gently reaches down to pull it from the water. Lifting the fish, the 8-year-old angler grins from ear to ear, while Dad gets out the camera and quickly takes pictures. It's a two-pounder, but for the young angler it might as well be a state record. Finally, Dad helps remove the hook, and the boy carefully places the fish back in the water. With catch-and-release fishing, it's a good bet that another boy and his father will have the opportunity to enjoy the great fishing at Lacassine National Wildlife Refuge.

HISTORY

Native Americans left behind six middens (areas where they disposed of food waste) from their occupation here hundreds of years ago. They were not the only living creatures who found the resources of the marsh bountiful. The original landscape of coastal prairie and freshwater marsh attracted large numbers of migrating waterfowl. The land was eventually drained for cattle and farming. Oil

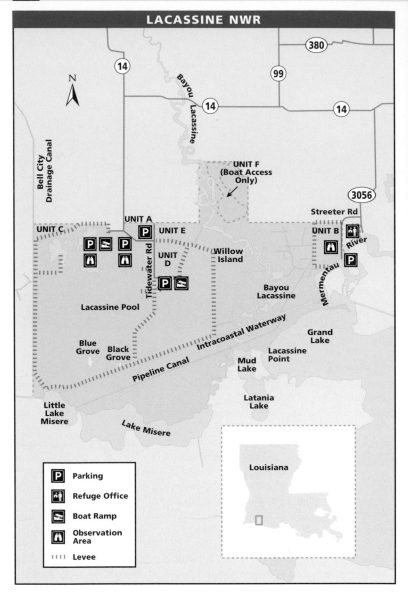

LACASSINE NWR

drilling operations were built. Lacassine National Wildlife Refuge was established in 1937 to provide winter habitat for migrating waterfowl. In the early 1940s, a network of levees was build as part of an effort to restore wetlands. These levees divide the refuge into several management units.

Today the 35,000-acre refuge is considered among the top birding spots in America. A small tract of land north of the refuge, the Vidrine Unit, is being restored as natural prairie. Future plans include the possible addition of 22,000 acres of marsh and agricultural lands on the north side of the refuge.

GETTING THERE

The refuge office is located a short distance outside the refuge, about 16 mi. from

Lake Authur. To get there from Lake Arthur, go west on LA 14 for 7 mi. to LA 3056, turn south, and go 4.5 mi.

To get to Unit B, turn west on Streeter Rd. on LA 3056 a short distance before reaching the headquarters. Go 2 mi. to the observation area.

To get to Lacassine Pool and the main refuge from Lake Arthur, go west on LA 14 for 15 mi. Turn south on Illinois Plant Rd. for 4 mi.

■ **SEASON:** The refuge is open year-round.

■ **HOURS:** The office is open weekdays, 7:30 a.m.–4 p.m. The Lacassine Pool and the observation area at Unit B are open from 1 hour before sunrise to 1 hour after sunset.

■ **ADDRESS:** Lacassine NWR, 209 Nature Rd., Lake Arthur, LA 70549

Cattle egret

■ **TELEPHONE, FAX, AND EMAIL:** 318/774-5923; fax: 318/774-9913; e-mail: r4rw_la.lcs@ fws.gov

TOURING LACASSINE

■ **BY AUTOMOBILE:** Only 4 miles of roads are available in the refuge. Most of these roads lead to access points or parking areas. ATVs are not allowed.

■ **BY FOOT:** There are no designated trails, but you can walk on any of 30 miles of levees and service roads that crisscross the refuge.

■ **BY CANOE, KAYAK, OR BOAT:** Two boat-launch areas at the end of Illinois Plant Road provide boat access to the many miles of canals, bayous, and waterways. Powerboats are limited to a maximum of 25 hp in Lacassine Pool, and only poling or paddling are allowed in the marsh areas. Private boat-launch facilities near the headquarters provide access to other parts of the refuge.

WHAT TO SEE

■ **LANDSCAPE AND CLIMATE** Most of the refuge is freshwater marsh typical of coastal Louisiana. Here, an important ingredient in the creation of the marsh is the clay soil, which prevents water from readily seeping deeper into the earth. Man-made levees help maintain water levels.

A marshy lake, Lacassine Pool, makes up the center of the refuge. The Gulf Intercoastal Waterway and the American Louis Pipeline Canal cross the southern part of the refuge in a southwest-northeast direction.

Grand, Latania, Mud, Misere, and Little Misere lakes form the refuge's southern border. Grand Lake is part of the Mermentau River. A marshy area south of the pipeline canal and north of Lake Misere is a designated Wilderness Area.

THE AMERICAN ALLIGATOR Once alligators were considered endangered. Now healthy populations exist throughout Louisiana and other southern and south-central states. National wildlife refuges have played a key role in making the recovery of the "king of the marsh" possible. Alligators can get quite big—10- to 12-footers are common; the record is 19 feet, 2 inches. These large reptiles will eat just about anything. Nutria are a favorite food, but they also eat fish, ducks, egrets, and turtles. Some have been known to gulp down cottonmouth water moccasins.

Alligators mate in the spring. The bull alligator's mating call is a loud bellowing roar that carries across the marshes. The female makes a similar roar, but not as loud. She also makes piglike grunts to call the young. Both sexes make hollow hissing noises when threatened.

When the female alligator is ready to lay her eggs in early summer, she makes a large, mound-shaped nest of vegetation. She may lay anywhere from 20 to 80 eggs in the nest. Young alligators hatch in late summer and may stay with their mother until the following spring. Mother gators are very protective of their young. Refuge visitors should give a wide berth to females guarding nests or their young.

The climate at Lacassine is typical of southern Louisiana: hot and humid in the summer and mild and wet in the winter. Tornadoes have been known to occur in fall and winter, and hurricanes can be a threat in late summer and early fall.

■ PLANT LIFE

Wetlands Almost 90 percent of the refuge is freshwater marsh and wetland. Lacassine Pool comprises 16,000 acres of this wetland. Lacassine Pool is covered almost entirely with emergent plants. The dominant plants here are maidencane and bulltongue. At slightly higher elevations, black willow and the exotic and invasive Chinese tallow tree are the dominant species. The marshes outside of Lacassine Pool are dominated by maidencane, sawgrass, and bulltongue.

The 34-acre Vidrine Unit, located in Evangeline Parish, 40 miles northeast as the crow flies, is being restored as coastal prairie with a mixture of grasses and forbs. Few areas of original prairie remain in coastal Louisiana.

Open waters There are 3,434 acres of open water in the refuge. This includes a portion of Lacassine Pool where emergent plants do not grow, Lacassine Bayou, the Gulf Intracoastal Waterway, and some canals. Water lilies grow in open water, their stems anchored in the bottom sediment and their leaves floating on long stalks. Their conspicuous flowers produce nectar that attracts bees, butterflies, and moths. Between the lily pads are thousands of minute plants that are not rooted to the bottom, merely floating at the will of the wind and water currents. These are duckweed, some of the tiniest of all floating plants and an important food for waterfowl. Similar to water lilies but on a smaller scale is watershield. After a rain, its cupped leaves hold water, reflecting light and resembling pools of liquid mercury.

Forest Only 630 acres of the refuge may be considered forested, mostly bald cypress and gum. The refuge has 592 acres of wetland forests, usually found in close proximity to the upland forest. Among the dominant species are deciduous holly and Chinese tallow.

Croplands About 2,000 acres, mostly on the north side of the refuge, are man-

American alligator, Lacassine NWR

aged for moist-soil plants and agricultural crops to provide supplemental food for waterfowl (rice, wheat, and soybeans).

■ ANIMAL LIFE

Birds Lacassine is strategically located where the Central and Mississippi flyways meet. It attracts one of the largest concentrations of wintering ducks and geese of any of the national wildlife refuges. Hundreds of thousands of ducks and geese begin arriving in September and literally blanket the lake. Wood ducks, mottled ducks, and fulvous and black-bellied whistling ducks nest on the refuge.

In spring the nearby rice fields and crayfish ponds host tremendous numbers of shorebirds, and in fall these same fields provide habitat for early arriving waterfowl.

The refuge contains several rookeries for wading birds, including herons, little blue herons, great egrets, and white-faced and white ibis. One rookery (sometimes called a "heronry") at Lacassine is estimated to have up to 9,000 cattle egret, white-faced ibis, white ibis, and tricolored and little blue herons. The first breeding colony of cattle egrets in Louisiana was discovered here. Cattle egrets are egrets native to Africa and reached North America via South America only 100 years ago.

Other common marsh and water birds attracted to Lacassine include neotropic cormorants, anhingas, least bitterns, American bitterns, king rails, American coots, common moorhens, purple gallinules, and black-necked stilts. Eagles and peregrine falcons occasionally visit the refuge and feast on waterfowl and fish.

In all, 251 species of birds have been recorded on the refuge. Recent exciting finds included groove-billed ani and a male vermillion flycatcher, a strikingly beautiful red and dark brown bird of the Southwest.

Mammals Mammals typical for southern Louisiana marshes are found here. During the night, raccoons hunt the shallow waters for fish and crayfish. They also

HUNTING AND FISHING Waterfowl hunting is permitted on 6,400 acres in accordance with state and federal regulations, and there is an archery season for **white-tailed deer**.

    Fishing is very popular at Lacassine and is permitted in accordance with state and federal regulations. Most fishing takes place after the waterfowl have left, from March 15 to Oct. 15. The **largemouth bass** is the most sought-after fish, but other fish species include **bowfin** (choupique), **bream**, **crappie**, **catfish**, and **gar**.

have a taste for eggs of any kind—whether turtle, duck, or egret. Refuge staff have placed protection guards around wood duck nest boxes to prevent raccoons and snakes from getting the eggs.

    Nutria, muskrat, swamp rabbit, and white-tailed deer are common. Less seen are armadillos, skunks, and otters. Coyotes can be heard howling at night.

Reptiles and amphibians An inventory of reptile and amphibian species indicates the great diversity of wildlife living in the marsh—9 salamanders, 11 toads and frogs, 29 snakes, 17 turtles, and 7 lizards, and more. The refuge has one of the densest populations of American alligators in Louisiana. In 1995 there were an estimated 10,240 gators. The alligator plays an important role in the ecology of the wetlands. Alligators dig holes that provide water for fish and other wildlife in dry periods; they also eat sick and diseased animals (see sidebar).

Invertebrates A wide variety of invertebrates, including crayfish, aquatic insect larvae, and numerous terrestrial insects, provides food for wading birds, shorebirds, and many of the mammals that live on the refuge.

ACTIVITIES

■ **CAMPING:** Camping is not permitted on the refuge, but there are private campgrounds near the headquarters at the end of LA 3056.

■ **PHOTOGRAPHY:** A short walk down the levy to the west from the parking lot at the end of Illinois Plant Road leads to a rookery area. During the nesting season, approach this area with care so that you don't disturb the birds. Both Unit A, just north of the parking area at the end of Illinois Plant Road, and Unit B at the end of Streeter Road, offer good opportunities for photographing wading birds and ducks in season.

■ **SEASONAL EVENTS:** December/January: Youth Waterfowl Hunt; May: International Migratory Bird Day; June: National Fishing Week; December: Christmas Bird Count.

■ **PUBLICATIONS:** Refuge brochure with map; refuge fact sheet; refuge boat-trail map; bird list; fishing and hunting regulations.

Lake Ophelia NWR Complex
Lake Ophelia NWR and Grande Cote NWR
Marksville, Louisiana

Raccoon

The sister refuges of the Lake Ophelia NWR Complex certainly live up to the slogan etched on every Louisiana license plate: "Sportsman's Paradise." With its rich bottomland hardwood forests and open waters, Lake Ophelia NWR provides plenty of hunting and fishing opportunities. Grand Cote NWR offers fishing and crayfishing. Both areas are good places to observe waterfowl and other wildlife. The refuges are located in the Mississippi Alluvial Plain near Marksville in east-central Louisiana. The management office is in Grand Cote.

Lake Ophelia NWR
Marksville

HISTORY

Lake Ophelia NWR takes its name from the 350-acre lake near its center. The relatively new 15,500-acre refuge was established in 1988 to provide habitat for wintering waterfowl and other wildlife.

GETTING THERE

From Marksville, follow LA 452 northeast 22 mi. to the refuge.
■ **SEASON:** Open year-round, although portions may be closed seasonally due to flooding or as a wildlife sanctuary.
■ **HOURS:** Sunrise to sunset.
■ **FEES:** None.
■ **ADDRESS:** Lake Ophelia NWR Complex, 401 Island Road, Marksville, LA 71351
■ **TELEPHONE:** 318/253-4238

WHAT TO SEE

Lake Ophelia NWR lies in the floodplain of the Red River, an area that was once part of an extensive bottomland hardwood forest. Most of the land was cleared for agriculture, but flooding made farming minimally successful. Today the refuge staff is working to restore the forest.

Water is plentiful at the refuge. Lake Ophelia is a beautiful lake with majestic cypress trees scattered about. There are numerous other smaller lakes, some connected by bayous. The Red River forms a large arc around the northern portion of the refuge.

The climate is mild with subtropical conditions throughout the year. Summers are hot and humid with highs occasionally in the 100-degree range. Freezes are unusual.

With so much water it is not surprising that Lake Ophelia attracts tens of thousands of wintering waterfowl and numerous summering wading birds. It is also good habitat for many year-round residents. Throughout the refuge are bobcat, red and gray fox, otter, beaver, raccoon, mink, and nutria. Other animals more frequently seen include white-tailed deer, squirrel, and rabbit. The peregrine falcon is a rare winter visitor here, and bald eagles are beginning to nest successfully. The Louisiana black bear occasionally lumbers into the area. As the bear populations are reestablished at Tensas NWR to the north and Atchafalaya NWR to the south, Lake Ophelia will serve as an important link in the corridor connecting the refuges.

ACTIVITIES

Most visitors to Lake Ophelia are either hunters or anglers. The refuge is especially popular for hunting waterfowl, white-tailed deer, and squirrel.

Grand Lake Road and Buck Road provide access to the refuge interior. These are unimproved roads and may become too muddy to travel in the rainy season. There are numerous parking areas along these roads where visitors can stop and

Northern pintail

watch or listen to wildlife. Several miles of ATV and hiking trails provide access for hunters and may be hiked throughout the year. There are boat ramps at Lake Ophelia and Duck Lake.

Grand Cote NWR
Marksville

HISTORY

Grand Cote, which is French for "Big Hill," joined the refuge system in 1989 to help meet the goals of the North American Waterfowl Management Plan. Most of the 6,077-acre refuge lies in a slump, or shallow depression, to the south and east of the "grand hill." (This hill, with less than a hundred feet of relief, is not actually grand by most measurements.) Much of the refuge was once a farm and still is largely cropland. However, reforestation efforts are slowly bringing the area back to its natural state.

GETTING THERE

From Marksville, take LA 1 North to the small town of Fifth Ward and turn left (south) onto Rte. 1194 at the caution light. Proceed approximately 4 mi. to refuge.

■ **SEASON:** Open year-round, although some parts may be closed seasonally due to flooding or as a wildlife sanctuary.

■ **HOURS:** General refuge open sunrise to sunset. Complex office open weekdays from 7:30 a.m.–4 p.m.

■ **FEES:** None.

■ **ADDRESS:** Grand Cote NWR, Lake Ophelia NWR Complex, 401 Island Road, Marksville, LA 71351

■ **TELEPHONE:** 318/253-4238

ACTIVITIES

Crayfishing is a popular activity at Grand Cote. The crayfish can be found anywhere there is standing water, from mud puddles and ditches to Choctaw Bayou and Coulee des Grues. The season is variable, depending on water levels and weather conditions, but usually occurs from mid-April to mid-May. Fishing is permitted in the Coulee des Grues along Little California Road. Hunting is not allowed.

Shallow flooded habitat is provided annually for wintering waterfowl, especially northern pintail. A half-mile nature trail begins in back of the office complex. Visitors may also walk the levees to watch for wildlife. Numerous species of waterfowl and wading birds can be observed during winter and spring from refuge trails and levees.

Sabine NWR
Hackberry, Louisiana

Sabine NWR encompasses the largest coastal marsh on the Gulf Coastal Plain.

Eager to catch the morning light and the flurry of wildlife activity, a photographer is the first person to walk Marsh Trail this morning in Sabine NWR. In the alligatorweed, the photographer finds a cooperative subject. A big gator, maybe a 12-footer, lies motionless in shallow water. The huge reptile is coated with dried mud that has taken on a silvery sheen, contrasting with the reptile's dark hide. Baby alligators, about 16 inches long, surround the big gator. They are dark, like their mother, but have striking orange bands and stripes. Some of the young are perched on the big gator's back, where they rest motionless; others swim in the shallow water. The photographer, keeping a safe distance from the animals, clicks away.

HISTORY

The opportunities to observe and photograph wildlife at Sabine NWR are tremendous. Sabine, which stretches for 10 miles between Sabine and Calcaseiu lakes, is the largest coastal marsh on the Gulf Coastal Plain. Like most marshes, it provides habitat for numerous resident and migratory wildlife. Strategically located at the southern terminus of the Mississippi and Central flyways, it attracts huge concentrations of migratory waterfowl and other birds.

This 124,511-acre refuge was established in 1937 to preserve wetland and provide winter habitat for migrating waterfowl. Prior to becoming a refuge, the area was owned by the Orange-Cameron Land Company, which used the area for a hunting club and a muskrat operation. The company trapped the large aquatic rodent and processed the glossy pelts at an on-site plant. Eventually, the value of muskrat pelts declined, and the company sold the land to the federal government.

The land beneath the refuge contains oil and gas deposits. Oil companies have built petroleum canals and drilling sites throughout the refuge and extract the oil and gas.

Maintaining the natural integrity of the marsh at Sabine is a challenge. The many man-made canals through the refuge have altered the marsh hydrology and allowed salt water to intrude into freshwater lakes. The Intracoastal Waterway, north of the refuge, is a major culprit. It acts as an interceptor, keeping the natural southward flow of freshwater from reaching the marsh. Managers are constantly manipulating floodgates in an attempt to maintain the natural conditions of the marsh. Nevertheless, the Sabine marsh is one of the most productive and fertile areas of North America.

GETTING THERE

Sabine lies in the far southwest corner of Louisiana about 7 mi. from Hackberry and 10 mi. from Holly Beach. LA 27 cuts through the eastern end of the refuge. From Hackberry take LA 27 South. From Holly Beach, take LA 27 North.

■ **SEASON:** Open year-round. Refuge impoundments and canals closed mid-Oct. to mid-March.

■ **HOURS:** General refuge open sunrise to sunset. Visitor Center open weekdays from 7 a.m.–4 p.m. and weekends, noon–4 p.m. Office open weekdays from 7 a.m.–4 p.m. Both are closed on all federal holidays.

■ **FEES:** None.

■ **ADDRESS:** Sabine NWR, 3000 Holly Beach Highway, Hackberry, LA 70645

■ **TELEPHONE:** 318/762-3816

■ **VISITOR CENTER:** The highlight of the Visitor Center is Cajun Man, an automated mannequin that tells about the life of the marsh and how it has changed. Other exhibits describe the marshes and the animals that live in them.

TOURING SABINE

■ **BY AUTOMOBILE:** No roads lead into the heart of the refuge, but LA 27, which transverses the east side from north to south, provides places to stop, park, and sightsee. Use caution in this area; traffic may be heavy and oncoming drivers may be watching birdlife rather than the road. Sabine is on the Creole Nature Trail National Scenic Byway, an outstanding auto tour for birders.

■ **BY FOOT:** A short interpretive trail, one of the best in the national wildlife system, leads to an observation tower off LA 27.

■ **BY CANOE, KAYAK, OR BOAT:** Boating is allowed on the 150 miles of refuge canals, bayous, and waterways from mid-March to mid-October. Outboard motors are permitted in the canals and bayous, but only poling or paddling is allowed in the open marshes. Dragging boats across a levee is prohibited. Outboard motors up to 40 hp are permitted in management units 1A, 1B, and 3.

WHAT TO SEE

■ **LANDSCAPE AND CLIMATE** The refuge lies in a broad basin located between what was once a large interior coastal prairie and sandy oak-covered ridges, or *cheniers,* that parallel the coast. These ridges are actually the remains of old barrier beaches. Freshwater marshes occupy most of the basin but meld into brackish and almost sea-strength marsh at the southern rim. Man-made canals and natural bayous cut across the marshes.

Most of the terrain is flat and low-lying, only a few feet above sea level. But there are a few ridges and wooded islands in the marsh. Some of these elevated areas are the spoil from the digging of canals. Topography is an important element in this wetland. A change of just a few inches in elevation can mean the difference between a salt marsh and brackish marsh, between grass and shrubs.

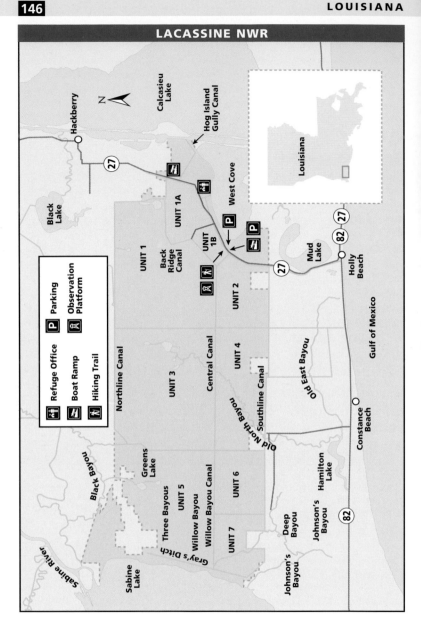

The marsh here was formed from silt deposited into the Gulf of Mexico by the Mississippi River. Over time, some of these deposits were carried westward by gulf currents and deposited in the region.

The climate is hot and humid in the summer, mild and wet in the winter. Hurricanes can occur in late summer and fall.

■ PLANT LIFE
Wetlands The most common plant of Sabine is salt-meadow cordgrass— sometimes called marsh-hay cordgrass—a salt-tolerant *Spartina*. It has little food value for wildlife but does provide good cover. *Spartina* is a climax plant and, if left

alone, would eventually take over the marsh. A management program of burning and grazing keeps the cordgrass from dominating the refuge and allows other, more nourishing plants to grow.

Other common plants of the marshes are bullwhip, Roseau cane, and alligatorweed. Bullwhip, a tall, slender member of the rush family, grows in waters of two feet or more. Roseau cane, or cane (*Phragmite*), is a tall reedlike grass that grows in thick clumps on slightly elevated areas and offers good places for wildlife to hide. Alligatorweed, an exotic from South America, floats in marsh waters. The plant is an excellent indicator of the salinity of water. Since it cannot tolerate even the slightest hint of salt, its occurrence indicates a freshwater area in the marsh. The plant has some nutritional value for deer and nutria.

Wax myrtle, groundsel tree, and high-tide bush are three shrubs that grow on ridges and levees throughout the refuge. They provide habitat for nesting birds and are the only plants strong enough to support wading bird rookeries.

Open waters Open water occurs in the 115 miles of canals that cut through the marsh.

■ ANIMAL LIFE

Birds Sabine is home to tens of thousands of migratory waterfowl. In winter large flocks of snow geese loaf in the marsh, feed in the fields, and eat grit at the Grit Site, a place where refuge staff dumps sand and gravel, which geese need for digestion. Dabbling ducks, including green- and blue-winged teal, wigeon, gadwall, and shoveler also winter here as do lesser scaups and other diving ducks. Wintering merlins and peregrine falcons often follow the waterfowl to the refuge.

Neotropical migrants visit the refuge in great numbers. Cold fronts in March, April, and May can produce spectacular fallouts of these birds when conditions are right. The shorebird migration often includes black-necked stilts, lesser yellowlegs, and white pelicans.

Black-necked stilt

Common moorhen

Thousands of double-crested and olivaceous cormorants nest at the refuge and large numbers of wading birds fish refuge marshes and mud flats including both white and white-faced ibis, herons, egrets, bitterns, and king and clapper rails. Spectacular flocks of roseate spoonbills roost at Sabine and can be seen almost every afternoon returning to their roosts from their feeding grounds. Another highlight for birders is the sighting of the regal wood stork, an uncommon species that occasionally stops by the refuge in late summer or early fall.

The common moorhen is one bird that is hard to miss (there are an estimated 50,000 in the refuge). The chicken-size bird is equally adept at swimming in marsh waters, scouting the mud banks for food, or walking on floating vegetation.

Closely related to the common moorhen but resplendently colored is the purple gallinule. This bird summers at the refuge and is quite popular with visitors, who enjoy watching it walk on lily pads using its large splayed-out toes to keep from sinking.

Mammals A number of mammals dwell in this vast marsh including nutria, raccoons, cottontail and swamp rabbits, skunks, muskrats, minks, white-tailed deer, and coyotes. Many of these mammals are active at night, so visitors may not actually see them. Yet they leave plenty of evidence of their presence, from scat, or droppings, to footprints, to tunnels and trails through marsh grasses.

If you don't spot any swamp rabbits, then look for the tunnels they leave through the thick marsh grasses. These tunnels are used by a variety of other animals in the marsh.

Reptiles and amphibians The undisputed "king of the marsh," the alligator inhabits this marsh in large numbers—some 9,000 strong—and alligator watching is easy to do; these reptiles can be found almost anywhere on the refuge.

Three closely related frogs, the bullfrog, bronze frog, and pig frog, inhabit the refuge. If you cannot see them, you can probably hear them. Their nighttime calls give them away. The bullfrog's call is a loud and deep bass, three-syllable *"jug-o-rum," "jug-o-rum."* The bronze frog's voice is a one-syllable, explosive baritone note: *"clung," "clung."* And the pig frog's voice is the easiest to remember; it sounds like the grunt of a pig or, when several are singing, a whole herd of hogs.

Invertebrates On the down side, the marshes spawn huge numbers of mosquitoes, "green-heads" (or deer-flies), and midges. On the up side, they support an abundance of crustaceans and other water-life that help sustain birds as well as butterflies, dragonflies, and damselflies.

How can you distinguish between a dragonfly and a damselfly? Dragonflies are usually larger and rest with their wings out straight; damselflies rest with their wings held together over their backs in an "up" position. Both of these insects prey on pesky people-biting insects. As they search for prey, they usually pick a favorite stick or blade of grass to return to and rest on. If you are trying to get a good look at or a picture of the dragonfly or the damselfly, be patient. It will return.

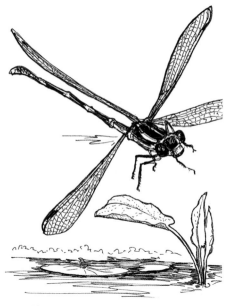

Damselfly

ACTIVITIES

■ **CAMPING:** Camping is not allowed on the refuge, but Sam Houston Jones State Park in Westlake has camping. There is also camping in Holly Beach.

■ **WILDLIFE OBSERVATION AND PHOTOGRAPHY:** Marsh Trail offers excellent opportunities to observe and photograph birds of all types. In addition, alligators and swamp rabbits are common along the trail and pose willingly for photographers of all skill levels and with all kinds of lenses. (Keep a good distance away from the gators, of course.) The normally shy moorhen has become accustomed to people on the trail and will often allow itself to be photographed.

A good place to see and photograph geese in winter the Grit Site just north of the Visitor Center on LA 27. The geese arrive every morning and peck at the grit, much like chickens pecking corn. A large wooden photo blind at the site is positioned to allow photographers to get great shots of the geese as they come in for a landing. It may be reserved by contacting the refuge office.

■ **HIKES AND WALKS:** The 1.5-mile Marsh Trail is located off LA 27 about four miles south of the Visitor Center and is wheelchair-accessible. This fine, well-maintained interpretive trail is a concrete-covered walk that traverses many types of marsh habitats with several footbridges over the wetter areas. About halfway around the trail, a short extension leads to an observation tower that offers a slightly elevated view of the marsh.

A self-guiding brochure describes plants and animals found along the trail. Allow plenty of time for the walk (a full two hours is not an unreasonable amount of time), and be sure to bring binoculars, field guides, and insect repellent. And leave your dog behind. Plenty of alligators hang out around the trail, and alligators do eat dogs.

> **HUNTING AND FISHING**
> Hunting for **waterfowl** is allowed; the season is set each year.
>
> Fishing throughout the refuge permitted, March 15 through Oct. 15; from the LA 27 bank, year-round.

■ **SEASONAL EVENTS:** April: Louisiana Ornithological Society spring meeting; July: Cameron Parish Fishing Rodeo; October: Louisiana Ornithological Society fall meeting; October: National Wildlife Refuge Week; December: Christmas Bird Count.

■ **PUBLICATIONS:** Refuge brochure with map; fishing regulations flyer; hunting regulations flyer; Marsh Trail guide; wildlife list; bird list; Young People's Checklist; Calendar of Events brochure.

Tensas River NWR
Tallulah, Louisiana

Tensas River NWR wetlands

Tensas River NWR is known for its spectacular bottomland forest, sparkling oxbow lakes, and remarkable wildlife. Sadly, however, the refuge may be best known for the wild animals that no longer live here.

The ivory-billed woodpecker, for example, the largest American woodpecker, formerly dwelled in bottomland forests throughout Louisiana. But timber cutting robbed the huge birds of the large mature hardwoods they needed to survive. Now, most scientists believe the bird is extinct in the United States (a remnant population may survive in Cuba). One of the last authenticated sightings of this spectacular bird was in what is now Tensas land.

Bachman's warbler, a yellow bird with a contrasting black bib, also thrived in bottomland forests throughout the southeastern United States and is now probably extinct (see Big Lake NWR). If it does exist, ornithologists believe Tensas would be the place to find it. The long-legged red wolf and the Florida panther once roamed the forests of Tensas. The last red wolves in Louisiana were captured in the early 1970s for a captive breeding program. The last Florida panther was seen in Louisiana in the 1960s. Hopes are that through captive breeding programs, these animals can someday be reintroduced to the region.

HISTORY

Tensas (pronounced TEN-saw) refuge straddles the Tensas River for 20 miles through northeast Louisiana. It was established in 1980 to preserve what was then the largest privately owned tract of bottomland hardwood forests remaining in the Mississippi Alluvial Plain. Owned by the Chicago Mill and Lumber Company, this 66,325-acre tract was destined to be clear-cut and converted to farmland. But citizens persuaded the U.S. Army Corps of Engineers to buy the land and turn it over to the U.S. Fish & Wildlife Service.

Today Tensas remains a priceless stretch of bottomland forest in a sea of agri-

Yellow-crowned night-heron

cultural land. It provides sanctuary for native wildlife and migratory birds. For easier management, it is divided into two units, the Judd Brake Unit to the north and the Fool River Unit to the south. The refuge sits atop oil and gas deposits, and oil drilling operations are scattered throughout the South Unit.

GETTING THERE

The refuge is located just off I-20 about 60 miles from Monroe. From Monroe, take I-20 East to the Waverly exit. Then follow LA 577 North for 1.5 mi., LA 80 East for 4 mi., and turn south on Quebec Road for 10 mi. to the Visitor Center.

■ **SEASON:** Open year-round.

■ **HOURS:** General refuge open 24 hours. Visitor Center open weekdays from 8 a.m.–4 p.m., Sat., 10 a.m.–4 p.m., Sun., 1 p.m.–4 p.m.

■ **FEES:** No entrance fee. $10 ATV user fee.

■ **ADDRESS:** Tensas River NWR, Rte. 2, Box 295, Tallulah, LA 71282

■ **TELEPHONE:** 318/574-2664

TOURING TENSAS RIVER

■ **BY AUTOMOBILE:** Automobiles are permitted on about 25 miles of refuge roads. Parking within 100 feet of an active oil-well site is prohibited. ATVs are permitted only on designated trails, all but two of which are closed from early February to mid-September.

■ **BY FOOT:** Two hiking trails include a short (.25-mi.) wildlife trail near the Visitor Center and a 4-mile trail at Rainey Lake. In addition, visitors can walk the many miles of old unimproved trails or ATV trails.

■ **BY BICYCLE:** Biking is permitted on the main entrance road.

■ **BY CANOE, KAYAK, OR BOAT:** Boating is allowed on the Tensas River and refuge lakes. A primitive launching site for canoes is located on the Tensas at the north end of the refuge. Only electric motors are allowed in refuge lakes.

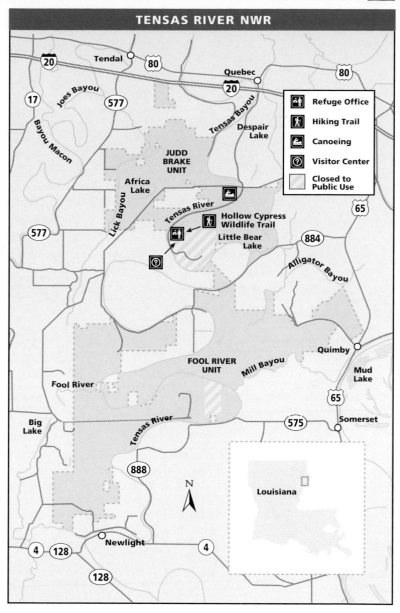

TENSAS RIVER NWR

Refuge Office

Hiking Trail

Canoeing

Visitor Center

Closed to
Public Use

WHAT TO SEE

■ **LANDSCAPE AND CLIMATE** The Tensas River meanders through the
Tensas River Basin, one of five large basins in the Mississippi Alluvial Plain.
(Atchafalaya River Basin, farther south, is the largest of these basins.) The basin
is bounded on the east by the Mississippi River and on the west by the Ouachita
River. The topography here is ridge and swale, caused by periodic flooding and
changes in the river's course. The shallow swales, or depressions, usually hold
standing water and are often flooded during the wet season.

The climate at Tensas is mild. Winter temperatures range from lows in the

Louisiana black bear peers through grass at the edge of the forest.

40s to highs in the 60s. Summers are hot and humid with highs occasionally in the 100-degree range. In wet periods the refuge can flood.

■ PLANT LIFE

Forests More than 80 percent of the refuge (54,808 acres) is bottomland hardwood forest. Species found here include towering white, water, willow, and overcup oak, willow, bald cypress, sweet gum, and Hercules club, also known as the toothache tree.

A variety of smaller trees, shrubs, and other plants grow beneath the tall trees including fan-shaped dwarf palmetto and red haw. Greenbrier, a thorny vine, winds itself around and up many trees, and Spanish moss hangs from branches. Projects are under way to reforest about 2,413 acres of former agricultural land.

Croplands About 4,000 acres of the refuge are kept open to provide a diversity of habitat for wildlife. Croplands (3,000 acres) farmed on a share basis with local farmers and moist-soil units (1,000 acres) provide food for wintering waterfowl. Clearings in the forest are managed by mowing or discing.

Open water The Tensas River and several cypress-lined bayous and oxbow lakes contain about 1,500 acres of open water.

■ ANIMAL LIFE

Birds Large concentrations of ducks and geese (as many as 40,000), raptors, and shorebirds winter at Tensas. Bald and golden eagles are rare winter visitors. In spring, the wet refuge attracts gray-cheeked, Swainson's, hermit, and wood thrushes, whose flutelike songs drift melodiously through the densest parts of the forest. In spring and fall, large numbers of warblers swoop through to feed on the many insects the dense bottomlands harbor.

Throughout the year, blue-gray gnatcatchers, Carolina wrens, tufted titmouse, and Carolina chickadee flit through the trees and undergrowth. Barred owls and red-shouldered hawks navigate the woods in search of prey. Scarlet-crested

THE STORY OF TEDDY BEARS We have the Louisiana black bear and an ex-president to thank for the stuffed toy teddy bears beloved by children. In 1907, while on a hunt just north of Tensas (bear populations were higher then), Theodore Roosevelt, perhaps the nation's greatest conservation-minded president, was given the opportunity to bag a bear cub that had been rather unsportingly tied to a tree. Although he could have easily added the bear to his trophy wall, Roosevelt was a true sportsman and refused to shoot the tethered bear. The incident became news and the subject of many cartoons. Seizing on a marketing opportunity, a couple began manufacturing and selling "Teddy Bears." The rest, as they say, is history.

pileated woodpeckers pummel old trees searching for insect larvae. Wild turkeys roam the forests and occasionally come out into open fields to feed.

The abundant water attracts a variety of waders including little blue herons, yellow-crowned night-heron, and cattle egret. Several wading-bird rookeries are located in the refuge, one not far from a trail.

Mammals Tensas also supports a huge population of mammals (43 species have been confirmed, including nine species of bats and 16 rodent species). Among the more common mammals are white-tailed deer, beaver, muskrat, raccoon, river otter, mink, woodchuck, and opossum. Bobcats and coyotes scout the refuge for small prey.

Louisiana black bears, one of 16 black bear subspecies, once roamed freely throughout the hardwood forests and swamps of the Mississippi Alluvial Plain (see sidebar.) Unfortunately, as farmers and loggers drained swamps and felled forests, the bears, which need large territories to survive, began to disappear. Now, thanks to habitat preservation and restoration, the Louisiana black bear is making a slow comeback. An estimated 100 to 200 bears inhabit the forests of Tensas, nearby refuges, and the natural corridor between them.

Reptiles and amphibians Sixty species—19 amphibians and 41 reptiles—have been confirmed in the refuge, among them three species of poisonous snakes (copperheads, cottonmouths, and timber rattlesnakes). Alligators hang out around refuge lakes and along the riverbanks. Occasionally the roar of a bull alligator breaks the forest quietude.

ACTIVITIES

■ **CAMPING:** Camping is not allowed in the refuge but is possible on nearby private campgrounds.

■ **WILDLIFE OBSERVATION:** Canoeing the Tensas can be rewarding. As you slowly and quietly drift down the river, you can approach wildlife more closely than by foot. Besides an abundance of birds in the trees that overhang the river, look for deer and other mammals who come to the water's edge to drink. The many miles of old unimproved refuge trails also provide visitors with opportunities to hear and see wildlife.

The Tensas River Refuge Association (TRRA) offers a variety of programs for students and refuge visitors, including popular night hikes called "Tensas Night Maneuvers."

■ **PHOTOGRAPHY:** A photography blind is available at the refuge; check with the staff for location and permission. Projects are under way to construct several bridges and wildlife observation blinds that will also be suitable for photography.

TENSAS RIVER HUNTING AND FISHING SEASONS

Hunting
(Seasons may vary)

	Jan	Feb	Mar	Apr	May	Jun	Jul	Aug	Sep	Oct	Nov	Dec
deer (bow)	■										■	■
deer (youth hunt)											■	
deer (gun)											■	■
deer (muzzleloader)											■	
rabbit										■	■	■
squirrel									■	■	■	■
raccoon	■	■										■
woodcock	■											■
feral hog	■									■	■	■

Specific deer hunting dates include: youth hunt, Nov. 14-15; gun season, Nov. 27–28 and Dec. 19–20. Raccoon hunting is allowed late Dec. through early Feb. Hunting for woodcock permitted, late Dec. through Jan. Turkey hunting is allowed in spring; season set each year. Hunting for ducks and coots is allowed Tues., Thurs., Sat., and Sun. during the season, which is set annually. Hogs may be hunted during squirrel, rabbit, and deer (archery) seasons. Regulations and seasons change yearly; contact the refuge for current dates and regulations.

Fishing (warm-water species) is allowed in Africa, Judd, Buck, and Rainey lakes year-round and in the remainder of the refuge, March through Oct.

■ **HIKES AND WALKS:** A short boardwalk wildlife trail begins at the Visitor Center and leads to an observation tower overlooking a marshy area where deer feed at dusk and waterfowl congregate in winter. The 4-mile trail at Rainey Lake traverses a bottomland area and leads to a fishing pier. The first quarter-mile and fishing pier are handicapped-accessible.

■ **SEASONAL EVENTS:** May: Migratory Bird Day; June: Founder's Day; September: National Hunting and Fishing Day, featuring shooting and fishing seminars, canoeing, wild game cooking, and dog demonstrations; October: National Wildlife Refuge Week; December: Christmas Bird Count.

■ **PUBLICATIONS:** Refuge fact sheet; refuge brochure with map; hunting regulations; *Living with the Louisiana Black Bear.*

Upper Ouachita NWR
Haile, Louisiana

Green-winged teal

It is a typical spring day a Ouachita NWR. At one of the refuge's small cypress-lined lakes two fishermen slip brand-new aluminum johnboats into the water, armed with the latest high-tech spinning rods and reels. Following in the footsteps of ancestors who long fished here, they hope to snag a few crappies. They are not disappointed—these waters teem with fish. By day's end the fishers have caught their limit.

A mile or so away three teenagers are canoeing down the Ouachita River. They've come to have fun on the river and enjoy the beautiful views, but as dusk approaches they chance upon a rare sight. A mink, its rich brown coat glistening in the late afternoon light, slinks out of a tangle of roots and limbs along the bank. The mink raises up on hind legs for a moment to check for danger. Not noticing the teenagers in the canoe, the mink determines that the area is free of predators and calls out. From under the tangle of roots four young minks emerge. The youngsters climb on the mother's back, and she carries them across the river.

HISTORY

Upper Ouachita NWR (pronounced WASH-i-taw), located in the Ouachita River Basin just south of the Arkansas-Louisiana line, is a remote, do-it-yourself refuge with few facilities and only limited access. It was established in 1978 to provide habitat for migratory and resident wildlife and is managed as part of the Northeast Louisiana Refuge Complex, with headquarters at D'Arbonne NWR.

The 43,000-acre refuge consists largely of dense bottomland hardwood forest and reforested farmland and has long been recognized for its abundant wildlife resources. As early as the 1700s, the French established settlements for hunters and trappers in the area. Earlier, Native Americans used the area.

In the early 1800s immigrants from the southeastern states came here to settle. After settlement, the area was farmed for cotton and corn, logged for oak and

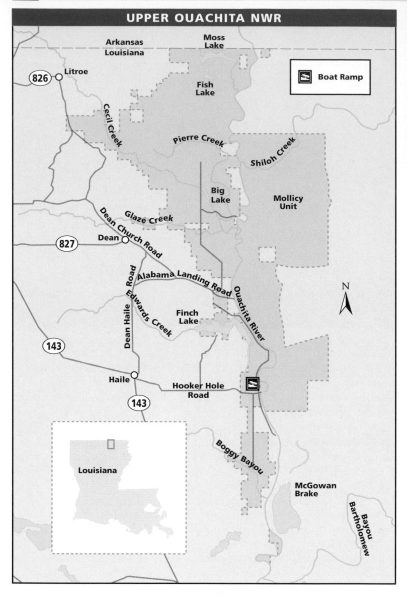

pecan, and finally tapped for gas. Several lumber, paper, and chemical companies exchanged ownership over the years. About 320 active gas wells remain on the refuge.

GETTING THERE

Upper Ouachita is located about 30 mi. north of Monroe. From Monroe, take LA 165 North to LA 2, go west through Sterlington and then north on LA 143 to the small town of Haile. From Haile, take Hooker Hole Rd. east about 5 mi. to the refuge maintenance shop and boat launch area. Or take Finch Lake Rd. north off Hooker Hole Rd. to a commercial boat ramp that provides access to Finch Lake and the refuge.

■ **SEASON:** Refuge open year-round.
■ **HOURS:** Open 24 hours a day.
■ **FEES:** None.
■ **ADDRESS:** Upper Ouachita NWR, % N. Louisiana Wildlife Refuges, 11372 Hwy. 143, Farmerville, LA 71241
■ **TELEPHONE:** 318/726-4222

TOURING UPPER OUACHITA

■ **BY AUTOMOBILE:** About 12 miles of roads provide access to the refuge. River Road can be reached from the boat ramp near the maintenance shop and leads north along the river. It is a beautiful drive through tall moss-draped trees and offers spectacular views of the river. An estimated 20 miles of ATV trails cross the northern side of the refuge and follow the western boundary.
■ **BY FOOT:** There are no foot trails, but many old logging, gas well, and secondary roads are still in place, allowing visitors to explore the interior forest. Most of these roads become impassable during the wet season, which usually lasts from late November to late May.
■ **BY BICYCLE:** Bicycling is allowed on the old roads.
■ **BY CANOE, KAYAK, OR BOAT:** Boating is the best way to see the refuge. Three boat-launch facilities provide access to the Ouachita River and Finch Lake. Small boats and canoes are the easiest and most enjoyable way to see the interior of the refuge.

WHAT TO SEE

■ **LANDSCAPE AND CLIMATE** The Ouachita is a 600-mile-long river originating in the Ouachita Mountains of Oklahoma and Arkansas and flowing southwest across Arkansas and into Louisiana. The refuge extends for 20 miles along the river just downstream of the Arkansas-Louisiana state line. The refuge is about 10 miles across at its widest point and consists mainly of bottomland hardwood forest. As much as 80 percent of the refuge may be flooded during wet seasons.

The climate for the area is typical of northern Louisiana, with mild winters and hot, humid summers; spring and fall can be wet. The average rainfall for the area is 48 inches. An inch or two of snow may fall every four to five years.

■ **PLANT LIFE**
Forests The most representative habitat at Upper Ouachita is its 14,500 acres of bottomland hardwood forest. The dominant tree is overcup oak, but bitter pecan, persimmon, American elm, cedar elm, water elm, green ash, swamp post oak, and willow oak are also found. The understory consists of seedlings of these species plus American snowbell and deciduous holly.

In addition to the spectacular bottomland forest, there are 5,000 acres of upland forest consisting mostly of mixed hardwoods and pine. Loblolly and shortleaf pine and southern red and post oaks are the common canopy species; blackberries, huckleberry, greenbrier, American beauty berry, and hawthorns make up the understory.

Reforestation is a major project at the refuge. Some 4,000 acres of farmland have been reforested, and another 13,500 acres will be.
Croplands Former croplands are being allowed to revert to natural vegetation.
Wetlands The refuge contains about 3,000 acres of shrub and wooded swamp. The dominant tree here is bald cypress and the dominant shrub is buttonbush. Swamp privet, water elm, red maple, and black willow are also present.

Open waters The Ouachita River, which on average is about 300 feet wide, and Finch, Big, and Harrell lakes provide about 1,200 acres of open water.

■ ANIMAL LIFE

Birds Ouachita attracts large concentrations of migratory waterfowl, wading birds, raptors, and a small wintering population of bald eagles. Red-cockaded woodpeckers nest in the upland forest on the western edge of the refuge where loblolly pine and shortleaf pine are the dominant species. Wood ducks, mallards, pied-billed grebes, double-crested cormorants, and anhingas are aquatic species that nest here. Wild turkeys, bobwhite quail, and woodcock comb the forest and open areas for food year-round. Shy wood storks are seasonal visitors.

The habitat is ideal for migrating warblers and other songbirds. Perky northern parula, yellow-throated, pine, prairie, black-and-white, prothonotary, worm-eating, Kentucky, and hooded warblers have all nested in the dense forest, as have Louisiana water thrush, common yellowthroat, and yellow-breasted chat.

Mammals Furbearers like beavers, muskrats, raccoon, otter, and minks traditionally attracted hunters and trappers to the region. The voracious mink has poor eyesight, using instead its excellent sense of smell to hunt from root to root and cranny to cranny for frogs, mice, and other creatures. Occasionally it will attack animals its size or larger, including rabbits, squirrels, and muskrats. Nutria escaped from cages during a hurricane in southern Louisiana, where they were being raised for their fur. Today, they have spread as far north as Virginia. Other mammals who inhabit the refuge include white-tailed deer, opossums, skunks, coyotes, feral hogs, and several bat and mice species.

Reptiles and amphibians Like most Louisiana bottomlands, Upper Ouachita is home to a wide variety of reptiles and amphibians. Bullfrogs and green frogs hang out in the muck at the edges of ponds and backwaters and lend their voices to the chorus of forest birds. Salamanders slither quietly under leaves on the

Nutria

Anhinga

damp forest floor. Tree frogs cling to branches and trill on summer evenings. Five-lined skinks ply forest debris in search of insects, spiders, and earthworms. Snapping turtles, painted turtles, sliders, and Ouachita map turtles paddle through refuge waters and sometimes climb up on fallen logs to sun. Cottonmouths glide effortlessly through refuge waters or join mud snakes along muddy banks.

> **HUNTING** The refuge currently allows hunting for **deer, squirrel, rabbit, quail, woodcock, waterfowl,** and **raccoons**.

ACTIVITIES

■ **CAMPING:** No camping facilities are located on the refuge, but the nearby Finch Bayou Recreation Area, operated by the U.S. Army Corps of Engineers, has camping facilities.

■ **WILDLIFE OBSERVATION AND PHOTOGRAPHY:** Look for wildlife as you slowly drive the roads or boat the waterways. Finch Lake is a good place to begin, whether by car or boat tour.

■ **HIKES AND WALKS:** Although there are no maintained foot trails per se, an intrepid hiker can enjoy walking the many miles of ATV trails and secondary roads or bushwhacking through the refuge in the drier season.

■ **PUBLICATIONS:** Refuge fact sheet; refuge hunting and fishing regulations; North Louisiana NWRs bird list.

Big Muddy NF & WR
Columbia, Missouri

Lesser scaups

It's the kind of natural disaster that happens only once every 500 years. The Great Flood of '93 (1993) brought devastation and destruction to the floodplain of the Missouri River. Homes, farms, and towns that had been protected by a system of serpentine levees were left with only rooftops above brown swirling water. When the levees broke, charging waters buried the farmland under deep sand that was carried 1,000 miles downriver.

With their property in ruin, landowners considered selling. Engineers and public officials considered ways to control flooding. In the end it was decided that managing floods nature's way—letting the land within the floodplain act like a sponge, slowly absorbing, then slowly releasing the water—might be the best solution. An old concept was born again. The U.S. Fish & Wildlife Service purchased land here to create Big Muddy National Fish & Wildlife Refuge, where the experiment is under way.

HISTORY

In September of 1994, the refuge's main goals were to restore and conserve habitat for fish and wildlife resources and to restore natural floodplain and riverine functions of public lands. By 1999, about 7,000 acres of a planned 60,000 had been acquired. When completed, the refuge will be a chain of beads stretching along the Missouri River from Kansas City to St. Louis. At present Big Muddy is small and undeveloped, with only about 650 people visiting each year.

GETTING THERE

The refuge will offer numerous boat access points along the river. Request a current map from the refuge office and information about boat launching.
- **SEASON:** Open year-round.
- **HOURS:** Open 24 hours daily.

■ **ADDRESS:** Big Muddy National Fish & Wildlife Refuge, 4200 New Haven Rd., Columbia, MO 65201
■ **TELEPHONE:** 573/876-1826

TOURING BIG MUDDY

The only viable way to visit most of the refuge is by powerboat from the Missouri River. (Foot trails, biking paths, roads, and other developed facilities do not yet exist.) Not all refuge boundaries are marked; to avoid trespassing on private land, use a refuge map. Boaters on the Missouri should use caution. Avoid flood stage and watch for high winds. Also steer clear of tow barges and their wakes.

WHAT TO SEE

■ **LANDSCAPE AND CLIMATE** The Missouri River divides the tallgrass prairies of northern Missouri from the Ozark highlands to the south. Once, this river was wide and muddy (hence the nickname "Big Muddy") and blessed with islands. Whole trees, washed from the ever-changing bank, floated downstream or became anchored in the sand to become "sawyer" capable of piercing the hulls of steamboats carrying people and goods.

The river valley was rich with virgin bottomland hardwood forest (mostly sycamore and cottonwood) and oxbow lakes and marshes, where migrating waterfowl found abundant food. The islands provided small backwaters and shallow areas where fish could spawn and their young had a good chance to escape predators.

Due to extensive human development of the floodplain, the river is now more like a canal. Rock dikes jut into the river, increasing current, scouring the river bottom so that barges can pass. Banks are lined with rocks (revetments) to help keep the river in place and to eliminate the historic meanderings of the stream across the floodplain.

The floodplain is flat and can be several miles wide. Tan and buff-colored limestone and dolomite bluffs, 100 to 200 feet high, box in the floodplain. Tributaries have cut their way through the bluffs, flowing into the Big Muddy.

Hot and humid in summer with days over 100 degrees, the area's winters can be bitterly cold. Spring and fall are the rainy seasons, and heavy rains upstream can cause the river to rise and even flood.

■ **PLANT LIFE**
Forest Remnant stands of bottomland hardwood forest consist mostly of sycamore and cottonwood. Willows grow thick along the banks of the river.
Open water In places, the river can be a mile wide. At lower levels, some sandbars

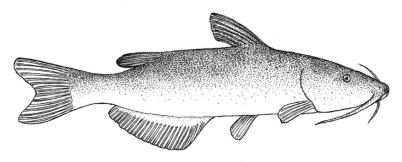

Catfish

BIG MUDDY HUNTING AND FISHING SEASONS

Hunting
(Seasons may vary)

	Jan	Feb	Mar	Apr	May	Jun	Jul	Aug	Sep	Oct	Nov	Dec
deer (bow)	■	□	□	□	□	□	□	□	□	■	■	■
deer (muzzle-loader)	□	□	□	□	□	□	□	□	□	□	■	□
waterfowl	■	□	□	□	□	□	□	□	□	□	■	■
dove	■	□	□	□	□	□	□	□	■	■	■	■

Fishing

	Jan	Feb	Mar	Apr	May	Jun	Jul	Aug	Sep	Oct	Nov	Dec
bass	■	■	■	■	■	■	■	■	■	■	■	■
catfish	■	■	■	■	■	■	■	■	■	■	■	■

Waterfowl hunting is permitted from early Nov. to early Jan., and **dove** hunting season runs from Sept. to mid-Jan. Archery hunting for **deer** is allowed Oct. 1 to Jan. 15, except during an 11-day period in mid-Nov. when deer may be hunted with muzzle-loaders. Contact the refuge for current regulations and seasons.

and islands emerge. Rock dikes provide habitat for fish and resting places for great blue herons. At high water, the dikes may lie just below the surface; boaters beware.
Wetlands Most of the marshes and wetlands in this stretch of river have been drained or filled, but the flood of '93 created some small ponds and lakes.

■ **ANIMAL LIFE** Among migrating diving ducks here you may see redhead, canvasback, lesser scaup, and ring-necked (on the big water of the river) and mallard, teal, and gadwall in shallow marshy areas and flooded fields in the floodplain. Wood ducks are year-round residents throughout the river valley.

Beaver are common; their gnawed trees are easily seen. Beavers don't build lodges here (the lodges would not withstand the river currents); rather, they dig tunnels beneath log jams. White-tailed deer, venturing into fields to poach soybeans, wheat, and corn, find protection in the forested areas along the river.

Several threatened and endangered species and a number of candidate species are found at Big Muddy: pallid sturgeon, least tern, gray bat, Indiana bat, decurrent false aster, lake sturgeon, blue sucker, paddlefish, sicklefin chub, sturgeon chub, flathead chub, plains minnow, western silvery minnow, and eastern Massasauga rattlesnake.

ACTIVITIES

■ **CAMPING AND SWIMMING:** No camping is allowed on the refuge. Swimming is not advised because of the strong river currents.
■ **WILDLIFE OBSERVATION:** Boating on the river provides the best opportunities to see wildlife. With binoculars or quiet paddling and patient waiting, you can see waterfowl flying overhead or resting on the river; look also for eagles perched in tall sycamores along the bank or deer coming to the water's edge to drink.
■ **PUBLICATIONS:** Refuge fact sheet, hunting and fishing information.

Clarence Cannon NWR
Annada, Missouri

Wetlands in changing light at Clarence Cannon NWR

The smallest of Missouri's wildlife refuges does not overpower the visitor with hundreds of thousands of waterfowl. Rather, Clarence Cannon NWR is a gentle, understated landscape that reflects an ecosystem in harmony. Stand on the observation platform on a warm, sunny fall day and scan the marsh and distant tree line with a pair of tack-sharp binoculars. At ground level in the marshy areas north of the platform, dabbling ducks swim contentedly and occasionally stretch to reach seeds underwater. Great blue herons, poised stock-still nearby, silently watch for the minuscule movement of fish. A few feet above the marsh, northern harriers bank and turn, sending ducks scurrying. A pair of wood ducks disappears behind stands of dead trees. Above the trees large flocks of ducks and geese head out to feed in nearby fields. Higher still are red-tailed hawks riding a thermal—a rising body of warm air—as they search for prey below.

HISTORY

The 3,747-acre Clarence Cannon NWR, named after a congressman from nearby Elsberry, is a marshy place along the ever-flooding Mississippi River in northeastern Missouri. Fox and Sauk Indians hunted and fished the rich Mississippi River valley. In early Colonial times, Spain and France vied for control of the area; the region was ultimately absorbed by the United States in the Louisiana Purchase, in 1803. Early boundaries of the French and Spanish land grants still influence property boundaries and roads of the area.

Following the Louisiana Purchase, settlers from Kentucky, Tennessee, Virginia, and the Carolinas established farms in the fertile floodplain, producing tobacco, apples, corn, wheat, and timber. The refuge property was privately farmed until 1964, when it was reverted to habitat for migratory birds and other wildlife. Funds for the purchase were raised from the sale of federal duck stamps.

Clarence Cannon is a part of the larger 45,000-acre Mark Twain NWR

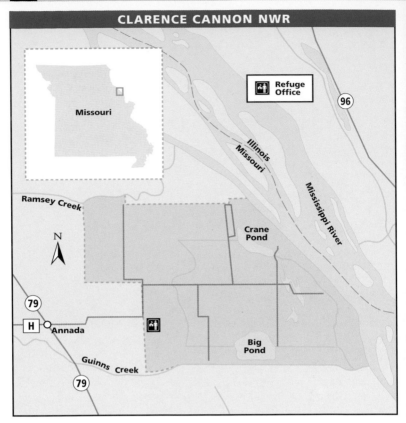

Complex (for migratory birds), a string of wetlands scattered along 350 miles of the Mississippi River. The complex is divided into three administrative districts and is headquartered in Quincy, Illinois. Approximately 24,000 people visit this refuge each year.

GETTING THERE

The refuge is an hour's drive north of St. Louis. From St. Louis take I-70 West to US 79, go north on US 79 for approximately 35 mi. to the small town of Annada. At Annada, follow signs to the refuge (1.5 mi. east).

■ **SEASON:** Open year-round, but access is restricted during periods of peak waterfowl use (Nov.–Dec. and Feb.–April).

■ **HOURS:** General refuge: dawn to dusk (April–Oct. and Dec.–Jan.). Visitor Center open weekdays, 7:30 a.m.– 4 p.m.; however, during peak waterfowl season, hours may vary.

■ **FEES:** None.

■ **ADDRESS:** Clarence Cannon NWR, Box 88, Annada, MO 63330

■ **TELEPHONE:** 573/847-2333

TOURING CLARENCE CANNON

■ **BY AUTOMOBILE:** There is no official auto tour but a little better than 4 miles of gravel road make most of the refuge accessible to cars during all but the peak waterfowl-use months.

■ **BY FOOT:** Visitors are encouraged to walk the refuge roads (there are no established hiking trails). A half-mile nature trail is planned.

■ **BY BICYCLE:** Bikes are permitted on all refuge roads open to automobiles.

■ **BY CANOE, KAYAK, OR BOAT:** Boating is not permitted at Clarence Cannon, and there is no access to the refuge from the Mississippi River.

WHAT TO SEE

■ **LANDSCAPE AND CLIMATE** Lying in the floodplain of the Mississippi River, the refuge is generally flat. It is wet here much of the year. The Lincoln Hills to the west and bluffs on the eastern boundary of the Mississippi floodplain are visible across the river. The refuge borders the Mississippi (although access is not possible because of the thick stands of willows and lack of roads). An access and overlook are planned.

Where the refuge borders the river, there are narrow bands of bottomland forest. Another strip of forest occurs along a drainage ditch near the center of the refuge. Elsewhere you will see seasonally flooded grasslands, cultivated fields, small ponds, and mudflats. Low levees inside the refuge form pools, while larger levees outside the refuge protect adjacent farms and communities from flooding.

Three small ponds provide water for wildlife during the summer months. Crane and Big ponds are the largest and usually contain water except in the very driest years. At Clarence Cannon, the river is actually "Pool 25," a man-made pool formed by a locks and dam structure downstream that regulates water depth for barge traffic.

The climate at Clarence Cannon is generally temperate with cold winters and long, hot, humid summers. Most of the rain occurs in the spring and fall. Tornadoes are a possibility, especially in the spring.

■ **PLANT LIFE**

Forests The bottomland hardwood forest here consists mainly of cottonwood and silver maple, pin oak, and pecan. The den trees and snags in these woods provide habitat for woodpeckers, wood ducks, and other wildlife. Unfortunately, about 80 percent of

Red-bellied woodpecker

the trees in the refuge's bottomland forest were killed during the Great Flood of 1993 (see Big Muddy NWR). A reforestation project is under way.

Cropland Some old farmland on the refuge is planted in corn and wheat to serve as a supplemental high-energy food for migrating waterfowl.

Black-bellied plover

Wetlands Almost all of the refuge is managed as marsh or moist-soil units, flooded in fall and winter and drained in early summer to allow a regrowth of fox-tail, millet, smartweed, and nutgrass. These plants provide seeds for migrating waterfowl in the fall.

■ ANIMAL LIFE

Birds During spring and fall migration, the refuge, under the Mississippi Flyway, hosts thousands of waterfowl, shorebirds, wading birds, songbirds, and raptors. Shorebirds to look for include black-bellied plovers, greater and lesser yellowlegs, and spotted, least, and pectoral sandpipers. American woodcock are found in good numbers as they probe for worms in the mudflats. In spring, a sharp-eyed birder may spot the occasional peregrine falcon zooming past overhead.

The refuge is one of the few places in Missouri to find the king rail, which appears occasionally in spring. These rails, on the Missouri endangered species list, are often easier to hear than to see. Near a marshy area at dawn or dusk, listen for their short, musical *tick-tick-tick*.

In spring and fall, the waterfowl population at the refuge reaches 80,000, including mallard, northern pintail, American wigeon, gadwall, northern shoveler, and both Canada and snow geese. This stretch of the Mississippi River also hosts the largest winter concentration of eagles in the South Central region. Eagles must have open water (not frozen) for fishing. Water discharged through locks and dams on the Mississippi helps keep portions of the river ice-free even in the coldest winters. Eagles also feed on fish killed or injured as they pass through locks and dams. The best time to see eagles: the coldest day of winter, often late December or January, when the surrounding waters are iced over. At the refuge, you may see eagles feeding on weak and dying waterfowl. One pair of bald eagles has nested here since 1992.

In winter, the Eurasian tree sparrow appears on the refuge. Unique to the area, this bird was introduced by German immigrants 120 years ago and has expanded its range northward along the Mississippi River. Ask a refuge manager to help you find the bird in small flocks in grassy and brushy areas.

Among common year-round residents are several species of woodpeckers as well as the tufted titmouse, white-breasted nuthatch, and American goldfinch. Red-tailed hawks are common most of the year. In wooded areas look for great-crested flycatcher, Carolina wren, American redstart, and wood duck.

Least bitterns, a species less frequently seen in Missouri, nest on this refuge. Their call (a series of four soft, low coos) won't be confused with that of the king rail. Killdeer can't be missed on the mudflats in spring and summer and are even occasionally seen in winter.

Mammals Although usually secretive and not easy to spot, raccoon, muskrat, beaver, mink, skunk, opossum, and coyotes are found on the refuge. The chances of seeing deer and

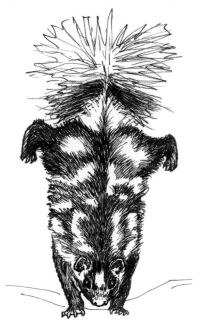

Spotted skunk

squirrel are better. River otter are occasionally seen on the refuge.

ACTIVITIES

■ **CAMPING AND SWIMMING:** There is no camping or swimming permitted on the refuge.

■ **WILDLIFE OBSERVATION:** The observation deck near the Visitor Center is an excellent place to look for wildlife. With a spotting scope it is possible to scan almost all of the flooded fields. There is a fixed spotting scope aimed at a bald eagle's nest in the Visitor Center. Wildlife of all forms may also appear anywhere on refuge roads. Great blue herons and other waders are abundant along the first mile of the auto route. Also commonly seen from the road along the muddy edges of water are common snipe and other shorebirds.

> **HUNTING AND FISHING**
> There is no hunting or fishing allowed at Clarence Cannon NWR.

■ **PHOTOGRAPHY:** At 1.7 miles into the refuge, turn left and go .5 mile. Look to the northeast for a large bald eagle's nest. From January through June, you cannot approach closer to the nest than the road, but this is close enough to get pictures (with a zoom lens) of the nesting eagles.

■ **HIKES AND WALKS:** Although there are no established trails in the refuge, you may walk on the roads or along levees throughout the property, most of the year. Some areas may be temporarily closed for wildlife management.

■ **PUBLICATIONS:** Refuge brochure and fact sheet; bird checklist.

Mingo NWR
Puxico, Missouri

Woodland scene along hiking trail, Mingo NWR

Missourians call it the "boot heel"—that slab of land in deep southeast Missouri that steals a ragged bite of the Mississippi Alluvial Plain from the northeast corner of Arkansas. This land was once all prime bottomland hardwood forest, rich with timber, waterfowl, and wildlife. Today, driving through most of the boot heel, you will see suntanned farmers astride John Deere tractors working as much as 18 hours a day. These farmers mix sweat, fertilizer, herbicides, and pesticides with the soil to produce some of the finest soybeans and rice in the nation.

But in the northwest section of this managed checkerboard of square fields and straight rows, with barely a trace of an errant weed, an island of green cypress and tupelo trees breaks the horizon. At Mingo NWR rare amphibians slither beneath leafy muck, cavity-nesting birds gather moss for nests in hollow den trees, and wildlife of all types seek sanctuary. The 21,676-acre refuge is the only remaining significant tract of Missouri's bottomland hardwood forests. People seem to appreciate this fact: Nearly 120,000 visitors use the refuge each year.

HISTORY

The Ozark hills tumble 1,000 feet into the lowlands of Missouri's boot heel. These lowlands are as flat as a pool table. At one time the Mississippi River ran between the Ozark hills and a serpentine rise to the east known as Crowley's Ridge. About 18,000 years ago, the Mississippi broke through Crowley's Ridge to its present channel, leaving a swamp. Trees grew dense and tall and attracted a plethora of wildlife. Shortly before European settlers arrived, Native Americans, including Quapaw and Osage and later Delaware and Shawnee, used the area as a winter hunting ground. The Delaware and Shawnee feared but respected swamps. Their trepidation was reflected in the name they gave the area: *Mingo,* meaning "treacherous" or "unreliable."

White settlers passed the area over for prairies and other lands that were easier to farm. In the early 1900s loggers began harvesting the boot heel's virgin timber. Mule teams and narrow-gauge railroads hauled the best logs out in only 15 short years. Mighty dredges then drained the wetlands, and farmers moved to the boot heel hoping to profit from the black-soil bottomlands.

But Mingo Swamp did not easily yield to domestication. It was too wet, too mucky for the men and machines of the early 1900s. The land speculators took their dredging machines elsewhere.Times remained tough in the 1930s, and Mingo Swamp yielded only a subsistence living for hard-scrabble farmers. The land became open range, with hogs and cattle roaming at will. People needed food, and hunting took place without respect for seasons or limits. Most of the land was tax delinquent, without clear ownership, and hungry men poached the remaining timber to sell to help feed their families.

In 1945, the U.S. Fish & Wildlife Service, aware of the area's former role as habitat for wildlife, purchased 22,000 acres of Mingo Swamp, mostly in terrible condition: overgrazed, burned, eroded, and overhunted. Happily, with good management practices and reforestation, much of Mingo Swamp has almost returned to its former self. About one-third of the refuge, essentially the entire southwestern section, is designated a Wilderness Area.

GETTING THERE

From Poplar Bluff take Hwy. 60 east about 12 mi. to US Hwy. 51. Go north on 51 about 15 mi. just past the town of Puxico to the main entrance. From Cape Giradeau take I-55 south 28 mi. to Hwy 60. Take US Hwy. 60 west for about 45 mi. to US Hwy. 51. Follow Hwy. 51 north for about 15 mi. through the town of Puxico to the main refuge entrance. A portion of the refuge parallels MO 51 between Puxico and Arab; the highway provides access points to the refuge.

■ **SEASON:** The refuge is closed to most activities from early Oct. to mid-March with these exceptions: auto tour open Sun. in April, Oct., and Nov.; board-walk trail, bluff road observation tower, some refuge roads, public hunting area, and area west of Ditch #6 open year-round (for photography, fishing, and horse-back riding).

■ **HOURS:** General refuge open one hour before sunrise to one-half hour after sunset. Visitor Center open weekdays, 8 a.m.–4 p.m. and weekends, 9 a.m.–4 p.m. mid-March–mid-June and mid-Sept.–mid-Nov.

■ **FEES:** Entrance fee $3 per car.

■ **ADDRESS:** 24279 State Hwy. 51, Puxico, MO 63960

■ **TELEPHONE:** 573/222-3589

■ **VISITOR CENTER:** Located 1.5 mi. north of Puxico on MO 51; remodeled in 1995, it offers exceptional educational displays.

TOURING MINGO

■ **BY AUTOMOBILE:** Vehicles are permitted on the 25-mile self-guided auto tour that skirts the refuge as well as on a few other refuge roads. Driving is not permitted on dikes, levees, or side roads.

■ **BY FOOT:** Three short trails, totaling about 2 miles, are developed for hiking. Walking is also permitted on all refuge roads as well as the tops of dikes and levees (50 miles in all). Hiking is permitted anywhere in the Wilderness Area, but in keeping with the wilderness theme, trails are not maintained.

■ **BY BICYCLE:** Visitors may bicycle the auto loop. Steep hills on the northwest side of the refuge make good brakes essential.

■ **BY CANOE, KAYAK, OR BOAT:** Canoe the Mingo River, Monopoly and

Mingo wetlands

Rockhouse marshes, Stanley Creek, and the many drainage ditches that cross the refuge. There is little current, but be sure to check weather conditions (especially wind) and water levels with the refuge staff. Gasoline-powered motors are not allowed on refuge waters; however, electric trolling motors may be used outside the Wilderness Area.

■ **BY HORSEBACK:** Horseback riders may follow the auto loop and the area west of Ditch #6. Horses must stay on existing roads and levees.

WHAT TO SEE

■ **LANDSCAPE AND CLIMATE** Mingo trends southwest to northeast along the abandoned channel of the Mississippi River. The refuge is flat and low in the center and has hills and limestone bluffs on both sides, offering overviews of the refuge. Monopoly and Rockhouse marshes are the two major standing bodies of water in the center of the refuge. The Mingo River drains both marshes, and Stanley Creek adds water from the hills to the northwest.

Mingo has relatively mild winters; snow is unusual and stays on the ground only a few days. In Mingo's hot summer, humidity of 90 percent or more can make the heat index unbearable. Spring and fall can be delightful, with warm, sunny days and fresh breezes. Tornadoes can occur almost anytime but are more frequent in spring.

■ **PLANT LIFE**
Forests Cypress and tupelo dominate Mingo's extensive bottomland forests. The 100-foot-tall cypress trees give Mingo its character. Young trees are plentiful, but the refuge is also home to 18 state and three national champion trees, including black gum, Carolina buckthorn, green hawthorn, and overcup oak. A severe storm in 1993 played havoc with the old forest; some trees were destroyed, and access to others is now almost impossible.

Beautiful wildflowers dot the bottomland hardwood forest; one, copper iris,

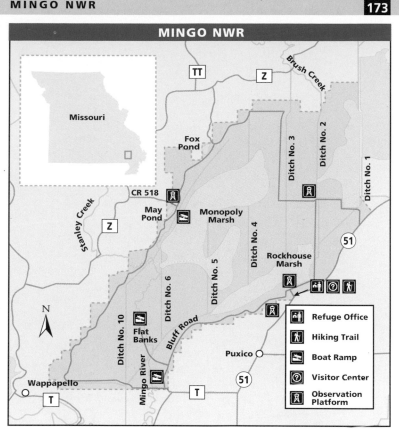

MINGO NWR

Missouri

Brush Creek

TT   Z

Fox Pond

Ditch No. 3

Ditch No. 2

Ditch No. 1

CR 518

Stanley Creek

May Pond

Z

Monopoly Marsh

Ditch No. 4

51

Ditch No. 5

Rockhouse Marsh

N

Ditch No. 6

Bluff Road

Ditch No. 10

Flat Banks

Mingo River

Puxico

Refuge Office

Hiking Trail

Boat Ramp

Visitor Center

Observation Platform

Wappapello

T

T

51

blooms in ditches along the roads. In July and August, wet areas are adorned in swamp buttercups, American lotus, and swamp hibiscus.

On the dry, limestone hills, white and black oaks and shagbark hickory trees typical of the Ozarks are dominant. Redbud and dogwood are characteristic understory trees. Here, wildflowers such as spring beauty, trillium, and phlox are abundant.

Croplands Crops, mostly winter wheat, are planted to provide additional food for migrating waterfowl, and it is common to see white-tailed deer grazing in the managed grasslands.

Wetlands Monopoly Lake (3,500 acres) is actually a shallow marsh averaging about 3 feet in depth; Rockhouse Cypress Marsh occupies 1,500 acres. Both are drawn down periodically. During peak flooding periods, these marshes act as a storage area for flood overflow.

Open waters Of Mingo's several small ponds, Red Mill Pond is a serene and scenic spot and the smaller Fox and May ponds provide open-water habitat.

Mingo River is fed by Stanley and Lick creeks from the north. In addition there is permanent open water in the numerous ditches and isolated forest pools. Several abandoned farm ponds dot the higher areas.

■ ANIMAL LIFE

Birds Mingo is one of Missouri's most popular places to birdwatch, and the refuge has an excellent checklist—246 species have been recorded here and another 35 have been seen as accidentals.

Least bittern can be viewed at Monopoly Marsh.

The refuge hosts a good mix of waterfowl during winter: mallard, Canada geese, snow geese, pintail, American wigeon, wood duck, and hooded merganser. Trumpeter swans stop by in winter. Wading birds are a common sight, except in winter, along the tour road as it skirts Monopoly and Rockhouse marshes. Least bitterns are especially abundant in Monopoly Marsh. Bird species more common to the marshes and bayous of the southern states have been seen at Mingo, including snowy egret, purple gallinule, and common moorhen. Fish crows and Mississippi kites, unusual this far north, are low in number but are usually present.

A project to fledge bald eagles here began in 1983. The refuge boasts the first successful fledgling in Missouri, born in 1985. Today, bald eagles are a prime attraction at Mingo.

Because of its islandlike nature, Mingo is a magnet for migrating spring warblers; 36 species of warblers have been recorded at the refuge, and sometimes yellow-rumped and orange-crowned warblers hang around in winter.

American crow, barred owl, great horned owl, white-breasted nuthatch, horned lark, and sedge wren can be seen year-round. The Carolina wren is a common year-round resident whose cheerful song can be heard in all habitats of the refuge.

Mammals Look around at ground level and in the trees to see Mingo's good variety of mammals. Opossum, raccoon, gray and red squirrels, flying squirrels, and cottontail and swamp rabbits are all here. At dusk, red bats and little brown bats twist and turn in midair to catch moths and other insects above the parking lots. Chipmunks scurry out of the way as you hike down Bluff Trail. Beavers are especially plentiful, and you will undoubtedly notice their gnawing, although they are nocturnal and require great patience to see.

In the white-tailed deer herds, look for majestic bucks with large racks in the fall and spotted fawns in early summer. Mink, red and gray fox, raccoon, striped skunk, and coyote are the most prevalent carnivores. Only a few lucky visitors will get a chance to see Mingo's elusive river otters or bobcat.

Reptiles and amphibians The warm, moist climate at Mingo makes reptiles and amphibians especially abundant. Showy marbled, spotted, and tiger salamanders are all present. With a flashlight you can locate them after dark, following the first warm rain in March, as they head to their breeding ponds.

The refuge holds one of the nation's largest populations of the western lesser siren, a 1-foot-long eel-like amphibian. Frogs are plentiful: Chorus, spring peeper, and cricket frogs herald spring as early as February. Bull, green, and bronze frogs add their deeper voices to the nighttime chorus later in the year. In early mornings and late evenings, the secretive narrow-mouth toad's call (a sheeplike *baaa*) emerges from a wastewater sewage lagoon 0.4 mile south of the Boardwalk Nature Trail's parking lot.

Mingo is a destination for herpetology classes from the University of Missouri. Each spring, students tour the area looking for the numerous timber rattlesnakes, western cottonmouths, and southern copperheads emerging from hibernation in the refuge's rocky bluffs. Visitors should be cautious about, but not afraid of, these pit vipers when visiting the refuge.

Invertebrates Ticks, chiggers, and mosquitoes abound in summer. Bring insect repellent.

ACTIVITIES

■ **CAMPING:** Camping is not allowed in the refuge, but there is camping at nearby Wapapello Lake.

■ **WILDLIFE OBSERVATION:** Wildlife observation (primarily to see deer and birds) has replaced hunting as the most popular activity at Mingo. Any season, except the dog-days of summer, offers good possibilities for observing wildlife here. Good places to spot wildlife are the Boardwalk Nature Trail in early morning and the auto route. Herds of deer (sometimes as many as 50) feed in grassy areas along the drive. From the boardwalk, which allows easy walking through an otherwise difficult area, you may hear the flutelike songs of the hermit and wood thrush. Prothonotary warblers dart in and out of hollow trees delivering food to their young.

Eagles, hawks, and water-

Great horned owl

BALD EAGLE NESTS The nest of the bald eagle is large, majestic, and imposing. Eagles usually choose to build their nests in the tallest and strongest tree in a forested area or a solitary tree in a plain or marsh. Cypress trees in shallow lakes are favorite nesting sites. Nests may be 30 to 60 feet above the ground. Both the male and female eagles contribute sticks and branches—generally several inches in diameter and up to 6 feet in length. Sticks are usually gathered from the ground but may be broken from dead trees. The nests are lined with smaller twigs, grass, sod, and other soft materials.

Bald eagles may use the same nest for several years with some reconstruction. After a few years of use the nest can become enormous—as much as 6 to 8 feet in diameter, 4 feet deep, and weighing more than a ton. Eventually eagle nests self-destruct because of their weight, or high winds may bring them crashing down.

The shape of an eagle's nest reflects the branch structure of the tree the bird chooses to call home. Common eagle nest shapes are cylindrical, bowl, inverted cone, and disk.

Bald eagle nest

MINGO HUNTING AND FISHING SEASONS

Hunting
(Seasons may vary)

	Jan	Feb	Mar	Apr	May	Jun	Jul	Aug	Sep	Oct	Nov	Dec
deer (gun)											■	
deer (bow)										■	■	■
deer (muzzle-loader)	■											
turkey (gun)				■						■		
turkey (bow)										■	■	■
waterfowl	■										■	■
squirrel					■	■	■	■	■			
turkey			■	■								

Fishing

	Jan	Feb	Mar	Apr	May	Jun	Jul	Aug	Sep	Oct	Nov	Dec
carp				■	■	■	■	■	■			
crappie				■	■	■	■	■	■			
bluegill				■	■	■	■	■	■			
catfish				■	■	■		■	■			

Waterfowl can generally be hunted Nov. to Jan.; contact the refuge for current regulations and seasons.

fowl can be observed from the observation towers and the Visitor Center, but they are distant, and a spotting scope is a necessity.

■ **PHOTOGRAPHY:** There are no permanent photo blinds at Mingo, but portable blinds are allowed. Take your camera in a canoe into the Wilderness Area and quietly drift up close to wildlife. Warblers will sing but stay hidden in the arching branches and Spanish moss overhead. The observation platforms overlooking Monopoly Marsh also provide a vantage point for sunrise and sunset pictures over the swamp.

■ **HIKES AND WALKS:** When you visit Mingo, allow time to walk the Boardwalk Nature Trail (1.1 miles) as it loops through the bottomland hardwood forest. There is an elevated spur leading to an observation tower overlooking a portion of Rockhouse Marsh.

Bluff Trail (0.5 mile), beginning at the Visitor Center and connecting with the Boardwalk Nature Trail, is short and steep but provides a good view of wildflowers in the spring and an opportunity to see the bluffs that once lined the Mississippi River.

The brief Hartz Pond Trail begins at the Visitor Center parking lot and leads to Hartz Pond, a small lake with picnic facilities and fishing.

There are no maintained trails in the Wilderness Area. However, there are paths and trails made by other animals, both two- and four-legged, that will cleverly lead you around obstacles. Exploring the wilderness area is the best way to get a feeling for what Mingo was like before Europeans settled the area.

■ **SEASONAL EVENTS:** Each winter, usually in February, the refuge, in cooperation with the Missouri Department of Conservation, hosts "Eagle Days" featuring displays, lectures, and the chance to see a live eagle at close range. The refuge also celebrates National Wildlife Refuge Week in October.

■ **PUBLICATIONS:** Refuge brochure with map; Boardwalk Nature Trail flyer.

Squaw Creek NWR
Mound City, Missouri

Canada and snow geese in flight at Squaw Creek NWR

It is almost sunset on Thanksgiving afternoon. About two dozen cars are parked along a gravel road at Squaw Creek NWR. It's an eclectic assortment of folks. A four-wheel-drive pickup, covered with mud, contains two hunters in camouflage. A van carries a family of four. A luxury car shelters a retired couple. Two photographers, both with lenses big enough to fend off a bear, wait patiently. They are all here for one reason, to watch some 380,000 snow and blue geese—enough birds to fill six or seven major league stadiums. The geese blanket the pool of water for almost a half-mile in each direction. Soon the geese will take off to travel to distant fields for their evening meal. Not all at once, however: If all the geese were to take off at one time, there would be collisions, broken wings, and mass confusion. The birds take flight in turns. One becomes airborne, then two, four, eight, and soon thousands are in the air at once.

A wave peaks at a few thousand geese, then fades as the birds settle back on the water. Each wave intensifies the anticipation. Suddenly, countless "*whouking*" geese are in the air, a flying layer of feathered bodies. It's a spectacle made even more dramatic as bald eagles move in to feed on the dead and dying.

HISTORY

Squaw Creek NWR, in the floodplain of the Missouri River in northwest Missouri, is one of the most popular refuges in the South Central region, attracting about 120,000 visitors annually. The 7,350-acre refuge was established in 1935 by President Franklin Roosevelt as a resting and feeding area for migratory birds and other wildlife. How Squaw Creek earned its name is a mystery. One theory holds that the creek's original name was Squaw Wood Creek, for the many small pieces of driftwood along the creek that squaws could easily gather.

LEWIS AND CLARK'S VOYAGE OF DISCOVERY Meriwether Lewis and William Clark began their exploration of the Louisiana Purchase in the summer of 1804 from St. Louis. In early June of that year, they passed through the area that was to become Big Muddy and Squaw Creek NWRs, finding the area "rich with wildlife," the "vegetation verdant." The June 7, 1804, entry in William Clark's journal contains a passage about Little and Big Manitou bluffs, near the mouth of Moniteau Creek, in the Big Muddy NWR area: "a Short distance above the mouth of this Creek, is Several Courious paintings and carving on the projecting rock of Limestone inlade with red & blue flint, of a verry good quality, the Indians have taken of this flint great quantities."

Traces of these paintings still exist, viewable from Katy Trail State Park, along the Missouri River. Wildlife was plentiful; Clark noted, "our Hunters brought in three Bear this evening." Bears are no longer found in Big Muddy refuge or in this part of Missouri.

On June 8, 1804, Clark describes the vegetation of the Missouri near the mouth of the Lamine River, also near Big Muddy: "...Capt. Lewis went out above the river & proceeded on one mile, finding the countery rich, the wedes & vines So thich & high he came to the Boat." Clark has an encounter with rattlesnakes: "We landed at the Inscription and found it a Den of Rattle snakes, we had not landed 3 Minites before three verry large Snakes was observed in the crevises of the rocks & killed."

July 11 and 12, 1804: Now farther upstream, Lewis and Clark camp at the mouth of the Big Nemaha River (on the Nebraska side of the river) near what was to become Squaw Creek NWR. "Nemaha" is a Sac or Fox Indian word meaning "no papoose," and Lewis and Clark surmised that it referred to the frequent outbreaks of malaria in the Indian population. Members of the expedition carved "Lewis and Clark 1804" in the bluffs here. Just upstream from Nemeha, the explorers were the first whites to observe and record the American white pelican, a bird that now frequents Squaw Creek refuge in great numbers.

GETTING THERE

The refuge is about 90 mi. north of Kansas City. From Kansas City, take I-29 north to MO 159, then go west 3 mi. to the refuge. The Visitor Center will be on the left, the entrance to the auto tour on the right.

■ **SEASON:** Open year-round.

■ **HOURS:** Refuge and auto tour open dawn to dusk. Office and Visitor Center open weekdays, 7:30 a.m.–4 p.m., and weekends, 10 a.m.–4 p.m. (mid-Oct.–early Dec. and mid-March –early May).

■ **FEES:** None.

■ **ADDRESS:** Squaw Creek NWR, Box 158, Mound City, MO 64470

■ **TELEPHONE:** 660/442-3187

■ **VISITOR CENTER:** Squaw Creek's Visitor Center features displays of mounted waterfowl, raptors, and mammals. Perched on the side of a loess hill, the building offers an outstanding overview of the main part of the refuge.

TOURING SQUAW CREEK

■ **BY AUTOMOBILE:** The only accessible road in the refuge is a 10-mile circular auto tour, the most popular feature of the refuge. The clockwise loop, which

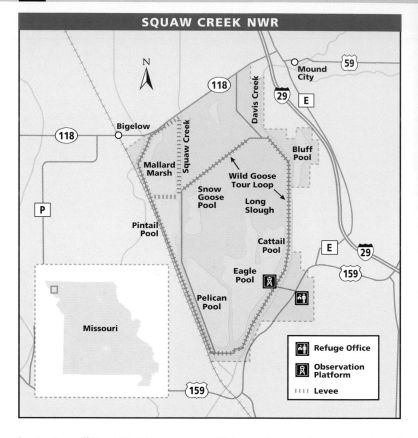

SQUAW CREEK NWR

Mound City
118
Bigelow
Davis Creek
Squaw Creek
Mallard Marsh
Wild Goose Tour Loop
Bluff Pool
Snow Goose Pool
Long Slough
Pintail Pool
Cattail Pool
Eagle Pool
Pelican Pool
Missouri

Refuge Office
Observation Platform
Levee

begins just off Rte. 159, takes you around lakes and pools, through woods and fields, and past a flooded bottomland hardwood forest, providing opportunities to see wildlife at close range. Ask for the auto-tour guidebook and allow at least one hour to make the loop.

■ **BY FOOT:** There are two short trails, and visitors may walk the auto-tour road.

■ **BY BICYCLE:** Bicycling is allowed on the auto-tour road.

■ **BY CANOE, KAYAK, OR BOAT:** Boating is not allowed in the refuge.

WHAT TO SEE

■ **LANDSCAPE AND CLIMATE** Most of Squaw Creek's topography is flat. The Missouri River cuts through the glaciated plains of the midwest, an area where "uplands" are tallgrass prairie and lowlands support bottomland hardwoods. Loess hills provide relief on the southeast boundary, rising steeply 100 feet above the floodplain floor; these hills are the remnants of windblown soil deposited during the last glacial period. The ruggedness of the hills has preserved some of the original prairie plants that once covered this area. The north slope of the loess hills receives less sunlight and holds moisture longer, supporting more trees than the south slopes—where you will see more prairie plants.

Several pools near the south end of the refuge are managed as marsh or wet-soil units for migrating waterfowl. The north side of the refuge has cropland and some forested areas. Both Squaw and Davis creeks flow south through the refuge into the man-made pools and then into the Missouri. (The refuge does not actually border on the Missouri River.)

The climate here can be very cold in winter, with temperatures reaching zero or below; winter winds blowing across the plains can create blizzardlike conditions when it snows. Missouri summers can be hot, with temperatures approaching 100 degrees. Spring and fall are often ideal times to visit.

■ PLANT LIFE

Forests Although it is probable that much of the Missouri River floodplain was originally forested with sycamore, cottonwood, and willow, only a few of these trees have survived agricultural and lumbering interests. The trees that remain can be found scattered throughout the refuge, especially near waterways. An unusual tree, the pawpaw grows along the base of the loess bluffs. All of the pawpaw's relatives are in the tropics. It blooms in the spring with a rich, dark red flower and produces a bananalike fruit that provides luscious food for wildlife and people.

Cedar trees constantly try to invade the loess hills. The proliferation of cedars had traditionally been suppressed through natural and man-made fires (by Native Americans). Now refuge staff control the cedars by cutting and burning.

Croplands About 500 acres of bottomland, mostly on the north and west sides of the refuge, are farmed for corn, soybeans, winter wheat, and clover to provide supplemental energy for waterfowl, deer, and upland birds.

Grasslands The loess hills were originally a tallgrass prairie that was sustained by natural and man-made fire. Although fire is allowed only as a management tool today, the prairies still contain a rich diversity of native species, including little bluestem, side-oats gama, and Indian grass. Forbs growing in the loess hills contain leadplant, snow-on-the-mountain, and skeletonweed. A mixture of warm-season grasses in the 2,000 acres of grasslands around the pools is managed by prescribed burning.

Wetlands The water levels of Eagle, Pelican, Pintail, Snow Goose, and Bluff pools and Mallard Marsh are all controlled by the refuge staff to maintain a healthy balance of aquatic vegetation. These shallow pools are ideal waterfowl habitat;

Ring-necked pheasants hide in the tall prairie grasses.

look for emergent plants such as cattails, river bulrush, arrowhead, and American lotus. There are 3,100 acres of managed marsh. Some areas are flooded and then drained, creating moist-soil units conducive to the important waterfowl food plants smartweed and wild millet.

■ ANIMAL LIFE

Birds Tremendous numbers of waterfowl begin arriving at Squaw Creek in October and peak in mid-November of most years. Severe weather will cause an earlier peak, and mild weather can cause a later one. Squaw Creek's amazing numbers of snow geese—in recent years as many as 380,000 have wintered here—is truly a spectacle. An additional 100,000 ducks may join the geese. As many as 300 bald eagles may follow the waterfowl and can be seen perched alone or in large numbers in tall cottonwood trees or sitting majestically on the hundreds of muskrat mounds throughout the marsh. Usually a few eagles remain after the refuge freezes and the geese have moved on. On rare occasions golden eagles and peregrine falcons join the bald eagles at Squaw Creek.

The piping plover and least tern are two other endangered birds that use the refuge. Ring-necked pheasants feed and hide in prairie grasses along the wildlife drive.

The refuge is located at a point where the ranges of eastern and western species of birds overlap. Golden eagles, prairie falcons, and Swainson's hawk are western raptors that hunt on the refuge along with red-tailed hawks, while cinnamon teal and Ross' goose are more typical western waterfowl that mingle with Canada geese and teal. Species that nest here include bobolink, scarlet tanager, rose-breasted grosbeak, cedar waxwing, and warbling vireo.

Birders have recorded some very rare or out-of-range species at Squaw Creek: Eurasian wigeon and ruff (from Europe), barnacle goose (from Greenland), and even a greater flamingo (from the Caribbean, unless it escaped from a zoo).

This all adds up to a remarkable 309 species of birds recorded on the refuge.

Mammals Mammals at Squaw Creek are plentiful (33 species), although many are shy or nocturnal and can be difficult to find. The more commonly seen include

White-tailed deer

fox squirrels in the woodlands near the loess hills and raccoons, opossums, and coyotes along the tour route.

The rich bottomland and nearby agricultural fields produce excellent crops that help the large deer herd (500 to 800 individuals) keep healthy. During the day most of the deer stay in the thick willows and cottonwood trees, but in the evening they come out to feed on the fields.

Some of Squaw Creek's mammals are unusual for Missouri. The Franklin ground squirrel is a rodent more common to the west. Look for it in vegetation along refuge roads in summer; it hibernates from early autumn to mid-spring. The southern bog lemming, the only member of the lemming family in Missouri, looks like a prairie vole but prefers wetter habitat. It has a habit of cutting grass stems and storing them to make "hay piles" along its runways in the tallgrass. Although not often seen or trapped, the number of remains found in the scat of long-eared owls indicate that the southern bog lemming is common here. The badger, a mammal more common to western prairies, is the largest member of the weasel family and feeds on mice and ground squirrels, which it ravenously digs from the ground.

Franklin ground squirrel

Reptiles and amphibians
Thirty-five species of reptiles and amphibians inhabit this refuge. One of rarest is the Massasauga rat-tlesnake. Squaw Creek may be the only place in Missouri with a healthy breeding population of this reptile. A small, timid snake (about 20 to 30 inches), its home is the wet prairie. The Massasauga rattlesnake are most likely to be encountered in the spring and fall crossing refuge roads while traveling from their denning areas to the marshlands. Drivers should keep an eye on the road to avoid running over this rare snake.

ACTIVITIES

■ **CAMPING:** No camping is permitted on the refuge; however, nearby Big Lake State Park has camping facilities.

■ **WILDLIFE OBSERVATION:** Near the entrance to the auto tour, an observation tower overlooks Eagle Pool. Many eagles can be seen here in winter, while green-winged teal feed in the shallow water near the road. As you continue on the auto-tour loop, look for more eagles in the tall trees on the southeast side of the road.

The loop heads south and continues on the levee bordering Pelican Pool, where thousands of American white pelicans appear during the spring and fall migrations. This pool may also be your best bet to see the hundreds of thousands of snow geese at Squaw Creek.

The tour next swings north, and a side extension will take you to Pintail Pool and Mallard Marsh, both good places to see ducks.

Continuing on the main route, about halfway through the tour and in a wooded area, is an excellent place to look for deer crossing the road or gathering in adjacent farm fields to feed. The tour route then heads south and passes by flooded bottomland hardwood forest, a good place to find wood ducks and raptors.

A favorite pastime of local residents is to drive the auto-tour route just before sunset for a look at the refuge's numerous white-tailed deer. Many are bucks with spectacular racks, and some of these bucks are seen on such a regular basis they have been given names by their human admirers.

■ **PHOTOGRAPHY:** On the auto-tour route, at peak migration, geese may be as close as 50 feet and bald eagles will perch in trees above the road. Stay in your car, using it as a photo blind. Eagle Overlook Trail leads to an area where eagles, geese, and ducks may fly overhead, offering good opportunities for pictures of birds in flight. Loess Bluff Trail is a fine place to photograph prairie wildflowers throughout the summer season.

> **HUNTING AND FISHING**
> Except for a brief muzzle-loader **deer** hunt (two days in mid-Jan.), there is no hunting on the refuge.
>
> Fishing (from shore areas only) is permitted year-round for **carp**, **catfish**, and **crappie**.

■ **HIKES AND WALKS:** Both Eagle Overlook Trail, a 1.5-mile roundtrip, and the Loess Bluff Trail, a .5-mile circuit with a 200-foot gain in elevation, provide good—if brief—walks. Ask for the guidebook on Loess Bluff Trail; it describes eight wildlife observation stations along the way. Parts of this trail are steep and require effort, but the view from the top of the loess hills overlooking the Missouri River valley is exquisite.

■ **SEASONAL EVENTS:** March 15–May 4 and October 11–December 7: Open House Weekends; October: National Wildlife Week; December: Eagle Days, cosponsored by the Missouri Department of Conservation; December: Christmas Bird Count.

■ **PUBLICATIONS:** Refuge brochure; bird and mammal flyers; Loess Bluff Trail Guide; auto-tour guide; Massassauga Rattlesnake flyer; Fall Migration of Snow Geese flyer.

Swan Lake NWR
Sumner, Missouri

White pelicans at Swan Lake NWR

It's a sunny April morning at Silver Lake. By now, the remnants of the winter's snow should be melted. In the distance, however, you see an island covered with white. Through the binoculars you realize that it is not snow but American white pelicans, maybe a thousand or more. They're here on their annual spring migration to Canada. On the gravel road on the east side of the lake, you can approach within 100 feet of the pelicans, which are busy swimming in a group and feeding on the rough fish of the lake, their basketlike bills dipping into the water. The birds snap their bills closed, water pours out, and, with luck, a few fish remain inside. One bird wades onto the mudbank, a catfish trapped in its bill.

HISTORY

Originally, most of the northwest corner of Missouri was tallgrass prairie. Bottomland hardwood forest grew along the natural waterways. By the early 1900s, the area was populated and tamed—by frontier standards. Land had been cleared, drained, and converted to farmland. Native game animals—deer, elk, bear, otter, and wild turkey—had all but disappeared.

But frequent flooding made farming here difficult at best. In the 1930s devastating floods robbed farmers of their crops and their mortgage payments. A 10,670-acre tract was sold to the U.S. Fish & Wildlife Service, and in 1937 Congress established Swan Lake NWR to provide habitat for migratory ducks and prairie chickens. The refuge contains two large man-made lakes, Swan Lake and Silver Lake, and the smaller, marshier South Lake. The Civilian Conservation Corps went to work building roads, structures, and wetlands. Farming continued, but crops were now grown to produce food for wildlife. In the years that followed, however, the prairie chicken disappeared from the region. But Swan Lake became an important wintering area for migrating Canada geese.

Ironically, swans rarely visit Swan Lake. The name possibly came from the

A family of Canada geese

explorers Lewis and Clark, who observed large flocks of swans about 30 miles south of the refuge.

GETTING THERE

Swan Lake NWR lies 100 mi. northeast of Kansas City. It has several entrances. To reach the main gate, from Kansas City take I-35 North to MO 36. Go east to Laclede, and follow MO 139 south about 11 mi. to the junction of Rte. RA in Sumner. The main entrance is on a gravel road one mi. south. To reach the east entrance, continue on MO 36 to Rte. 11. Go south to Rte. CC and turn west 1.9 mi.

■ **SEASON:** Office, observation tower, nature trails, and main entrance road open year-round. The interior of the refuge is closed mid-Oct.–early March.

■ **HOURS:** Interior parts of the refuge are open during daylight hours (in season); observation tower, nature trails, main entrance open all year. Refuge office and Visitor Center open weekdays, 7:30 a.m.–4 p.m., and occasionally on weekends when it is staffed by volunteers.

■ **FEES:** None.

■ **ADDRESS:** Swan Lake NWR, Route 1, Box 29A, Sumner, MO 64681

■ **TELEPHONE:** 660/856-3323

TOURING SWAN LAKE

■ **BY AUTOMOBILE:** Driving is permitted along 13 miles of gravel roads. An auto-tour road begins at the east entrance and makes an approximately 10-mile trip through the refuge.

■ **BY FOOT:** There is one short trail near the Visitor Center. A grain silo that has been converted to an observation tower is located next to the Visitor Center. It is not handicapped-accessible. Hiking is also permitted on service roads and atop levees.

■ **BY BICYCLE:** Biking is allowed on the gravel roads.

■ **BY CANOE, KAYAK, OR BOAT:** All refuge waters are open to nonmo-

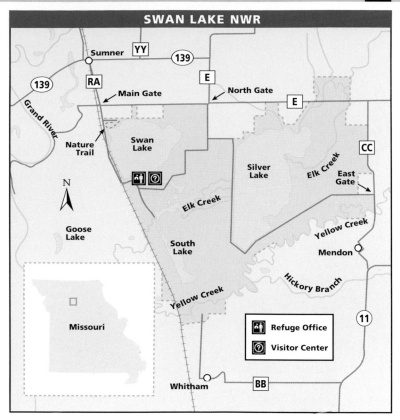

SWAN LAKE NWR

Sumner YY 139
139 RA E
Main Gate North Gate
Grand River E
Nature Trail Swan Lake
Silver Lake Elk Creek CC East Gate
Refuge Office Visitor Center
N
Goose Lake Elk Creek
South Lake Yellow Creek
Mendon
Yellow Creek Hickory Branch
Missouri 11
Refuge Office
Visitor Center
Whitham BB

torized boats. There is a boat launch on Silver Lake. The lake is shallow, and wind can be a problem; however, paddling along the edge to search the vegetation and trees for wading birds and songbirds can be rewarding. Motors of 10 hp or less may be used on Silver Lake only.

WHAT TO SEE

■ **LANDSCAPE AND CLIMATE** The refuge lies in the dissected till plains region of Missouri, an area north of the Missouri River that was once covered by glaciers. The terrain is flat, and all of the refuge lies in the floodplain of the Grand River near its confluence with the Missouri. Yellow Creek, a tributary of the Grand River, forms the southern border. Levees, control valves, and small canals facilitate control of water levels throughout the refuge.

The winter climate in northern Missouri can be cold and bitter, with frequent windy blizzards. Summers are hot and humid and subject to tornadoes. The best times to visit are spring and fall.

■ PLANT LIFE

Forests Bottomland hardwoods make up 1,000 acres. These forests grew naturally along Yellow and Elk creeks before settlement began. Species found here include pin oak, white oak, and sycamore.

Grasslands There is a small area of native prairie between Route CC and the south side of Elk Creek, north of the east entrance. Cordgrass and big bluestem are the most abundant of the tallgrass prairie species found here. At least one-half of the refuge consists of old fields in various successional stages. These fields were once cropland, but now native grasses and trees are beginning to reclaim the area.

Croplands The farming done at Swan Lake is carried out with minimal use of inorganic fertilizers and herbicides. Of the 1,250 acres in corn, sorghum, clover, and wheat, only 125 acres are farmed on shares, with a portion going to the farmer and a portion left in the field for the wildlife. The majority of the crops are left in the fields for geese and other wildlife.

Wetlands Water levels are manipulated on an additional 3,500 acres of marshy lowland to produce natural waterfowl foods such as millet and smartweed.

Open waters Silver Lake, a permanent body of open water, covers 3,000 acres; Swan Lake, about 1,100 acres; and South Lake, 1,850 acres. The lakes are connected by a system of canals and ditches. There are also areas of standing water in borrow pits where material was removed to construct levees. The three lakes have dead snags that provide roosts for double-crested cormorants in summer and dozens of bald eagles in winter. American lotus grows from the shallower portions of the lakes, while marsh grasses and cattails prefer the wettest soil around the lakes.

■ ANIMAL LIFE

Birds Canada geese have found Swan Lake to be ideal for their needs, making the refuge one of the best places in America to see tremendous numbers of this familiar species. Other waterfowl present in the winter include snow geese and large numbers of a wide variety of ducks. They are accompanied by up to 100 bald eagles.

One of the earliest migrants to return in the spring is the killdeer. This highly vocal shorebird announces his presence by repeating his name: *Killdeer, Killdeer, Killdeer.*

Pied-billed grebes and least bittern have been found nesting in spring and early summer in the marsh vegetation along the inlet to Swan Lake. They can be heard from the bridge over Elk Creek; the bittern chirps a series of "KOK" notes that sound much like Morse Code, and the grebe makes low, slurred whistles.

By mid-August there may be a good variety of southward-migrating shore-

Killdeer

Badger

birds, terns, and gulls, but the numbers of birds depend on the presence or absence of mudflats, which occur at the margin of the lakes as they naturally dry up during late summer and before the fall rains fill them again.

American white pelicans are attracted by the thousands to the large lakes on the refuge. Flycatchers like the combination of open grasslands and scattered trees; they roost in the trees. Resident flycatchers include eastern wood peewee, eastern phoebe, great-crested flycatcher, and eastern kingbird. The horned lark, dickcissel, indigo bunting, and loggerhead shrike are among the year-round residents. Altogether, more than 230 species of birds have been recorded at Swan Lake.

Mammals White-tailed deer grow large and healthy in this ideal habitat. You will see them on almost any visit. Muskrat, woodchuck, coyotes, red and gray fox, river otter, raccoon, and gray and fox squirrels are found here, but you may have to look hard or wait patiently to see them. Resident badgers are even more elusive.

Reptiles and amphibians Forty-three species of reptiles and amphibians call Swan Lake refuge home. One of the prettiest is the red milk snake, aka the "candy-cane snake," for its white skin mottled with red blotches. Folk legends contend that these snakes milk cows. The tale most likely originated from the fact that since the snakes eat mice and rats, they are often found in cow barns.

Invertebrates Several freshwater mussels with intriguing names like giant floater, mapleleaf, flat floater, and pink papershell inhabit the Grand River area. These and other freshwater mussels are important members of the Grand River ecosystem, but due to sediment runoff and chemicals from agriculture and other pollution sources, they face an uncertain future.

ACTIVITIES

■ **CAMPING:** Camping is not permitted on the refuge, but excellent facilities are available at Pershing State Park (Rte. 130, 7 miles north).

■ **WILDLIFE OBSERVATION:** Along the shore of Silver Lake you may find green-backed heron and sora rails poking their heads from the vegetation, while great-crested flycatchers snatch insects from the air. Killdeer can be seen in the fields, near the water, and on mudflats. They lay their well-camouflaged eggs on the ground in the fields or even on the gravel roads. Killdeer are masters of the old "I'm a very injured bird, see my broken wing" trick to lure predators or humans away from their nest.

■ **PHOTOGRAPHY:** South Lake is a good spot to photograph wading birds, shorebirds, and ducks. Climb the observation tower for panoramic shots of the whole refuge. (The tower is not handicapped-accessible.) The auto-tour road, near the east gate, can be good for ducks, cormorants, and pied-billed grebes. Pelicans make a spectacular sight at sunrise on Silver Lake in the fall and spring. Swan Lake Drive in the winter is good for photographing Canada geese, ducks, and bald eagles. With permission, photographers may use some of the hunting blinds.

> **HUNTING AND FISHING**
> Hunting is prohibited on the refuge except for a special primitive weapons **deer** hunt (permits issued by lottery) and a **goose** hunt from late Oct. to late Nov.
>   Fishing for **catfish**, **carp**, **bullhead**, and **crappie** is permitted March through mid-Oct.

■ **HIKES AND WALKS:** A 0.5-mile (round-trip) walking trail located immediately east of the Visitor Center passes through a strip of forest and offers a view of Swan Lake. A primitive trail, about 8 miles in length, begins near the Visitor Center and runs atop levees on the south side of the refuge to a point near the east entrance.

To explore an area with mature bottomland hardwoods and clearings where breeding land birds are often visible, drive from the east entrance to where the refuge road turns sharply northwest; park and walk a short distance—less than a mile—along an access road parallel to the southern boundary of the refuge.

Two miles farther on the auto road is another side road closed to vehicles that goes to the left along a levee. Bell's vireos and willow flycatchers are usually found north of the beginning of the side road in the small trees by a pond.

■ **SEASONAL EVENTS:** October: During National Wildlife Refuge Week there is a specially marked auto-tour route. Guided group tours are available on request.

■ **PUBLICATIONS:** Refuge brochure and fact sheet; "Birds of Swan Lake NWR" checklist; "Fall Migration of Canada Geese" pamphlet.

Little River NWR
Broken Bow, Oklahoma

Meandering waterway on Little River NWR

The route to Little River refuge leads through sparsely settled hills of southeastern Oklahoma where roads have no names or numbers but are known in the community by which family lived there the longest. It's a landscape from another time. As you enter the refuge, tree limbs crowd the car into the center of what was once a two-lane road. Roadside blackberry bushes and poison ivy provide thick, protective cover for small birds as their songs drift into the air. Old logging roads, now deep with ruts and tall with grass, invite you to explore. Kentucky warblers call from the low brush; ruby-crowned kinglets sing from a tangle of wild grapes. Tall grass moving in a line indicates that something is fleeing—perhaps a rabbit, perhaps a skunk, perhaps a box turtle.

HISTORY

Established in 1987, Little River refuge protects the finest example of bottomland hardwood forest remaining in this part of Oklahoma and provides habitat for wood ducks and migratory waterfowl, particularly mallards. The refuge is still in the acquisition stage. There are currently 12,029 acres (of a projected 15,000) managed by the refuge. Prior to becoming a wildlife refuge, some sections had been clear-cut and replanted as pine plantations, while other areas were left as large open fields. The refuge plans to establish a variety of habitat types to benefit a diversity of wildlife.

GETTING THERE

The refuge is situated at the northwest edge of Ouachita National Forest. From Idabel, take US 70 north. Cross the Little River, continue 4 mi. to a crossroads and turn right. At this writing there is no sign to the refuge. From this point, go 1 mi. on a blacktop road and turn right; after another mi. turn left onto a gravel road; go 0.6 mi. to a fork; bear right, and follow this gravel road to the refuge. From

Broken Bow, take US 70 south for 2 mi. and turn left to get to the refuge. Follow the directions above after leaving the highway. Check with headquarters for help with directions and road conditions.

■ **SEASON:** The refuge is open year-round.

■ **HOURS:** Refuge open from sunrise to sunset. Headquarters (in Broken Bow) open weekdays, 7:30 a.m.–4 p.m.

■ **FEES:** None.

■ **ADDRESS:** Little River NWR, P. O. Box 340, Broken Bow, OK 74728

■ **TELEPHONE:** 580/584-6211

TOURING LITTLE RIVER

■ **BY AUTOMOBILE:** Ten miles of primitive roads are open to automobiles, and, except during spring floods, most are passable. However, campers, motor homes, and buses are not recommended. Refuge roads offer good opportunities for viewing wildlife, but check with headquarters for advice on directions and road conditions

■ **BY FOOT:** There are no developed trails, but hikers may use miles of old roads closed to vehicles.

■ **BY CANOE, KAYAK, OR BOAT:** The refuge has no established boat launches, but there are places where you can carry a boat down a steep bank to the river. You can rent a canoe and get advice on planning a canoe trip from Riverside Canoe (580/835-7130).

WHAT TO SEE

■ **LANDSCAPE AND CLIMATE** Little River refuge is just south of the Ouchita Mountains. Two rivers, Little and Mountain Fork, intersect on the refuge. The Little River terrain is flat to gently rolling with swampy ground (subject to flooding), punctuated by old oxbows and sloughs. The rivers are generally clear, with steep banks. The climate is hot and humid in summer and cool to cold and humid in winter.

■ **PLANT LIFE**

Forests This is densely forested land, in spite of the commercial logging that went on here prior to its protection as a refuge. Along the river, bottomland species such as sweetgum, cypress, and white oak dominate. On higher ground, loblolly pine, hickory, and walnut prevail. Deciduous holly is the principal understory, but dogwoods (flowering gorgeously in spring) are also present.

Wetlands A small man-made marsh is located at the first road junction. Cattails, sedges, and bulrushes cover most of the wet area. In several other low areas with standing water, cypress are the predominant trees.

Open waters Twenty miles of Little River, with a few scattered islands, twist and turn through the refuge.

■ **ANIMAL LIFE**

Birds Mallards and wood ducks seek the seasonally flooded bottomland hardwood habitat of Little River to feed on acorns and other mast produced by these forests. Other ducks found in smaller numbers here are the wigeon, green-winged teal, and gadwall.

In winter, several bald eagles feast on fish and waterfowl. Herons and egrets use the refuge and nest together in colonies called rookeries. The anhinga may also nest with them. At Little River, this bird is at the northern edge of its breeding range. Sometimes called "snakebirds," they swim with only their heads and necks above water, looking something like a snake. Anhingas' feathers become waterlogged, so they are often seen perched on a snag above the water with their head held high and their wings outstretched to dry in the sun. (They lack the water-resistant oils that most shorebirds and seabirds have.) The anhinga eats mostly insects that it finds by walking on the ground, flipping over leaves, and probing the ground with its heavy bill. It nests, usually, near ground level at the edge of a dense growth of cane, near or over water.

The refuge is said to have the largest number of nesting warblers in the state, including parula, Kentucky, hooded, black-and-white, and Louisiana water-thrush. The rare Swainson's warbler (brown-olive and gray in color), whose numbers are declining from the clearing of bottomland forests, is often found here in dense stands of cane. This secretive bird is not shy when it comes to singing—you will hear it more often than see it.

Mammals The refuge is thought to hold approximately 43 mammal species, although some have not actually been seen. Traveling the gravel roads of the refuge, look for the beavers' stick-and-mud dams on small creeks. Their natural hydroengineering provides additional waterfowl habitat.

Reptiles and amphibians Wet, forested habitat is ideal for amphibians and reptiles. Amphibians species here total about 29; reptile species total 51, including 27 types of snakes.

The refuge is at the northern edge of the range for the American alligator, mud snake, and three-toed amphiuma.

An isolated population of bird-voiced tree frogs lives at Little River near open water, marsh, and forested habitats. Normally this frog is not found west of central Louisiana. The frogs look something like the gray tree frog, but their voice sounds like someone whistling for a dog. The similar-looking gray tree frog is present, but its voice is more of a trill, similar to the call of a red-bellied woodpecker.

Cottonmouth water moccasins are abundant throughout the refuge; local residents call the young "rusties" because of their color.

ACTIVITIES

■ **CAMPING AND SWIMMING:** Not permitted on the refuge.

■ **WILDLIFE OBSERVATION:** In winter, a boat trip on the river will be highlighted by the sight of several bald eagles waiting in the large trees to feed on fish and waterfowl. The same trip in summer will reveal herons and egrets; look for their rookeries on predator-free islands or high in trees.

■ **PHOTOGRAPHY:** With its large population of warblers, Little River offers photographers plenty of opportunity to capture the flighty subjects on film. In the marsh, look for yellow-crowned night-herons, common yellowthroats, and the well-hidden American bittern. Graceful, white spider lilies are among the better wildflower subjects here.

HUNTING AND FISHING
Squirrel hunting is permitted here from mid-May through Jan., and **rabbits** can be hunted Oct. through mid-March. Check with the refuge for special conditions and seasons for hunting **deer**, **turkey**, and **waterfowl**.

Fishing is permitted on the refuge's waters. **Catfish** are the most sought-after species on the river; **bass** and **panfish** are popular in the lakes and oxbows.

■ **PUBLICATIONS:** Refuge brochure; mammal, reptile and amphibian, fish, and bird checklists, and hunting and fishing regulations.

Salt Plains NWR
Jet, Oklahoma

Visitors are drawn to the great salt flat at Salt Plains NWR.

Salt Plains NWR is one of the most popular refuges in Oklahoma, with annual visitation reaching almost 150,000 people. Its appeal is broad-based. For bird-watchers, the large lake bustles with the comings and goings of thousands of ducks and geese in the winter migration. For novice wildlife enthusiasts, a vege-tated area beneath the shade of mature cottonwoods offers glimpses of deer and songbirds. And the huge white salt flat attracts novice geologists armed with shovels and buckets, seeking essentially worthless but nonetheless captivating selenite crystals (see sidebar).

During migration, shorebirds are drawn to the salt flats of the refuge, which has been named a Western Hemisphere Shorebird Reserve Network Regional Site. Such sites in the United States, Canada, Mexico, and South America protect vital wetlands used by shorebirds for resting and feeding during migration. Strategically placed stopovers are critical for shorebirds needing to replace depleted energy reserves for their long journeys. The loss of any of these sites as a result of development or pollution could have disastrous effects on whole popu-lations of shorebirds. Salt Plains NWR is also a Registered Natural Landmark, and has been designated as critical habitat for whooping cranes.

HISTORY

Located in north-central Oklahoma and established in 1930, Salt Plains NWR is just 15 miles from the Kansas border. The 32,000-acre refuge got its name from the wafer-thin layer of salt that lies on the surface of the sandy soil comprising the flats.

The salt found in the Great Salt Plains has made it an important habitat for mammals, who need salt to maintain the proper balance of body fluids. Game animals were drawn here to satisfy their need for salt; as a result the land became an important Indian hunting ground. The 1828 treaty between the United States and the Cherokees states that "The right is reserved to the U.S. to allow other tribes of red men to get salt on the Great Salt Plains in common with the Cherokee tribe." Cattlemen traveled from as far away as Texas and western Kansas to haul away wagonloads of the mineral. Salt deposits were also important to early settlers, who used the salt to cure and preserve meat through the summer.

The National Atmospheric Deposition Network has used the refuge as an acid-rain analysis site since 1980. Oklahoma State University's wildlife research unit studies terns and shorebirds, which use the salt flats here.

GETTING THERE

Salt Plains lies about 40 mi. northwest of Enid. From Enid, take US 81 North to Rte. 64 West. At Jet take Rte. 38 North 13 mi., then go 1 mi. west to the Visitor Center and headquarters.

■ **SEASON:** The refuge is open year-round.

■ **HOURS:** Refuge open dawn to dusk. Visitor Center open weekdays, 7:30 a.m.–4 p.m., and weekends, 11 a.m.–6 p.m. (early April–mid-Oct.).

■ **FEES:** None.

■ **ADDRESS:** Salt Plains NWR, Rte. 1, Box 76, Jet, OK 73749

■ **TELEPHONE:** 580/626-4794

■ **VISITOR CENTER:** A slide show features seasonal changes on the refuge, and a diorama depicts the least tern in its nesting habitat. A spectacular selenite crystal, about the size of a football, is the second-largest found on the refuge, especially impressive because most crystals measure just a couple of inches long.

TOURING SALT PLAINS

■ **BY AUTOMOBILE:** Although Oklahoma state highways completely encircle the refuge, roads into the refuge itself are scarce. The one-way Miller Auto Tour Route, 2.5 miles, has numbered stops with interpretive signs. It begins near the Visitor Center and exits on OK 11 after meandering past tree-lined refuge ponds and farm fields. Visitors are asked to stay in their cars except when walking the trails.

Rte. OK 11, within the refuge boundaries, also provides good view of habitats and wildlife.

■ **BY FOOT:** Visitors may hike 2 miles of nature trails. Caution: Temperatures on the salt flat can easily exceed the century mark in summer and the white salt reflects the sunlight upward. Wear protection; a hat and sunscreen are strongly advised. Bring water.

■ **BY CANOE, KAYAK, OR BOAT:** A boat ramp at the Jet Recreation Area and one off OK 38 north of Nescatunga provide access to Salt Plains Lake. A buoy line, an extension of OK 38, divides the lake; boating is permitted year-round east of the line. Ralstin Island, a rookery island in the middle of the lake, is usually closed to boats.

Whooping crane

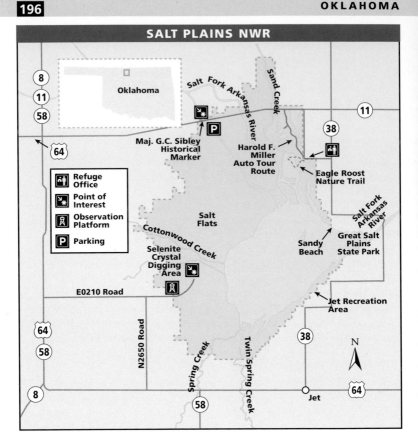

SALT PLAINS NWR

Map legend:
- Refuge Office
- Point of Interest
- Observation Platform
- Parking

Map labels: Oklahoma; Salt Fork Arkansas River; Sand Creek; Maj. G.C. Sibley Historical Marker; Harold F. Miller Auto Tour Route; Eagle Roost Nature Trail; Salt Flats; Cottonwood Creek; Sandy Beach; Great Salt Plains State Park; Salt Fork Arkansas River; Selenite Crystal Digging Area; E0210 Road; N2650 Road; Spring Creek; Twin Spring Creek; Jet Recreation Area; Jet; N

WHAT TO SEE

■ **LANDSCAPE AND CLIMATE** Salt Plains NWR lies in the Central Lowland Plains of Oklahoma, an area of rolling hills. The western third of the refuge is an amazing 11,000-acre salt flat 7 miles long and about 3 miles wide. Pool-table flat, the white surface is desertlike when the summer heat shimmers and mirages appear and disappear. Ancient seas covered the area millions of years ago. The seas were eventually cut off from the ocean and evaporated, leaving the salt behind. Later, salt layers were covered by sediment eroded from distant mountain ranges. The salt crust on the surface forms when capillary action through the salt-saturated sand causes groundwater to travel upward, come to the surface, and evaporate.

In the southern two-thirds of the refuge lies Great Salt Plains Reservoir, formed when the U.S. Army Corps of Engineers dammed the Salt Fork of the Arkansas River in 1941. The western shore of the lake rises ever so gently, yielding to the salt flats. With such a gradually sloping shore, varying water levels will greatly determine the ratio of lake to salt flat in this refuge.

The remaining third of the refuge is a complex of waterways, low grasslands, and marshy areas. Areas of invading brush and forest and crop fields are interspersed with small freshwater ponds and marshes engineered as part of the waterfowl management program.

The climate is warm and dry. Most rain occurs in spring. Tornadoes are most likely in the spring, when warm Gulf of Mexico air clashes with cool air from the north. Expect strong winds, especially in spring and fall.

■ PLANT LIFE

Forest Most of the trees grow at the north end of the refuge along Sand Creek and on the boundary. Few trees can tolerate salt levels in the salt flats. Cottonwoods are dominant, but black willow and elm grow on the banks of the lake and waterways. There are thousands of acres of salt cedar that grow on the edge of salty areas around the lake.

Croplands Approximately 1,200 acres are planted in winter wheat, milo, Austrian winterpeas, millet, and occasionally corn and sunflowers to provide food for wintering migratory birds and other wildlife.

Marshes Several man-made impoundments at the north end of the refuge are flooded in fall, then drained in spring and allowed to grow up with wild millet, alkali bulrush, smartweed, and other native plants, again to provide needed food for migratory waterfowl. The impoundments, which can be seen on the auto tour, are Little, Intermediate, School, Mink Run, Casey, North Casey, Wilson's Pond, and Big Marshes.

Open waters Great Salt Plains Lake (not to be confused with the similarly named lake in Utah) has varied greatly in size—from 8,690 acres to 27,730 acres—with corresponding changes in shoreline length and the size of salt flats during periods of flooding. The lake's one major island, Ralstin, sits in the north-central end. Rivers on the refuge generally drain from northwest to southeast and include the Salt Fork, Sand Creek, and Clay Creek.

■ ANIMAL LIFE

Birds From fall through spring Salt Plains is especially busy, with thousands of ducks and Canada geese on Sand Creek Bay at the north side of the refuge. The refuge is a migration stopover point for 40,000 sandhill and whooping cranes; these large, stately birds fly with their long necks and legs fully extended. In spring, watch for their famous courtship ritual "dance," complete with leaps, the flapping of wings, and ardent calls. The springtime pass-through of the cranes is fairly quick; however, in fall they are traveling with their young and tend to stay at the refuge longer.

Other long-distance travelers, shorebirds, need Salt Plains for survival. Some have come from Tierra del Fuego at the tip of South America all the way to the Arctic Circle

Sandhill crane

Selenite crystal

and back, an unbelievable distance of 20,000 miles. They may be half-starved when they arrive at Salt Plains, but the refuge's rich food sources allow them to double their weight in just a few weeks.

The threatened snowy plover and the endangered interior least tern nest on the salt plains during the summer along with American avocets. Least terns build a shallow, unlined nest in the bare sand, while American avocets build a shallow nest lined with dried grass in the vegetation below a low-growing brush. Thousands of egrets, herons, and white-faced ibis nest on Ralston Island in the Great Salt Plains Lake.

Mammals Beaver are common in the marshes and ponds. Signs of their presence include gnawed tree stumps, felled logs, and smooth, narrow trails, an imprint of their tails dragging the ground. Deer take shelter in the woods during the day but come out to feed in the fields and grasslands in the morning and evening.

Reptiles and amphibians Turtles, frogs, and snakes inhabit Eagle Roost and other ponds and marshes in the refuge.

Invertebrates When water is available, salt brine flies hatch and become food for shorebirds. The mudflats along Sandpiper Trail are home to worms, crustaceans, insects, and mollusks that also help to fuel the shorebird migration.

ACTIVITIES

■ **CAMPING:** Primitive camping is available at Jet Recreation Area on the southeast side of the refuge from early April to mid-October.

■ **SWIMMING:** There are no swimming beaches operated by the refuge, but boaters often swim or wade in the reservoir. Swimmers and waders should use caution as there are no lifeguards on duty.

■ **WILDLIFE OBSERVATION:** Driving the auto tour at a leisurely pace with

SELENITE CRYSTALS Great Salt Plains is the only national wildlife refuge where you are allowed to dig for selenite crystals. Selenite is the name for a unique form of gypsum. Chemically, both gypsum and selenite are calcium sulphate, but the arrangement of their molecules are different, forming different types of crystal (like diamonds and coal—both are carbon but have different crystal structures).

On the southwest corner of Great Salt Plains, the crystals form just below the surface, seldom more than 2 feet deep. Crystals take on the characteristics of their environment; the finer the soil, the clearer the crystals. Iron oxide gives the crystals a chocolate brown color. Sand and clay particles form the "hourglass" shape that is unique to the crystals of the Great Salt Plains.

Single crystals, penetration twins, and clusters are typical shapes. Exceptional cluster specimens up to 36 inches long and weighing 100 pounds have been found. A brochure available at the refuge headquarters provides information on how to dig for the crystals. Everyone will be successful.

frequent stops allows you to listen to the four-note song of the Carolina chickadees and the musical whistle of the cardinal while you watch the many ducks on the pond.

From OK 11 you can spot waterfowl, shorebirds, and other waterbirds in roadside ponds and streams. At times, thousands of wigeon will take advantage of a temporary body of water in a flooded field.

The island in Salt Plains Lake attracts lots of wading birds and can be viewed from the boat launch south of the turnoff to the Visitor Center on OK 38. Wading birds such as egrets, herons, and ibises can be seen at closer range feeding on refuge wetlands and grasslands.

American white pelicans peak from late summer through October. The number of pelicans visiting the lake has increased in the last few years, with peak numbers in the 25,000 to 60,000 range. Snowy plovers run across the salt flats along the road to the crystal digging area. Wilson Pond is a brood pond for mallard and wood duck. Look for ducklings in the spring and summer, where they sometimes can be photographed hiding beneath the large leaves of the American lotus. In early morning and evening, beaver may be spotted in the marshes along the auto-tour route and nature trail.

■ **PHOTOGRAPHY:** Casey Marsh Tower stands a few hundred feet from the auto tour and overlooks an outstanding area for photographing birds. School Marsh Overlook is another good place for capturing pictures of wading birds.

■ **HIKES AND WALKS:** The 1.25-mile-long Eagle Roost Nature Trail is open year-round. This mostly flat trail starts along Sand Creek Bay with an overlook equipped with a 20-power scope for watching rafts of ducks, hundreds of swallows, or a lone osprey feeding over the water of the bay. Geese nest on the small islands of Puterbaugh Pond. The trail gains slightly in elevation and passes through a wooded area before looping back to the parking lot.

Sandpiper Trail is a three-eighths-mile trail open year-round. A well-maintained gravel path through grassland with shallow water and mudflats and nesting least terns nearby, it starts on the south side of Hwy. 11 near the western edge of the refuge. An observation platform with a 20-power scope offers outstanding shorebird and waterfowl viewing on the salt flats.

The easy 0.25-mile walk to Casey Marsh Tower ends at a man-made wall constructed to conceal the viewer's presence from the waterfowl on the other side. (Peepholes arranged at strategic levels let you view wildlife without their knowing you are watching.) Best viewing times are from October to April. During late fall and winter, thousands of ducks and geese mingle with bald eagles in the trees in the distance. Overhead, pelicans circle. In spring, flocks of avocets sweep the water with their long, upturned beaks.

HUNTING AND FISHING Controlled **deer** hunting is allowed, and there are 1,200 acres open for **upland game** and **waterfowl** hunting.

Fishing is permitted April to mid-Oct., but portions of the refuge may be closed to fishing during the waterfowl migration season. There is a designated fishing pond (Bonham Pond) near the Visitor Center for children 14 and under and the disabled.

■ **SEASONAL EVENTS:** Mid-January: Bald eagle viewing day from the OK-38 bridge; first weekend in May: Annual birding and crystal festival, including seminars and boat trips to Ralston Island rookery; October: Pelican Viewing Weekend with boat trips to see the rafts of pelicans on the lake.

■ **PUBLICATIONS:** Flyers on Eagle Roost Nature Trail, Miller Auto Tour Route, and whooping cranes; brochures on refuge birds and Great Salt Plains Lake (good map); "Whooping Cranes: The Road to Survival" brochure.

Sequoyah NWR
Vian, Oklahoma

Newly planted field at Sequoyah NWR

It's a peaceful and quiet early spring day on Sequoyah NWR. Tractor engines hum in the distance as bottomland is turned in preparation for planting. A few anglers sit in lawn chairs by the slough, hoping to catch a mess of channel catfish. Shorebirds dally on the waters. There's no hint of the area's tormented human history.

Great sadness prevailed when the Cherokee, Chickasaw, Choctaw, Creek, and Seminole Indians were ripped from their ancestral homes in the East and relocated to the hills and grasslands of eastern Oklahoma. The Arkansas and Canadian rivers became the boundary line between Cherokee to the north and Chickasaw and Choctaw tribes to the south. Then came the Civil War, and the Arkansas River became a natural barrier between Union and Confederate forces. The pastoral landscape was filled with the sights and sounds of war.

Peace did not come to the area after the war. Eastern Oklahoma was a magnet for outlaws in the 1880s. Fifty years later, during the Great Depression, outlaw Pretty Boy Floyd preyed on the rich and "helped" the poor in this troubled area.

But today, all is calm on the refuge.

HISTORY

Sequoyah NWR, located in east-central Oklahoma, was established in 1970 with the completion of Kerr Reservoir, which dams the Arkansas River. The reservoir dwarfs the refuge and gives it some of its varied habitat and character. Sequoyah's 20,800 acres provide habitat for waterfowl and other migratory birds and food and cover for resident wildlife.

The refuge is named in honor of Sequoyah, the extraordinary Cherokee who was a silversmith and trader in the tribe's home country (in what had become the state of Georgia). Sequoyah converted the Cherokee language to writing. About 1821, he visited the removed Cherokee in Arkansas and taught thousands to read and write their own language. He then moved with his people when they were

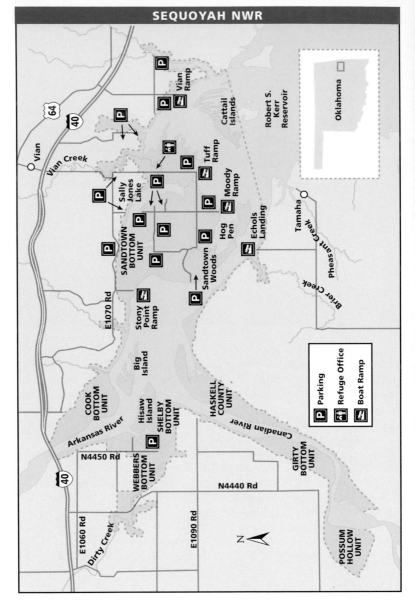

SEQUOYAH NWR

removed again to what is now Oklahoma and there helped to found a weekly Cherokee newspaper.

GETTING THERE

Sequoyah is located on the western side of Kerr Reservoir, between I-40 and OK 9. From Oklahoma City, take I-40 to the Vian exit. Follow the county road south for 3 mi. to the refuge.

■ **SEASON:** General refuge: Open year-round. Parts of the Sandtown Bottom Unit are closed to all entry (except on designated hiking trails) from early Sept. to mid-March. Adjacent areas, bordering the reservoir, are closed from early Oct. to mid-Feb. The Sandtown Unit 1 is closed during special deer hunts in Oct. or Dec. (usually held midweek).

■ **HOURS:** Main refuge open from sunrise to sunset. Headquarters open weekdays, 7:30 a.m.–4 p.m.

■ **FEES:** None.

■ **ADDRESS:** Sequoyah NWR, Rte. 1, Box 18A, Vian, Ok 74962

■ **TELEPHONE:** 918/773-5251

TOURING SEQUOYAH

■ **BY AUTOMOBILE:** Six miles of gravel auto-tour roads are open for year-round touring in the Sandtown Bottom Unit (closest to the headquarters building). Buses and recreational vehicles have no problems navigating this road, but travel may be restricted during wet and icy weather.

To reach the Webbers Bottom and Girty Bottom units, return to U.S. 40, go west and look for the first road to the left after crossing the Arkansas River. (Ask at the headquarters for specific directions and a map.) Webbers Bottom has a 2-mile drive and a fishing access.

■ **BY FOOT:** There are two 1-mile footpaths: Horton Slough and Sandtown Woods trails. Girty Bottom Unit has no maintained trail, but you may walk along the Canadian River through the woods and farm fields.

■ **BY BICYCLE:** Refuge tour roads are flat and graveled and make for pleasant biking. However, roads can be very dusty during dry spells.

■ **BY CANOE, KAYAK, OR BOAT:** Dirty Creek, the Arkansas River, and the northern end of Kerr Reservoir offer plenty of places for boating. The Arkansas and Canadian rivers' delta is also within refuge boundaries. When boating in this area, stay alert for submerged stumps, logs, and sandbars. A portion of the reservoir east of Tuff Ramp is a roosting area for waterfowl and is closed to all entry from early October to mid-February. There are five boat ramps (most are located near the refuge headquarters) that provide access to the lake.

WHAT TO SEE

■ **LANDSCAPE AND CLIMATE** The Prairie Plains Region of Oklahoma has the gently rolling foothills of the Ozarks as a backdrop. Sequoyah NWR is a mixture of croplands, wetlands, bottomland hardwood, and open lake. The refuge lies at the confluence of the Arkansas and Canadian rivers, on the upper end of Kerr Reservoir. Summers here are warm to hot with periodic but not sustained cold in winter.

■ PLANT LIFE

Forests Common tree species include water and Shumard oak, cottonwood, and willow. There are areas of bottomland hardwood forest, with more forest restoration occurring as a focus of habitat restoration.

Croplands and grasslands Much of the refuge is planted in wheat and other grain crops to provide supplemental food for the migrating waterfowl. Refuge staff are working to remove Johnson grass, plant switch grass, and big and little bluestem grass.

Wetlands Natural vegetation is allowed to grow in wetland areas.

■ ANIMAL LIFE

Birds Mallards winging up and down the Central Flyway are attracted to Sequoyah in great numbers. You can also see here gadwall, wigeon, pintail, and

MIGRATING MONARCH BUTTERFLIES Monarchs are the most well-traveled butterflies in the world and are among the most beautiful. The adult's 4-inch wingspan is a handsome reddish-brown, with black veins and borders dotted by white spots. Monarchs are seen worldwide but fly primarily in North America; they are also known as the milkweed butterfly (its caterpillars feast on milkweed plants).

Unlike other migrants, there may be several life cycles over the entire migration route. A single monarch makes one leg of the trip, stops, and dies off but reproduces itself as a new butterfly (preserving its DNA where migration route information is stored), then carries on for the next leg, before the process repeats.

Monarchs west of the Rocky Mountains travel to groves of trees along the California Coast. Those east of the Rockies fly a great distance to the mountains of central Mexico (where hosts of monarchs may completely cover the trees). As the eastern population gathers to migrate south, geography, climate, and food supply funnel them through Oklahoma, where you can see them at Sequoyah NWR.

Monarchs are usually solitary animals, but as the winter migration season approaches they huddle together at night and then begin their southwesterly journey during the day. They stop to feed on their way south and actually gain weight as they migrate. But they cannot linger: As winter approaches, their food supply dwindles and, because they are cold-blooded, the falling temperatures affect their ability to survive.

teal—and the largest concentration of snow geese in Oklahoma. Migrating bald eagles join the resident population, bringing the winter total up to 5 dozen.

Mammals Bobcats are seen more often at Sequoyah than at any of the other refuges in this region. Your best chance for spotting one is in early morning. The cat could be lounging idly in a tree, legs hanging leopardlike over the branches. Or it might be hunting rabbits in the fence rows. Bobcats can even be seen at the edge of water searching for frogs and fish.

Armadillos are in abundance at Sequoyah. About the size of a large house cat, these ancient mammals are covered with a protective armor with coarse hair straggling out from between the plates. They are fairly nearsighted, so you can approach closely if you are very quiet. When they finally do sense your presence,

Monarch butterfly

they will scuffle off remarkably fast to one of their burrows or a dense thicket in which to hide.

Reptiles and amphibians Many varieties of turtles, such as the red-eared slider, can be seen in wetlands regularly during the warmer seasons. They bask for hours on logs, stumps, or snags, sometimes two and three deep. Watch from a distance—because as soon as you try to approach them on foot, they quickly slide into the water and out of sight. Diamondback water snakes bask on logs or hang on branches over the

SEQUOYAH HUNTING AND FISHING SEASONS

Hunting
(Seasons may vary)

	Jan	Feb	Mar	Apr	May	Jun	Jul	Aug	Sep	Oct	Nov	Dec
rabbit	■	■								■	■	■
goose	■	■									■	■
duck	■										■	■

Fishing

	Jan	Feb	Mar	Apr	May	Jun	Jul	Aug	Sep	Oct	Nov	Dec
white bass	■	■	■	■	■	■	■	■	■	■	■	■
striped bass	■	■	■	■	■	■	■	■	■	■	■	■
crappie	■	■	■	■	■	■	■	■	■	■	■	■
black bass	■	■	■	■	■	■	■	■	■	■	■	■
catfish	■	■	■	■	■	■	■	■	■	■	■	■
sunfish	■	■	■	■	■	■	■	■	■	■	■	■

Hunting is limited to designated areas, including Sandtown Bottom, Webbers Bottom, and Girty Bottom. Contact the refuge for current regulations and seasons.

water. They are also quite shy and will quickly disappear into the water if approached.

Invertebrates Sequoyah is a major stopover for migratory monarch butterflies in early fall (see sidebar). They congregate in fields of wildflowers.

ACTIVITIES

■ **CAMPING AND SWIMMING:** No camping or swimming is allowed on the refuge.

■ **WILDLIFE OBSERVATION:** The auto tour offers many opportunities to see wildlife. Winter is the best time to see large numbers of waterfowl and white-tailed deer in wetlands or fields along the route. Refuge staff can provide suggestions about particular spots to find monarch butterflies in the fall.

■ **PHOTOGRAPHY:** On winter mornings and late evenings, fields of soybeans and winter wheat along the auto-tour road are good places to photograph snow geese in abundant numbers. During the rest of the day, look for them as they rest on Kerr Reservoir.

■ **HIKES AND WALKS:** Horton Slough Trail, a 1-mile loop, starts from the information kiosk at refuge headquarters. In spring, the trail leads through blooming redbuds and plums on the north side of Horton Slough. It crosses a narrow, swinging bridge where you may have good views of wood ducks. Armadillos root in the leaf litter for food The trail returns along the south bank of the slough. Be on the lookout for poison ivy.

Sandtown Woods Trail starts at spot # 21 on the auto-tour route map. Along this 1-mile trail, you'll see the wooden tower once used as a release site for bald eagles. Today, some of these birds are permanent residents, and their massive stick nests can be seen along the shores of the Arkansas and Canadian rivers.

Check with refuge headquarters about access to Cook Bottom, Shelby Bottom, Haskell County, and other units of Sequoyah NWR.

■ **PUBLICATIONS:** Refuge brochure; hunting and fishing brochures; bird checklist.

Tishomingo NWR
Tishomingo, Oklahoma

Beaver dam at Tishomingo NWR

The tailwaters of Lake Texoma (half in Texas, half in Oklahoma) follow the Washita River northward into Oklahoma and finally settle at Tishomingo NWR. This is the same Washita River that flows through Washita NWR in western Oklahoma. The refuge provides a haven where both wildlife and people can enjoy peace and quiet.

Visit on a hot summer evening, and in the haze you may well see doe and fawns feeding contentedly along the forest's edge, flicking flies with their short white tails. Fishing boats float leisurely on Cumberland Pool, while under the surface, crappie and channel catfish wait expectantly for a morsel of food to drift their way.

HISTORY

Tishomingo NWR, in south-central Oklahoma, was established in 1946 to provide wintering habitat for migratory waterfowl using the Central Flyway. Consisting of 16,464 acres, Tishomingo is named for a Chickasaw chief, as is the nearby town of Tishomingo-the old tribal capital of the Choctaw-Chickasaw Nation. Before this area became a refuge, it was a large agribusiness operation known as Chapman Farms. A small community existed here, with 53 houses, a school, a church, a silo, and a store. Some of these structures now lie under the dammed-up waters of Lake Texoma, but others are still standing and can be seen scattered throughout the refuge. When the government purchased land for Lake Texoma, a portion of the property was dedicated as the wildlife refuge.

GETTING THERE

From downtown Tishomingo, follow OK 78 East to the edge of town. At the high school, turn south on Refuge Road (watch for sign), and go 3 mi. to the refuge.
■ **SEASON:** General refuge open year-round. Wildlife Management Unit is closed for limited hunting Oct. through Feb.

■ **HOURS:** Main refuge open seven days a week, sunrise to one-half hour after sunset, except for night fishing and camping. Headquarters office open weekdays 7:30 a.m.–4 p.m.
■ **ADDRESS:** Tishomingo NWR, 12000 S. Refuge Rd., Tishomingo, OK 73460
■ **TELEPHONE:** 580/371-2402

TOURING TISHOMINGO

■ **BY AUTOMOBILE:** Fifteen miles of roads wind through various habitats of Tishomingo. Nida Point and Bell Creek roads are good choices for viewing wildlife.
■ **BY FOOT:** Craven Nature Trail, north of headquarters, goes through a mile of woodlands and out to a small deck on Dick's Pond.
■ **BY BICYCLE:** Bicycling is allowed on all refuge roads.
■ **BY CANOE, KAYAK, OR BOAT:** Boating is permitted March 1 to Sept. 30. Boaters should watch for floating debris and submerged concrete structures in Cumberland Pool.

WHAT TO SEE

■ **LANDSCAPE AND CLIMATE** At Tishomingo rolling uplands give way to the vast expanse of Lake Texoma. Tishomingo NWR lies at the upper Washita arm of Lake Texoma. Washita River, murky with sediment, flows through the western portion of the refuge.

Summers are hot and winters are usually mild, but dress warmly for winter visits. The winds off the lake can be bitter.

■ **PLANT LIFE**
Forests Almost 11,000 acres of the refuge are dense hardwood forest with oaks and hickories the dominant species. These trees produce excellent mast crops for white-tailed deer and wild turkey. Near the water, cottonwood, willow, and box elder are the common species. On the edges of the forest are fragrant plum thickets that give way to grasslands.
Croplands Corn, milo, and winter wheat are grown on approximately 900 acres near the refuge headquarters. These crops are left in the field to provide grain and forage for geese, deer, and other wildlife.
Open waters A quarter of the refuge is 4,500-acre Cum-

Wild turkey

berland Pool, a part of Lake Texoma. Its murky waters don't let in enough light to support the growth of large aquatic plants, but its abundant nutrients nourish microscopic plants and animals to sustain a healthy fish population. Moist-soil units in the refuge are flooded seasonally for waterfowl.

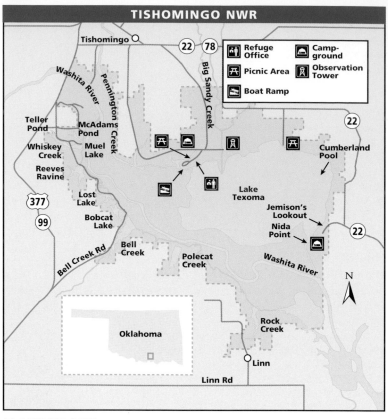

■ ANIMAL LIFE

Birds Up to 100,000 mallards, teal, and other dabbling ducks begin gathering on Cumberland Pool in September and peak between mid-December and late January. Snow geese make up most of the 45,000 geese, but Canada and white-fronted geese can also be seen on the lake or nibbling wheat in the fields near the roads. In winter, 20 to 30 bald eagles may also be present. Unless the weather is severe, some waterfowl will stay all winter.

The woods are alive with neotropic migrants in fall and spring. On the lake, up to 30,000 Franklin's and ring-billed gulls and impressive flocks of white pelicans take a break from their journeys to rest and feed.

In summer scissor-tailed flycatchers, the state bird of Oklahoma, line the fences, darting up to catch insects. The blue grosbeak's husky warbles emanate from the thickets and hedgerows. When seen in the shadow the male looks quite drab, but when the sun hits him, he turns a deep, rich, and dazzling blue. The dense cover also hides the painted bunting, a bird that proves you can have everything—a beautiful song and the most colorful body of any North American songbird. The refuge checklist names 252 species that have been seen at Tishomingo.

Mammals White-tailed deer seek cover in the dense hardwood forest by day. In the mornings and evenings hundreds come to feed, alongside the geese, on the crops. Spring Creek, west of headquarters, has beaver dams that you can see from the road. Skunks, opossums, raccoons, and armadillos are other common mammals here.

Snow geese feeding

Invertebrates The willows by Cumberland Pool take on an orange cast in the fall from the countless migrating monarch butterflies that cling to them.

ACTIVITIES

■ **CAMPING:** Limited camping is available for fishermen.

■ **SWIMMING:** Swimming is prohibited on the refuge.

■ **WILDLIFE OBSERVATION AND PHOTOGRAPHY:** The observation tower east of Big Sandy Creek overlooks a field and is a good place to observe or photograph large flocks of ducks and geese in winter. Jemison's Lookout, near Nida Point, provides a beautiful view of the Cumberland Pool year-round. From the pier at Dick's Pond, you may see beaver and herons in the summer and waterfowl in the winter.

■ **SEASONAL EVENTS:** Special events to provide something for everyone: wildflower and plant walks, historical tours, geology field trips, spring bird walks; eagle tours, and a pontoon boat tour of the lake. Contact the refuge staff for information and reservations.

■ **PUBLICATIONS:** Refuge brochure with map; birds of Tishomingo flyer.

HUNTING AND FISHING Hunting for **waterfowl**, **white-tailed deer**, **dove**, **upland game**, and **wild turkey** is permitted Oct. through Feb. on the Wildlife Management Unit. Hunting is restricted to archery and shotgun only.

Fishing from a boat is allowed March through Sept.; pole fishing is permitted in other months. Some species popular with sportsmen include **crappie**, **bass**, **channel catfish**, **flathead catfish**, and **blue catfish**.

Washita NWR
Butler, Oklahoma

Black-tailed prairie dog

Standing on the observation platform atop the hill behind the contact station of Washita NWR (pronounced wa-SHE-ta), it's easy to see why the refuge is a magnet for migrating waterfowl. Thousands of Canada cluster together feeding in this man-made restaurant. It might be difficult for a human to understand why the geese choose one spot over another in acre after treeless acre of winter wheat, all still emerald green in color, in which to feed. For the geese it makes no difference: This must be goose heaven.

HISTORY

Washita NWR contains the northern portion of Foss Reservoir in western Oklahoma and includes a section of the muddy Washita River. Established in 1961 in cooperation with the Bureau of Reclamation, Washita provides 8,200 acres of feeding and resting area for migratory waterfowl and sandhill cranes.

When the reservoir was in its early stages, an abundance of aquatic vegetation and animal life supported peak numbers of 150,000 ducks in the winter. At the current high-water level, the aquatic plants have suffered, which has caused a reduction in the number of ducks using the refuge. Currently, moist-soil units are being developed to provide additional food to supplement that lost to high water.

GETTING THERE

Washita is located about 115 mi. west of Oklahoma City. From Oklahoma City, take I 40 west to Clinton, then US 183 north for 9 mi. to OK 33. Go west 13 mi. to Butler. Continue through Butler another 5 mi., then turn north on a paved road for 1 mi., then west on another paved road for 0.5 mi. to the refuge contact station.

■ **SEASON:** Portions of the general refuge open year-round, but a large area of the southern end is closed to protect wildlife.

■ **HOURS:** General refuge open dawn to dusk. Headquarters open weekdays, 7:30 a.m.–4 p.m.
■ **FEES:** None.
■ **ADDRESS:** Washita NWR, Rte 1., Box 68, Butler, OK 73625
■ **TELEPHONE:** 580/664-2205; fax: 580/664-2206

TOURING WASHITA

■ **BY AUTOMOBILE:** Ten recreation areas ("R.A." on refuge maps), or access points, mostly along the Washita River and Foss Reservoir, can be reached from OK 33 and unnamed gravel roads off the highway. These are marked on the refuge map.
■ **BY FOOT:** Visitors may walk anywhere within the open areas of the refuge year-round. There is a designated trail from the Owl Cover Recreation Area to the Turkey Flats Recreation Area.
■ **BY CANOE, KAYAK, OR BOAT:** Boating is permitted from mid-March to mid-Oct. Boaters should avoid excessive speed on refuge waters.

HUNTING AND FISHING
Hunting for **quail** and **cottontail rabbits** is permitted on certain portions of the refuge, while **geese** and **sandhill cranes** may be hunted by special permit. Only shotguns are allowed. (No deer, turkey, dove, or duck hunting is permitted.)

Fishing is allowed on the Washita River and Foss Reservoir from mid-March to mid-Oct.

WHAT TO SEE

■ **LANDSCAPE AND CLIMATE** Washita lies in an area of gently rolling hills where intermittent streams have cut deep ravines and gullies. The Washita River winds through the northwestern portion of the refuge before adding its waters to Foss Reservoir. Several small creeks also feed the reservoir. The upper reservoir and river comprise about 2,000 acres of open water.

Although weather is generally mild, severe thunderstorms and tornadoes are possible, especially in the months of April through June. The winds are strong in this part of Oklahoma. Be prepared for extremes in all seasons.

■ **PLANT LIFE** There are 3,000 acres of mixed-grass prairie and 1,200 acres of bottomland forest along the creeks. Crops are planted on 2,100 acres in cooperation with farmers who leave a share of the winter wheat, milo, and legumes for wildlife.

■ **ANIMAL LIFE** Up to 100,000 geese may be on the refuge in November or December. Of these, 95 percent are Canadas. They roost on the open waters of Foss Reservoir, where they are safe from predators. In the morning and evening, the birds fly out to feed in the fields.

Ducks are also present in the winter. More than 1,000 common mergansers may be seen in January as they dive to catch fish, their main food. Hooded and red-breasted mergansers also show up.

Swainson's hawks migrate from the Great Plains to South America in the fall. In October flocks of hundreds of these hawks have been seen in a single field feeding on insects—mainly grasshoppers and caterpillars. The hawks catch insects in the air or run them down on the ground. Watch for them as they perch on fence posts, their sharp eyes scanning the ground.

On the hillside between the refuge headquarters and the road is a black-tailed prairie dog town. The antics of the prairie dog can easily be seen from inside your car. Badgers are present and can sometimes be spotted early in the morning. They feed mainly on ground squirrels and kangaroo rats that they dig easily from the ground. Look in the trees, especially at McClure Recreation Area, for porcupines. They feed on buds, small twigs, and the inner bark of the trees; trees with bark chewed away near the top are a sure sign of porcupines.

ACTIVITIES

■ **CAMPING AND SWIMMING:** Not allowed on the refuge.

■ **WILDLIFE OBSERVATION:** There are many good places to observe wildlife, mostly from the roads that wind through the refuge. Croplands have many grazers, both birds and mammals. From Riverside Recreation Area you can watch the geese as they fly up the Washita River to their feeding grounds. Or watch them return in early afternoon at Lakeview Recreation Area.

From Owl Cove Recreation Area where the Washita River joins Foss Reservoir, walk up the river for 1.2 miles to an area of shallow marshes. This is a good place to see mallard, blue-winged teal, and northern pintail. Dabbler ducks also congregate at Pitts Creek Recreation Area, where they are sheltered from the winter winds. Diving ducks prefer the deep open water of the lake, and large rafts can be seen from Lakeview Recreation Area.

■ **PUBLICATIONS:** Refuge brochure and fact sheet; mammal and bird checklists.

SATELITTE REFUGE

■ **Optima NWR**   Here, in the middle of Oklahoma's panhandle in an area known as the Cimarron Territory, Optima NWR was established in 1975 at a size of 4,333 acres. The refuge consists of a small canyon surrounded by rolling grasslands on the southwest arm of Optima Reservoir. The reservoir struggles to fill because of the upstream demands on the water supply. Coldwater Creek flows through the refuge. About half the grasslands are characterized by Sandsage-Bluestem Prairie; the remainder is blue gama and buffalo grass. The woodlands along the creek are dominated by cottonwoods and tallgrass species such as little bluestem and sand lovegrass.

Optima was established for Canada geese and mallards, but shorebirds, least terns, and western grebes are also found here. This area is

HUNTING AND FISHING
Only limited hunting is permitted.

more likely to have western raptors such as the golden eagle, prairie falcon, and rough-legged hawk than the other Oklahoma refuges. Scaled quail and the Rio Grande turkey are two southwestern game birds found on the refuge.

To reach Optima, located in Guymon, take OK 3 northwest of Hardesty for 2 mi. to a parking lot. There are no public facilities.

■ **ADDRESS:** Optima NWR, Rte 1., Box 68, Butler, OK 73625

■ **TELEPHONE:** 580/664-2205

■ **PUBLICATIONS:** Refuge brochure; bird list.

Wichita Mountains NWR
Indiahoma, Oklahoma

Elk, Wichita Mountains NWR

Once more than 60 million bison roamed the prairies of the Great Basin. Over time, the huge beasts were slaughtered by the thousands to feed railroad workers and for their skins. By 1900 no more than a thousand survived.

The loss of the bison was not acceptable to everyone. President Theodore Roosevelt and William T. Hornaday were among them. Hornaday and others organized the American Bison Society to pressure Congress to act. In 1907 Congress appropriated $15,000 to fence an area in the Wichita National Forest and Game Preserve for bison. The New York Zoological Society donated 15 bison to be shipped by train to the Cache railhead in October 1907. After a week of travel, seven bulls and eight cows had been safely returned to the wild. Later, other game and large mammals were similarly transplanted to the region. Today herds of free-roaming bison, elk, deer, turkey, and longhorn cattle offer every visitor the opportunity to glimpse a lost part of their natural heritage.

HISTORY

The 59,020-acre Wichita Mountains NWR is a true crown jewel among refuges in the South Central region. It is the only refuge where mammals are the main attraction and the only one with spectacular mountain and prairie scenery. It is the oldest-managed wildlife preserve in the United States. The refuge wilderness area covers 8,570 acres in two units: Charon's Garden Unit, in the southwestern section of the refuge; North Mountain Unit (limited access), in the north-central part of the refuge. The Special Use Area (inside the game fence), comprising 36,620 acres, is restricted to big game, eagles, and other wildlife that need large undisturbed areas. This area is open to the public only for refuge-directed tours.

There is much more water on the refuge now than there was in the past. During the 1930s the Civilian Conservation Corps constructed dams on 20 streams to create several lakes.

WICHITA MOUNTAINS NWR

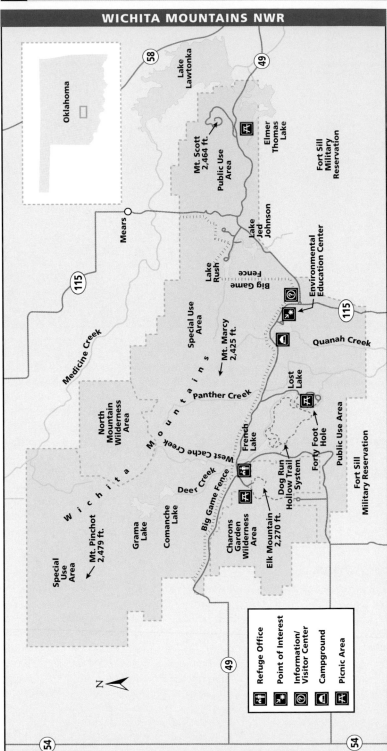

Oklahoma

58

49

Lake Lawtonka

Mt. Scott 2,464 ft.

Public Use Area

Elmer Thomas Lake

Fort Sill Military Reservation

Mears

115

Lake Jed Johnson

Environmental Education Center

Lake Rush

Big Game Fence

115

Medicine Creek

Special Use Area

Mt. Marcy 2,425 ft.

Quanah Creek

Panther Creek

Lost Lake

North Mountain Wilderness Area

West Cache Creek

French Lake

Public Use Area

Forty Foot Hole

Deer Creek

Dog Run Hollow Trail System

Fort Sill Military Reservation

W i c h i t a   M o u n t a i n s

Big Game Fence

Charons Garden Wilderness Area

Grama Lake

Comanche Lake

Elk Mountain 2,270 ft.

Mt. Pinchot 2,479 ft.

Special Use Area

49

N

54

54

Refuge Office

Point of Interest

Information/ Visitor Center

Campground

Picnic Area

GETTING THERE

Wichita abuts Ft. Sill Military Reservation. From Oklahoma City, take I-44 South to Medicine Park, then OK 49 west 14 mi. to the refuge. From Lawton, take US 62 west to Cache exit, then OK 115 north 6 mi.

■ **SEASON:** Open year-round.

■ **HOURS:** General refuge: open daylight hours. The Visitor Center is open daily 10 a.m.–5:30 p.m., except Tues. and major holidays. Headquarters is open week-days, 8 a.m.–4:30 p.m.

■ **ADDRESS:** Wichita Mountains NWR, Rte. 1, Box 448, Indiahoma, OK 73552

■ **TELEPHONE:** 580/429-3222

■ **VISITOR CENTER:** Enter the state-of-the-art Visitor Center: A croaking frog and stuffed buffalo welcome you. Dioramas with exquisitely mounted animals represent the refuge's four major habitats. Interactive displays test your wildlife knowledge. A film depicts refuge history and management practices. A "night exhibit" allows you to gaze at the stars as you listen to the sounds of the night.

TOURING WICHITA MOUNTAINS

■ **BY AUTOMOBILE:** More than 50 miles of paved roads provide access to almost all of the refuge. Drive defensively and be alert for wandering animals.

■ **BY FOOT:** Fifteen miles of hiking trails traverse every habitat.

■ **BY BICYCLE:** Bicycles are restricted to developed roads; biking off-road or on closed roads is prohibited. A dirt road behind Mt. Scott is open to mountain biking.

■ **BY CANOE, KAYAK, OR BOAT:** Nonmotorized boats are permitted on Jed Johnson, Rush, Quanah Parker, and French lakes, and sailboats are permitted on Elmer Thomas Lake. Electric trolling motors are permitted on boats under 14 feet on Jed Johnson, Rush, French, and Quanah Parker lakes. Any size boat or motor is permitted on Lake Elmer Thomas, but there is a no-wake rule across the entire lake.

Mt. Scott

WHAT TO SEE

■ **LANDSCAPE AND CLIMATE** From Mt. Scott (2,464 feet) you will enjoy a panoramic view and get a sense of the terrain. What you will see are mainly the Osage Plains, part of the Central Lowlands that was never glaciated. At Wichita, mixed-prairie intersperses with sparkling lakes, strips of oak forest, peaks over 2,000 feet high, and huge, rounded, red granite boulders covered with chartreuse-colored lichens. Several ponds and lakes provide open water for fishing or watch-

Blooming Wichita cactus

ing aquatic wildlife. Elmer Thomas, Jed Johnson, Quanah Parker, Lost, French, Comanche, and Grama lakes are all in the refuge; Lake Lawtonka lies just to the east of the refuge.

Rounded granite cobbles that can be seen around the refuge and that were used in many of the local houses were rounded and deposited by erosion about 250 million years ago, as were other granite gravel deposits. Today, the granitic rocks form the high mountains. The gabbro underlies much of the lowland along OK 49 west of Quanah Parker Lake. It can be seen on the brush-covered lower slopes of Mt. Sheridan and around Doris Campground. A thick soil forms on the gabbro, and buffalo love to roll in this dirt. From the summit of Mt. Scott, look down the south slope at the boulder slide. There are more boulder slides throughout the refuge in the drainage depressions on many of the steep slopes. The granite actually saved the prairie from ever being turned by a plow: It makes the ground far too rocky.

The climate is temperate, with generally mild temperatures and moderate rainfall. Temperature extremes vary from minus16 degrees to 117 degrees, with an average annual temperature of 61. Average annual rainfall is about 30 inches, with spring and fall seasons being the wettest.

■ PLANT LIFE
Forests Patches of oak forest throughout the refuge (fingers of black jack and post oak) are remains of a ecological system known as the "Cross Timbers." Cross Timbers once formed a dense natural barrier marking Native American tribal boundaries and making passage difficult for travelers heading west. The 1885 land run and the arrival of settlers marked the beginning of the assault on the trees— they fell to the axe to make passageway for pioneer wagons heading west.

Walnut, pecan, ash, elm, hackberry, cottonwood, and other woody species typical of this portion of Oklahoma grow along streams. A small grove of live oak, typically more southern, represents the northern extent of this species in the plains country.

Grasslands Large mammal herds are supported entirely by grazing on 59,000 acres of lush prairie, with buffalo and gama grasses typical of western shortgrass prairies as well as both of the bluestems, Indian grass, and switch grass more common in eastern tallgrass areas. Wildflowers such as Indian blanket, blue phlox, and prairie clover bloom among the grasses and are also an important component of the grazing animal's diet.

Mountains Although they seem bare, the red granite rocks in the mountains are actually home to a unique plant. Lichens—an algae and fungus growing together in a symbiotic relationship—slowly break down granite into new soil. Look for a variety of colorful lichens: shades of green and gray, chartreuse, yellow, and red.

■ ANIMAL LIFE

Birds No fewer than 278 species of birds have been recorded here, including turkeys transplanted from Missouri and Texas. The big mammals are obviously not the only show in town. The Wichita Mountains have the largest breeding population in Oklahoma (620 adults) of the endangered black-capped vireo. This small olive bird with a glossy black cap and white spectacles is found from Kansas to central Texas; however, its population is declining from nest parasitism by the brown-headed cowbird and the loss of suitable nesting habitat. On the refuge, cowbirds are trapped and removed from the nesting area. Controlled burning is used to make more nesting habitat. To find the vireo, walk through the oaks in the spring and listen for a two- or three-note song. Sometimes the vireo hangs upside-down to search for insects.

Mammals You can count on seeing some of the many large mammals on the refuge. Remember: Although refuge mammals may appear tame or harmless, they are wild and should not be approached closely, teased, fed, or frightened. Not only are these actions illegal, they are dangerous. Bison can be especially dangerous (see sidebar). Mountain lion are also present in the refuge.

The elk at Wichita are descendants of Rocky Mountain elk brought in from Jackson Hole, Wyoming. Wichita's original subspecies of elk, Merriam's elk, had

Black-tailed prairie dog

AMERICAN BISON Today, an estimated 200,000 bison—the symbol of the Great Plains—roam in national parks, state parks, and national wildlife refuges, but most are owned by private individuals. The bison is the largest land animal to live in North America since the end of the Ice Age. Bulls can stand 6 feet tall at the shoulder and weigh a ton or more. Cows are smaller, and calves weigh about 60 pounds at birth. The normal bison life span is 20 to 30 years, but a few live to be older.

The bison is well adapted to withstand extreme temperature variations (subzero winters to 100-degree-plus summers) in its native territory. It grows a thick, shaggy coat in the winter and sheds it come summer. During the winter the bison uses its large head to scrape away snow to reach grass underneath.

Bison have good senses of smell and hearing, but their eyesight is extremely poor. This is why they can be dangerous. When a person gets too close, the bison suddenly becomes aware of a presence *in its territory* and defends itself. Every year at a park or refuge in America, people are gored by these massive and powerfully strong animals. In addition to their size and strength, buffalo are extremely fast and can outrun a horse for both short and long distances. Admire them from afar; they are a marvel even at a safe distance.

been hunted to extinction by 1881. Texas longhorns, which numbered 10 million at the close of the Civil War, were replaced by better meat-producing breeds. The steers produce the longest horns—many of them 6 feet or more from tip to tip. The longhorn herd is maintained at a minimum of 280 animals. The cattle are selected for length of horns and variety of color.

Reptiles and amphibians The collared lizard can be greenish, yellowish, brownish, or bluish, but it always has a black collar. It lives in hiding places among the boulders and will quickly duck out of sight if you approach. These lizards can run on all fours and on their hind legs.

ACTIVITIES

■ **CAMPING:** Doris Campground includes sites from primitive to full electric hookup. Groups are welcome, with reservations; otherwise it's first come, first served. Backcountry camping in Charon's Garden Wilderness Area is by permit only. Length of stay: three days and two nights. Inquire at refuge headquarters.

■ **SWIMMING:** Swimming is not permitted on the refuge.

■ **WILDLIFE OBSERVATION:** A drive though the refuge offers plenty of chances to see wildlife. The refuge staff also offers many wildlife tours, including some into the Special Use Area (seasonal, by reservation).

The huge bison with their massive heads and shaggy hair are usually seen in herds as they graze close to roads and along hiking trails, even to the top of the mountains. They can also be found resting in the shade of trees or behind boulders.

Most of the 380 elk are in the Special Use Area, but they can also easily be seen from the road. Rutting season starts in September. At this time males have handsome, gigantic racks and spend their time and energy gathering and guarding harems of cows from other bulls. Listen for their haunting buglelike call, especially at dawn and dusk. Calving occurs in June.

Texas longhorn cattle are kept in the Public Use Area of the refuge for easy viewing by visitors.

American bison

Prairie dogs cavort near the road on the south side of Quanah Parker Lake and on the south side of OK 49 between the refuge headquarters and the turnoff to Sunset Recreation Area.

On a winter visit to the refuge, search the trees around Gama and Comanche lakes for roosting bald eagles. The number of wintering eagles varies from three to six in most years.

■ **PHOTOGRAPHY:** The windy drive through huge granite boulders to the top of Mt. Scott offers panoramic shots. Want more wilderness? Walk to the top of Elk Mountain for golden sunset views. Fall color is provided by the eastern sugar maple and the big-toothed maple of the Rockies. Big-game animals can be found "posing" amost anywhere.

■ **HIKES AND WALKS:** There are 15 miles of good, well-maintained hiking trails. At French Lake trailhead, choose among several trails: Elk (1 mile), Longhorn (2 miles), or Buffalo (8 miles)—all in Dog Run Hollow trail complex.

Buffalo Trail allows the hiker access to Kite Trail (1.5 miles) between Lost Lake Recreation Area and Boulder Recreation Area. These trails wind through rocky prairie, oak forest, and along French Lake. The lake is especially pleasant at evening with geese honking overhead, swallows circling to catch insects on the wing, and startled wood ducks crying *wheeoook* as they take off from their hiding places.

The 2-mile trail leading around the west end of Elk Mountain traverses Charon's Garden Wilderness Area from Sunset Recreation Area to Post Oak and Treasure Lake parking area. A side trail from Sunset Recreation Area leads to the top of Elk Mountain. This trail has vertical rock hopping, but no technical climbing skills are necessary. Look down over the prairie at a herd of deer frolicking by. As you climb, the landscape changes from grass to trees to boulders. Multicolored wildflower gardens nestle between rocks. At the top, rock wrens and rufous-crowned sparrows appear around boulders, occasionally perching in the open to sing.

Little Baldy Mountain Trail runs 1.5 miles along the western edge of Quanah Parker Lake with a side trail leading to the summit of Little Baldy Mountain. Access from the Quanah Parker Visitor Center or Quanah Parker dam. From the western side of the lake, use your binoculars to view ducks and geese swimming, or look south and watch the prairie dogs in their town watching you.

The Environmental Education Interpretive Trail (0.25 mi., handicapped-accessible) has interpretive signs. Access from the Quanah Parker Visitor Center parking lot.

■ **ROCK CLIMBING:** The refuge has good-quality granite, multipitch routes, wilderness settings, and fine weather for good rock climbing. Technical climbing is allowed during daylight hours in the Public Use Area (south and east of the big-game fence) of the refuge. However, short rappelling is prohibited in the area along West Cache Creek downstream of Boulder Cabin. Rock faces are closed to climbing activity on the north and east sides of West Cache Creek downstream of Boulder Cabin. This area is known as "The Narrows." Approval from the refuge manager is needed before placement or replacement of fixed anchors.

HUNTING AND FISHING
There is a lottery drawing for permits to hunt **white-tailed deer** and **elk**, the only two game animals hunted on the refuge.

Fishing is permitted year-round. **Largemouth bass**, **sunfish**, **crappie**, and **catfish** can be found in refuge lakes. Handicapped-accessible fishing piers are available near the Environmental Education Center and Elmer Thomas Lake.

■ **SEASONAL EVENTS:** Autumn: Longhorn and bison roundups and auction.
■ **PUBLICATIONS:** Refuge general brochure, and specific brochures or fact sheets on the following Wichita NWR topics: backcountry camping, birds, botany, buffalo herd, Doris Campground, environmental education, fish, geologic history of Wichita Mountains, mammals, rock climbing, Texas longhorns, vascular plants. Visit the bookshop in the Visitor Center for other publications.

Appendix

NONVISITABLE NATIONAL WILDLIFE REFUGES

Below is a list of other national wildlife refuges in the South Central region. Even though these refuges are closed to the public, these refuges are important sanctuaries for wildlife, plant habitats, and endangered or threatened species.

Logan Cave NWR
c/o Holla Bend NWR
Rt. 1, Box 59
Dardanelle, AR 72834-9704
501/229-4300

Little Sandy NWR
c/o Little River NWR
P.O. Box 340
Broken Bow, OK 74728
405/584-6211

Pilot Knob NWR
c/o Mingo NWR
24279 State Highway 51
Puxico, MO 63960
573/222-3589

Ozark Plateau NWR
c/o Sequoyah NWR
Route 1, Box 18A
Vian, OK 74962
918/773-5251

FEDERAL RECREATION FEES

Some—but not all—NWRs and other federal outdoor recreation areas require payment of entrance or use fees (the latter for facilities such as boat ramps). There are several congressionally authorized entrance fee passes:

■ ANNUAL PASSES

Golden Eagle Passport Valid for most national parks, monuments, historic sites, recreation areas and national wildlife refuges. Admits the passport signee and any accompanying passengers in a private vehicle. Good for 12 months. Purchase at any federal area where an entrance fee is charged. The 1999 fee for this pass was $50.00

Federal Duck Stamp Authorized in 1934 as a federal permit to hunt waterfowl and as a source of revenue to purchase wetlands, the Duck Stamp now also serves as an annual entrance pass to NWRs. Admits holder and accompanying passengers in a private vehicle. Good from July 1 for one year. Valid for *entrance* fees only. Purchase at post offices and many NWRs or from Federal Duck Stamp Office, 800/782-6724, or at Wal-Mart, Kmart, or other sporting good stores.

■ LIFETIME PASSES

Golden Access Passport Lifetime entrance pass—for persons who are blind or permanently disabled—to most national parks and NWRs. Admits signee and any accompany passengers in a private vehicle. Provides 50 percent discount on federal use fees charged for facilities and services such as camping, or boating. Must be obtained in person at a federal recreation area charging a fee. Obtain by showing proof of medically determined permanent disability or eligibility for receiving benefits under federal law.

Golden Age Passport Lifetime entrance pass—for persons 62 years of age or older—to national parks and NWRs. Admits signee and any accompanying passengers in a private vehicle. Provides 50 percent discount on federal use fees charged for facilities and services such as camping, or boating. Must be obtained in person at a federal recreation area charging a fee. One-time $10.00 processing charge. Available only to U.S. citizens or permanent residents.

For more information, contact your local federal recreation area for a copy of the *Federal Recreation Passport Program* brochure.

VOLUNTEER ACTIVITIES

Each year, 30,000 Americans volunteer their time and talents to help the U.S. Fish & Wildlife Service conserve the nation's precious wildlife and their habitats. Volunteers conduct Fish & Wildlife population surveys, lead public tours and other recreational programs, protect endangered species, restore habitat, and run environmental education programs.

The NWR volunteer program is as diverse as are the refuges themselves. There is no "typical" Fish & Wildlife Service volunteer. The different ages, backgrounds, and experiences volunteers bring with them is one of the greatest strengths of the program. Refuge managers also work with their neighbors, conservation groups, colleges and universities, and business organizations.

A growing number of people are taking pride in the stewardship of local national wildlife refuges by organizing nonprofit organizations to support individual refuges. These refuge community partner groups, which numbered about 200 in 2,000, have been so helpful that the Fish & Wildlife Service, National Audubon Society, National Wildlife Refuge Association, and National Fish & Wildlife Foundation now carry out a national program called the "Refuge System Friends Initiative" to coordinate and strengthen existing partnerships, to jump start new ones, and to organize other efforts promoting community involvement in activities associated with the National Wildlife Refuge System.

For more information on how to get involved, visit the Fish & Wildlife Service Homepage at http://refuges.fws.gov; or contact one of the Volunteer Coordinator offices listed on the U.S. Fish & Wildlife General Information list of addresses below or the U. S. Fish & Wildlife Service, Division of Refuges, Attn: Volunteer Coordinator, 4401 North Fairfax Drive, Arlington, VA 22203; 703/358-2303.

U.S. FISH & WILDLIFE GENERAL INFORMATION

Below is a list of addresses to contact for more inforamation concerning the National Wildlife Refuge System.

U.S. Fish & Wildlife Service Division of Refuges
4401 North Fairfax Dr., Room 670
Arlington, Virginia 22203
703/358-1744
Web site: fws.refuges.gov

F & W Service Publications:
800/344-WILD

U.S. Fish & Wildlife Service Pacific Region
911 NE 11th Ave.
Eastside Federal Complex
Portland, OR 97232-4181
External Affairs Office: 503/231-6120
Volunteer Coordinator: 503/231-2077
The Pacific Region office oversees the refuges in California, Hawaii, Idaho, Nevada, Oregon, and Washington.

U.S. Fish & Wildlife Service Southwest Region
500 Gold Ave., SW
P.O. Box 1306
Albuquerque, NM 87103
External Affairs Office: 505/248-6285
Volunteer Coordinator: 505/248-6635
The Southwest Region office oversees the refuges in Arizona, New Mexico, Oklahoma, and Texas.

U.S. Fish & Wildlife Service Great Lakes–Big Rivers Region
1 Federal Dr.
Federal Building
Fort Snelling, MN 55111-4056
External Affairs Office: 612/713-5310
Volunteer Coordinator: 612/713-5444
The Great Lakes-Big Rivers Region office oversees the refuges in Iowa, Illinois, Indiana, Michigan, Minnesota, Missouri, Ohio, and Wisconsin.

U.S. Fish & Wildlife Service Southeast Region
1875 Century Center Blvd.
Atlanta, GA 30345
External Affairs Office: 404/679-7288
Volunteer Coordinator: 404/679-7178
The Southeast Region office oversees the refuges in Alabama, Arkansas, Florida, Georgia, Kentucky, Louisiana, Mississippi, North Carolina, South Carolina, Tennessee, and Puerto Rico.

U.S. Fish & Wildlife Service Northeast Region
300 Westgate Center Dr.
Hadley, MA 01035-9589
External Affairs Office: 413/253-8325
Volunteer Coordinator: 413/253-8303
The Northeast Region office oversees the refuges in Connecticut, Delaware, Massachusetts, Maine, New Hampshire, New Jersey, New York, Pennsylvania, Rhode Island, Vermont, Virginia, West Virginia.

U.S. Fish & Wildlife Service Mountain-Prairie Region
P.O. Box 25486
Denver Federal Center
P. O. Box 25486
Denver, CO 80225
External Affairs Office: 303/236-7905
Volunteer Coordinator: 303/236-8145, x 614
The Mountain-Prairie Region office oversees the refuges in Colorado, Kansas, Montana, Nebraska, North Dakota, South Dakota, Utah, and Wyoming.

U.S. Fish & Wildlife Service Alaska Region
1011 East Tudor Rd.
Anchorage, AK 99503
External Affairs Office: 907/786-3309
Volunteer Coordinator: 907/786-3391

NATIONAL AUDUBON SOCIETY WILDLIFE SANCTUARIES

National Audubon Society's 100 sanctuaries comprise 150,000 acres and include a wide range of habitats. Audubon managers and scientists use the sanctuaries for rigorous field research and for testing wildlife management strategies. The following is a list of 24 sanctuaries open to the public. Sanctuaries open by appointment only are marked with an asterisk.

EDWARD M. BRIGHAM III ALKALI LAKE SANCTUARY*
c/o North Dakota State Office
118 Broadway, Suite 502
Fargo, ND 58102
701/298-3373

FRANCIS BEIDLER FOREST SANCTUARY
336 Sanctuary Rd.
Harleyville, SC 29448
843/462-2160

BORESTONE MOUNTAIN SANCTUARY
P.O. Box 524
118 Union Square
Dover-Foxcroft, ME 04426
207/564-7946

CLYDE E. BUCKLEY SANCTUARY
1305 Germany Rd.
Frankfort, KY 40601
606/873-5711

BUTTERCUP WILDLIFE SANCTUARY*
c/o New York State Office
200 Trillium Lane
Albany, NY 12203
518/869-9731

CONSTITUTION MARSH SANCTUARY
P.O. Box 174
Cold Spring, NY, 10516
914/265-2601

CORKSCREW SWAMP SANCTUARY
375 Sanctuary Rd. West
Naples, FL 34120
941/348-9151

FLORIDA COASTAL ISLANDS SANCTUARY*
410 Ware Blvd., Suite 702
Tampa, FL 33619
813/623-6826

EDWARD L. & CHARLES E. GILLMOR SANCTUARY*
3868 Marsha Dr.
West Valley City, UT 84120
801/966-0464

KISSIMMEE PRAIRIE SANCTUARY*
100 Riverwoods Circle
Lorida, FL 33857
941/467-8497

MAINE COASTAL ISLANDS SANCTUARIES*
Summer (June–Aug.):
12 Audubon Rd.
Bremen, ME 04551
207/529-5828

MILES WILDLIFE SANCTUARY*
99 West Cornwall Rd.
Sharon, CT 06069
860/364-0048

NORTH CAROLINA COASTAL ISLANDS SANCTUARY*
720 Market St.
Wilmington, NC 28401-4647
910/762-9534

NORTHERN CALIFORNIA SANCTUARIES*
c/o California State Office
555 Audubon Place
Sacramento, CA 95825
916/481-5440

PINE ISLAND SANCTUARY*
P.O. Box 174
Poplar Branch, NC 27965
919/453-2838

RAINEY WILDLIFE SANCTUARY*
10149 Richard Rd.
Abbeville, LA 70510-9216
318/898-5969 (Beeper: leave message)

RESEARCH RANCH SANCTUARY*
HC1, Box 44
Elgin, AZ 85611
520/455-5522

RHEINSTROM HILL WILDLIFE SANCTUARY*
P.O. Box 1
Craryville, NY 12521
518/325-5203

THEODORE ROOSEVELT SANCTUARY
134 Cove Rd.
Oyster Bay, NY 11771
516/922-3200

LILLIAN ANNETTE ROWE SANCTUARY
44450 Elm Island Rd.
Gibbon, NE 68840
308/468-5282

SABAL PALM GROVE SANCTUARY
P.O. Box 5052
Brownsville, TX 78523
956/541-8034

SILVER BLUFF SANCTUARY*
4542 Silver Bluff Rd.
Jackson, SC 29831
803/827-0781

STARR RANCH SANCTUARY*
100 Bell Canyon Rd.
Trabuco Canyon, CA 92678
949/858-0309

TEXAS COASTAL ISLANDS SANCTUARIES
c/o Texas State Office
2525 Wallingwood, Suite 301
Austin, TX 78746
512/306-0225

BIBLIOGRAPHY AND RESOURCES

Animal Behavior Guides

Stokes, Donald W. *A Guide to Animal Tracking and Behavior: Stokes Nature Guides*, Boston: Little, Brown and Co., 1998.

Stokes, Donald W. *A Guide to Bird Behavior: Stokes Nature Guides*, : Vol. 1, 1983; Vol. 2, 1985; Vol. 3, Boston: Little, Brown and Co., 1989.

Stokes, Donald W. *A Guide to Nature in Winter: Stokes Nature Guides* , Boston: Little, Brown and Co., 1979.

Stokes, Donald W. *A Guide to Observing Insect Lives: Stokes Nature Guides*, Boston: Little, Brown and Co., 1983.

Tyning, Thomas F. *A Guide to Amphibians and Reptiles: Stokes Nature Guides*, Boston: Little, Brown and Co., 1990.

Aquatic Biology

Morgan, Ann Haven. *Field Book of Ponds and Streams: An Introduction to the Life of Fresh Water*, New York: G. P. Putnam's Sons, 1930.

Audio Recordings

Peterson, Roger Tory. *Field Guide to Bird Songs-Eastern/Central North America*, Boston: Houghton Mifflin Co., 1999.

Botany

Cobb, Boughton. *Peterson Field Guides: Ferns*, Boston: Houghton Mifflin Co., 1963.

Dennison, Edgar. *Missouri Wildflowers*, Jefferson City, Mo.: Missouri Conservation Department, 1989.

Niering, William A. *North American Wildflowers, Eastern Region*, New York: Alfred A. Knopf, 1979.

Peterson, Roger Tory and Margaret McKenny. *Peterson Field Guides: Wildflowers*, Boston: Houghton Mifflin Co., 1968.

Petrides, George A. *Peterson Field Guides: Trees and Shrubs*, Boston: Houghton Mifflin Co., 1972.

Sutton, Ann and Myron Sutton. *National Audubon Society Nature Guides: Eastern Forests*, New York: Alfred A. Knopf, 1985.

Birds

Ehrlich, Paul R., David S. Dobkin, and Darryl Wheye. *The Birder's Handbook, A Field Guide to the Natural History of North American Birds*, New York: Simon & Schuster, Inc., 1988.

Field Guide to the Birds of North America, 3rd Edition, Washington, D.C.: National Geographic Society , 1999.

Griggs, Jack. *American Bird Conservancy's Field Guide, All the Birds of North America*, New York: Harper Perennial, 1997.

Kaufmann, Kenn. *Lives of North American Birds*, Boston: Houghton Mifflin, 1996.

Palmer, Kay. *A Guide to the Birding Areas of Missouri*, Rocheport, Mo.: The Audubon Society of Missouri, 1993.

Peterson, Roger Tory. *Eastern Birds*, Boston: Houghton Mifflin, 1980.

Robbins, Mark B. and David A. Easterla. *The Birds of Missouri, Their Distribution and Abundance,* Columbia, Mo.: University of Missouri Press, 1992.

Webster Groves Nature Study Society. *Birds of the St. Louis Area,* Webster Groves, Mo.: Webster Groves Nature Study Society, 1995.

White, Mel. *A Birder's Guide to Arkansas,* Colorado Springs: American Birding Association, Inc., 1995.

Zimmerman, John L. and Sebastian T. Patti. *A Guide to Bird Finding in Kansas and Western Missouri,* Lawrence, Ks.: University Press of Kansas, 1988.

Geology

Bagnall, Norma Hughes. *On Shaky Ground, The New Madrid Earthquakes of 1811-1812,* Columbia: University of Missouri Press, 1996.

Penick, James, Jr. *The New Madrid Earthquakes, Revised Edition*, Columbia: University of Missouri Press, 1981.

Mammals

Burt, William H. and Richard P. Grossenheider. *Peterson Field Guide, Mammals*, Boston: Houghton Mifflin, 1976.

Schwartz, Charles and Elizabeth Schwartz. *The Wild Mammals of Missouri,* Columbia: University of Missouri Press, 1959.

Regional/State Guides

Missouri Nature Viewing Guide, Jefferson City, Mo.: Missouri Department of Conservation, 1995.

Oklahoma Department of Wildlife Conservation. *Oklahoma Watchable Wildlife Viewing Guide*, Helena, Mont.: Falcon Press, 1993.

Reptiles and Amphibians

Conant, Roger. *Peterson Field Guide, Eastern and Central Reptiles and Amphibians*, Boston: Houghton Mifflin, 1975.

Johnson, Tom R. *The Amphibians and Reptiles of Missouri,* Jefferson City, Mo.: Missouri Department of Conservation, 1992.

Invertebrates

Heitzman, J. Richard and Joan E. *Butterflies and Moths of Missouri*, Jefferson City, Mo.: Missouri Department of Conservation, 1987.

Opler, Paul A. and Vichai Malikul. *Peterson Field Guide, Eastern Butterflies*, Boston: Houghton Mifflin, 1992.

GLOSSARY

Accidental A bird species seen only rarely in a certain region and whose normal territory is elsewhere. *See also* occasional.

Acre-foot The amount of water required to cover one acre one foot deep.

Alkali sink An alkaline habitat at the bottom of a basin where there is moisture under the surface.

Alligators and crocodiles Alligators—wide, rounded snouts, no teeth showing when mouth is closed; fairly common, usually in fresh water, range from Everglades to coastal No. Carolina, have young that are yellowish with brown patterns; alligators bellow and roar. Crocodiles—tapered snouts, a tooth on each side that fits into a notch outside the skin; relatively rare, prefer salt water, range mostly south of Miami, have greenish young with black crossbands or spots; crocodiles grumble and grunt. Both species lay eggs in mounds of vegetation; female alligators guard nests, help the young hatch, and protect them for up to a year; female crocodiles visit nests only occasionally.

Alluvial Clay, sand, silt, pebbles and rocks deposited by running water. River floodplains have alluvial deposits, sometimes called alluvial fans where a stream exits from mountains onto flatland.

Aquifer Underground layer of porous water-bearing sand, rock, or gravel.

Arthropod Invertebrates, including insects, crustaceans, arachnids, and myriapods, with a semitransparent exoskeleton (hard outer structure) and a segmented body, with jointed appendages in articulated pairs.

ATV All-Terrain-Vehicle. *See also* 4WD and ORV.

Barrier island Coastal island produced by wave action and made of sand. Over time the island shifts and changes shape. Barrier islands protect the mainland from storms, tides, and winds.

Basking The habit of certain creatures such as turtles, snakes, or alligators to expose themselves to the pleasant warmth of the sun by resting on logs, rocks or other relatively dry areas.

Bayou Term used along central coast of Gulf of Mexico for a usually slow-moving stream or watercourse in a swamp or marsh.

Biome A major ecological community such as a marsh or a forest.

Blowout A hollow formed by wind erosion in a pre-existing sand dune, often due to vegetation loss.

Bog Wet, spongy ground filled with sphagnum moss and having highly acidic water.

Bottomland Low-elevation alluvial area, close by a river. Sometimes also called "bottoms."

Brackish Water that is less salty than sea water; often found in salt marshes, mangrove swamps, estuaries, and lagoons.

Brake Term used along lower Mississippi River for a crescent-shaped lake formed from an abandoned river course that became blocked from the main channel. *See also* oxbow.

Breachway A gap in a barrier beach or island, forming a connection between sea and lagoon.

Breaks Deep, sometimes broad openings in flat terrain, resulting from glaciation or erosion. As in "Missouri Breaks."

Bushwhack To hike through territory without established trails.

Cambium In woody plants, a sheath of cells between external bark and internal wood that generates parallel rows of cells to make new tissue, either as secondary growth or cork.

Canopy The highest layer of the forest, consisting of the crowns of the trees.

Carnivore An animal that is primarily flesh-eating. *See also* herbivore and omnivore.

Chiggers Larval form of some species of mites. Chiggers burrow into the skin of humans and other vertebrates (usually in warm, moist parts of the body), feed off blood and cells, and then drop off to continue their development.

Climax In a stable ecological community, the plants and animals that will successfully continue to live there.

Colonial birds Birds that live in relatively stable colonies, used annually for breeding and nesting.

Competition A social behavior that organizes the sharing of resources such as space, food, and breeding partners when resources are in short supply.

Coniferous Trees that are needle-leaved or scale-leaved; mostly evergreen and cone-bearing, such as pines, spruces, and firs. *See also* deciduous.

Cordgrass Grasses found in marshy areas, capable of growing in brackish waters. Varieties include salt-marsh cordgrass, hay, spike grass, and glasswort.

Crust The outer layer of the earth, between 15 to 40 miles thick.

Crocodiles *See also* alligators.

Crustacean A hard-shelled, usually aquatic, arthropod such as a lobster or crab. *See also* arthropod.

DDT An insecticide (C14H9Cl5), toxic to animals and human beings whether ingested or absorbed through skin; particularly devastating to certain bird populations, DDT was generally banned in the U.S. in 1972.

Deciduous Plants that shed or lose their foliage at the conclusion of the growing season, as in "deciduous trees," such as hardwoods (maple, beech, oak, etc.). *See also* coniferous.

Delta A triangular alluvial deposit at a river's mouth or at the mouth of a tidal inlet. *See also* alluvial.

Dominant The species most characteristic of a plant or animal community, usually influencing the types and numbers of other species in the same community.

Ecological niche An organism's function, status or occupied area in its ecological community.

Ecosystem A mostly self-contained community consisting of an environment and the animals and plants that live there.

Emergent plants Plants adapted to living in shallow water or in saturated soils such as marshes or wetlands.

Endangered species A species determined by the federal government to be in danger of extinction throughout all or a significant portion of its range (Endangered Species Act. 1973). *See also* threatened species.

Endemic species Species that evolved in a certain place and live naturally nowhere else. *See also* indigenous species.

Epiphyte A type of plant (often found in swamps) that lives on a tree instead of on the soil. Epiphytes are not parasitic; they collect their own water and minerals and perform photosynthesis.

Esker An extended gravel ridge left by a river or stream that runs beneath a decaying glacier.

Estuary The lower part of a river where fresh water meets tidal salt water. Usually characterized by abundant animal and plant life.

Evergreen   A tree, shrub, or other plant whose leaves remain green through all seasons.

Exotic   A plant or animal not native to the territory. Many exotic plants and animals displace native species.

Extirpation   The elimination of a species by unnatural causes, such as over-hunting or fishing.

4WD   Four-wheel drive vehicle. *See also* ATV.

Fall line   A line between the piedmont and the coastal plain below which rivers flow through relatively flat terrain. Large rivers are navigable from the ocean to the fall line.

Fauna   Animals, especially those of a certain region or era, generally considered as a group. *See also* flora.

Fledge   To raise birds until they have their feathers and are able to fly.

Floodplain   A low lying, flat area along a river where flooding is common.

Flora   Plants, especially those of a certain region or era, generally considered as a group. *See also* fauna.

Flyway   A migratory route, providing food and shelter, followed by large numbers of birds.

Forb   Any herb that is not in the grass family; forbes are commonly found in fields, prairies, or meadows.

Frond   A fern leaf, a compound palm leaf, or a leaflike thallus (where leaf and stem are continuous), as with seaweed and lichen.

Glacial outwash   Sediment dropped by rivers or streams as they flow away from melting glaciers.

Glacial till   An unsorted mix of clay, sand, and rock transported and left by glacial action.

Gneiss   A common and rather erosion-resistant metamorphic rock originating from shale, characterized by alternating dark and light bands.

Grassy bald   A summit area devoid of trees due to shallow or absent soil overlying bedrock (ledge).

Great Plains   Expansive grassy region of North America reaching extending from central Canadian provinces of Alberta, Saskatchewan, and Manitoba south to Texas. Cattle raising and wheat ranching are predominant farming activities.

Greentree reservoir   An area seasonally flooded by opening dikes. Oaks, hickories, and other water-tolerant trees drop nuts (mast) into the water. Migratory birds and other wildlife feed on the mast during winter.

Habitat   The area or environment where a plant or animal, or communities of plants or animals, normally live, as in "an alpine habitat."

Hammock   A fertile spot of high ground in a wetland that supports the growth of hardwood trees.

Hardwoods   Flowering trees such as oaks, hickories, maples, and others, as opposed to softwoods and coniferous trees such as pines and hemlocks.

Herbivore   An animal that feeds on plant life. *See also* carnivore and omnivore.

Heronry   Nesting and breeding site for herons.

Herptiles   The class of animals including reptiles and amphibians.

Holdfast   The attachment, in lieu of roots, that enables seaweed to grip a substrate such as a rock.

Hot spot   An opening in the earth's interior from which molten rock erupts, eventually forming a volcano.

Humus   Decomposed leaves and other organic material found, for instance, on the forest floor.

Impoundment   A man-made body of water controlled by dikes or levees.

Indigenous species   Species that arrived unaided by humans but that may also live in other locations.

Inholding   Private land surrounded by federal or state lands such as a wildlife refuge.

Intertidal zone   The beach or shoreline area located between low and high tide lines.

Introduced species   Species brought to a location by humans, intentionally or accidentally; also called nonnative or alien species. *See also* exotic.

Key   A small low island, such as Key West, FL. Term used mostly in Florida and the Caribbean.

Lichen   A ground hugging plant, usually found on rocks, produced by an association between an alga, which manufactures food, and a fungus, which provides support.

Loess   Deep, fertile and loamy soil deposited by wind, the deepest deposits reaching 200 ft.

Magma   Underground molten rock.

Management area   A section of land within a federal wildlife preserve or forest where specific wildlife management practices are implemented and studied.

Marsh   A low-elevation transitional area between water (the sea) and land, dominated by grasses in soft, wet soils.

Mast   A general word for nuts, acorns, and other food for wildlife produced by trees in the fall.

Meander   A winding stream, river, or path.

Mesozoic   A geologic era, 230-65 million years ago, during which dinosaurs appeared and became extinct, and birds and flowering plants first appeared.

Midden   An accumulation of organic material near a village or dwelling; also called a shell mound.

Migrant   An animal that moves from one habitat to another, as opposed to resident species that live permanently in the same habitat.

Mitigation   The act of creating or enlarging refuges or awarding them water rights to replace wildlife habitat lost because of the damming or channelization of rivers or the building of roads.

Moist-soil unit   A wet area that sprouts annual plants, which attract waterfowl. Naturally produced by river flooding, moist-soil units are artificially created through controlled watering.

Moraine   A formation of rock and soil debris transported and dropped by a glacier.

Neotropical   New world tropics, generally referring to central and northern South America, as in *neotropical* birds.

Nesting species   Birds that take up permanent residence in a habitat.

Occasional   A bird species seen only occasionally in a certain region and whose normal territory is elsewhere.

Oceanic trench   The place where a sinking tectonic plate bends down, creating a declivity in the ocean floor.

Old field   A field that was once cultivated for crops but has been left to grow back into forest.

Old-growth forest   A forest characterized by large trees and a stable ecosystem. Old growth forests are similar to pre-Colonial forests.

Omnivore   An animal that feeds on both plant and animal material. *See also* carnivore and herbivore.

ORVs Off-Road-Vehicles. *See also* 4WD and ATV.

Oxbow A curved section of water once a bend in a river that was severed from the river when the river changed course. An oxbow lake is formed by the changing course of a river as it meanders through its floodplain.

Passerine A bird in the Passeriformes order, primarily composed of perching birds and songbirds.

Peat An accumulation of sphagnum moss and other organic material in wetland areas, known as peat bogs.

Petroglyph Carving or inscription on a rock.

Photosynthesis The process by which green plants use the energy in sunlight to create carbohydrates from carbon dioxide and water, generally releasing oxygen as a byproduct.

Pictograph Pictures painted on rock by indigenous people.

Pit and mound topography Terrain characteristic of damp hemlock woods where shallow-rooted fallen trees create pits (former locations of trees) and mounds (upended root balls).

Plant community Plants and animals that interact in a similar environment within a region.

Pleistocene A geologic era, 1.8 million to 10,000 years ago, known as the great age of glaciers.

Pocosin Area in a swamp that is slightly higher than the surroundings and is spongy enough to retain water and to support hardwoods grow. Term used mostly in the Carolinas.

Prairie An expansive, undulating or flat grassland, usually without trees, generally on the plains of mid-continent North America. In the southeast, "prairie" refers to wet grasslands with standing water much of the year.

Prescribed burn A fire that is intentionally set to reduce the buildup of dry organic matter in a forest or grassland, to prevent catastrophic fires later on or to assist plant species whose seeds need intense heat to open.

Proclamation area An area of open water beside or around a coastal refuge where waterfowl are protected from hunting.

Rain shadow An area sheltered from heavy rainfall by mountains that, at their higher altitudes, have drawn much of the rain from the atmosphere.

Raptor A bird of prey with a sharp curved beak and hooked talons. Raptors include hawks, eagles, owls, falcons, and ospreys.

Rhizome A horizontal plant stem, often thick with reserved food material, from which grow shoots above and roots below.

Riparian The bank and associated plant life zone of any water body, including tidewaters.

Riverine Living or located on the banks of a river.

Rookery A nesting place for a colony of birds or other animals (seals, penguins, others).

Salt marsh An expanse of tall grass, usually cordgrass and sedges, located in sheltered places such as the land side of coastal barrier islands or along river mouths and deltas at the sea.

Salt pan A shallow pool of saline water formed by tidal action that usually provides abundant food for plovers, sandpipers, and other wading birds.

Scat Animal fecal droppings.

Scrub A dry area of sandy or otherwise poor soil that supports species adapted to such conditions, such as sand myrtle and prickly pear cactus, or dwarf forms of other species, such as oaks and palmettos.

Sea stack A small, steep-sided rock island lying off the coast.

Second growth Trees in a forest that grow naturally after the original stand is cut or burned. *See also* old-growth forest.

Seeps Small springs that may dry up periodically.

Shell mound A mound of shells built by coastal native Americans who ate shellfish and disposed of shells in a pile. Most shell mounds are now covered with trees and other vegetation. *See also* midden.

Shorebird A bird, such as a plover or sandpiper, frequently found on or near the sea shore.

Shrub-steppe Desert-like lands dominated by sagebrush, tumbleweed and other dry weather adapted plants.

Slough A backwater or creek in a marshy area; sloughs sometimes dry into deep mud.

Spit A narrow point of land, often of sand or gravel, extending into the water.

Staging area A place where birds rest, gather strength and prepare for the next stage of a journey.

Successional Referring to a series of different plants that establish themselves by territories, from water's edge to drier ground. Also, the series of differing plants that reestablish themselves over time after a fire or the retreat of a glacier.

Sump A pit or reservoir used as a drain or receptacle for liquids.

Swale A low-lying, wet area of land.

Swamp A spongy wetland supporting trees and shrubs (as opposed to a marsh, which is characterized by grasses). Swamps provide habitat for birds, turtles, alligators, and bears and serve as refuges for species extirpated elsewhere. *See also* extirpated.

Test The hard round exoskeleton of a sea urchin.

Threatened specie A species of plant or animal in which population numbers are declining, but not in immediate danger of extinction. Threatened species are protected under the Endangered Species Act of 1973. *See also* endangered.

Tuber A short, underground stem with buds from which new shoots grow.

Understory Plants growing under the canopy of a forest. *See also* canopy.

Vascular plant A fern or another seed-bearing plant with a series of channels for conveying nutrients.

Vernal pool Shallow ponds that fill with spring ("vernal") rains or snowmelt and dry up as summer approaches; temporary homes to certain amphibians.

Wader A long-legged bird, such as a crane or stork, usually found feeding in shallow water.

Wetland A low moist area, often marsh or swamp, especially when regarded as the natural habitat of wildlife.

Wilderness Area An area of land (within a national forest, national park or a national wildlife refuge) protected under the 1964 Federal Wilderness Act. Logging, construction, and use of mechanized vehicles or tools are prohibited here and habitats are left in their pristine states. "Designated Wilderness" is the highest form of federal land protection.

Wrack line Plant, animal, and unnatural debris left on the upper beach by a receding tide.

INDEX

ACKNOWLEDGMENTS

Without the dedicated professional staff who work for the U. S. Fish & Wildlife Service, there would be no sanctuaries for America's wildlife and no special places for the rest of us to visit. I would like to thank each of these men and women for their hard work and commitment to ensuring that our natural heritage remains intact for coming generations. Their warm hospitality and willing assistance on this project was very much appreciated. I hope that every reader of this book who visits a refuge takes the opportunity to join me in thanking them.

I would also like to express my thanks to David Emblidge, Series Editor, for his help and guidance through the project. The production staff at Balliett & Fitzgerald has been the epitome of professionalism and a pleasure to work with.

And finally, major thanks to my wife, Kay, for helping, listening, pushing, prodding, consoling, and mostly for just being there for the year it took to complete this book.

—William Palmer

ABOUT THE AUTHOR

With degrees in biology and environmental science, William Palmer has served as Director of State Parks in both Missouri and Texas and has been an environmental education coordinator in the Missouri Department of Natural Resources.

PHOTOGRAPHY CREDITS

We would like to thank the U. S. Fish & Wildlife Service for letting us publish photos from their collection, as well as the other contributing photographers for their wonderful imagery. The pages on which the photos appear are listed after each contributor.

Dan Gibson: 5, 141

John & Karen Hollingsworth: ii-iii, 4, 6, 39, 50, 56, 60, 65, 86, 109, 117, 135, 148, 151, 154, 165, 170, 182, 198, 201, 209, 217

Gary Kramer: xii, 7, 8, 14, 26, 34, 43, 47, 51, 57, 84, 89, 92, 104, 107, 122, 126, 129, 142, 152, 157, 161, 162, 168, 175, 181, 197, 210

Omni-Photo Communications: 24, 98, 119, 137, 167, 206

William Palmer: 18, 20-21, 28, 33, 36, 44, 48, 53, 54, 59, 66, 68, 71, 73, 76, 79, 83, 87, 94, 97, 110, 114, 121, 127, 130, 139, 144, 147,172, 178, 185, 186, 188, 191, 194, 213, 215

U.S. Fish & Wildlife Sevice: 23, 30, 40, 62, 75, 95, 101, 112, 132, 174, 216, 219

NATIONAL AUDUBON SOCIETY
Mission Statement

The mission of National Audubon Society, founded in 1905, is to conserve and restore natural ecosystems, focusing on birds, other wildlife, and their habitats for the benefit of humanity and the earthís biological diversity.

One of the largest, most effective environmental organizations, Audubon has more than 560,000 members, numerous state offices and nature centers, and 500+ chapters in the United States and Latin America, plus a professional staff of scientists, lobbyists, lawyers, policy analysts, and educators. Through our nationwide sanctuary system we manage 150,000 acres of critical wildlife habitat and unique natural areas for birds, wild animals, and rare plant life.

Our award-winning Audubon magazine, published six times a year and sent to all members, carries outstanding articles and color photography on wildlife and nature, and presents in-depth reports on critical environmental issues, as well as conservation news and commentary. We also publish Field Notes, a journal reporting on seasonal bird sightings continent-wide, and Audubon Adventures, a bimonthly childrenís newsletter reaching 500,000 students. Through our ecology camps and workshops in Maine, Connecticut, and Wyoming, we offer professional development for educators and activists; through Audubon Expedition Institute in Belfast, Maine, we offer unique, traveling undergraduate and graduate degree programs in Environmental Education.

Our acclaimed World of Audubon television documentaries on TBS deal with a variety of environmental themes, and our children's series for the Disney Channel, Audubon's Animal Adventures, introduces family audiences to endangered wildlife species. Other Audubon film and television projects include conservation-oriented movies, electronic field trips, and educational videos. National Audubon Society also sponsors books and interactive programs on nature, plus travel programs to exotic places like Antarctica, Africa, Australia, Baja California, Galapagos Islands, Indonesia, and Patagonia.

For information about how you can become an Audubon member, subscribe to Audubon Adventures, or learn more about our camps and workshops, please write or call:

National Audubon Society
Membership Dept.
700 Broadway
New York, New York 10003
212/979-3000
http://www.audubon.org/audubon

JOIN THE NATIONAL AUDUBON SOCIETY—RISK FREE!

Please send me my first issue of AUDUBON magazine and enroll me as a tempo-rary member of the National Audubon Society at the $20 introductory rate—$15 off the regular rate. If I wish to continue as a member, I'll pay your bill when it arrives. If not, I'll return it marked "cancel," owe nothing, and keep the first issue free.

____ Payment Enclosed   ____ Bill Me

Name _____

Street _____

City _____

State/zip _____

Please make checks payable to the National Audubon Society. Allow 4–6 weeks for delivery of magazine. $10 of dues is for AUDUBON magazine. Basic mem-bership, dues are $35.

Mail to:

> NATIONAL AUDUBON SOCIETY
> Membership Data Center
> PO Box 52529
> Boulder, CO 80322-2529